ALL ABOUT Dreams

Also by Gayle Delaney, Ph.D.:

LIVING YOUR DREAMS

IN YOUR DREAMS: FALLING, FLYING, AND OTHER DREAM THEMES

THE DREAM KIT: AN ALL-IN-ONE TOOL KIT FOR UNDERSTANDING YOUR DREAMS

SENSUAL DREAMING: HOW TO UNDERSTAND AND INTERPRET THE EROTIC
CONTENT OF YOUR DREAMS

BREAKTHROUGH DREAMING: HOW TO TAP THE POWER OF YOUR 24-HOUR MIND

NEW DIRECTIONS IN DREAM INTERPRETATION

ALL ABOUT Dreams

EVERYTHING YOU NEED TO KNOW ABOUT
WHY WE HAVE THEM, WHAT THEY MEAN,
AND HOW TO PUT THEM TO WORK FOR YOU

Gayle Delaney, Ph.D.

HarperSanFrancisco

A Division of HarperCollins*Publishers*

FIRST EDITION

Library of Congress Cataloging-in-Publication Data

Delaney, Gayle M. V.
All about dreams : everything you need to know about why we have them, what they mean, and how to put them to work for you /
Gayle Delaney. —1ˢᵗ ed.
p. cm.
Includes bibliographical references and index.
ISBN 0–06–251411–3 (pbk.)
1. Dreams. 2. Dream Interpretation. I. Title.
BF1091.D375 1998
154.6'3—DC21   97–45891

03 04 05 (RRD) 20 19 18 17 16 15 14 13 12

This book is dedicated to Charles Schulz, the creator of "Peanuts" and the quiet patron of the Redwood Empire Ice Arena in Santa Rosa, California. Thanks to Mr. Schulz's enthusiasm and generosity, my friends and I can continue our great passion for skating in a beautiful, friendly environment embellished by stained-glass images of Snoopy, pretty lights, murals of rural Switzerland, and wonderful food. If you have ever ice-skated indoors in America, you may appreciate how very unusual this is and how very lucky we are. Mr. Schulz has hired legends of the sport like "Mr. Debonair," Richard Dwyer, and the ever playful Skippy Baxter to run the rink and take wonderful care of our ice skates. He has also surrounded us with the greatest competitive and show skaters, whom he invites to practice among us and to skate in his famous *Christmas Show on Ice*. This gentle, forever creative man is also a star of the hockey team the Diamond Icers. It is my hope that this dedication will convince him to let us form a cheerleading team for the Icers, none of whom is under seventy years old. Thank you, Sparky, for the good times and the good care you take of us all.

ACKNOWLEDGMENTS IX

INTRODUCTION TO MY DREAM WORLDVIEW 1

One

HOW OTHERS HAVE INFLUENCED WHAT YOU THINK ABOUT
DREAMS 9

Two

THE ARCHITECTS OF TWENTIETH-CENTURY DREAM
INTERPRETATION 65

Three

SIX DIFFERENT WAYS TO INTERPRET DREAMS 88

Four

THE DREAM INTERVIEW 102

Five

FOLLOWING THE STEPS OF THE INTERVIEW 123

Six

COMMON DREAM THEMES 145

Seven

DIRECTING YOUR DREAMS 198

Eight

WHAT'S NEW IN DREAMS AND PROBLEM SOLVING? 228

Nine
EXPLORING YOUR DREAMS ALONE OR WITH OTHERS 251

APPENDIX:
HOW TO RECALL YOUR DREAMS MORE VIVIDLY AND RECORD
THEM MORE EFFECTIVELY 269

NOTES 273

RESOURCES: GOOD BOOKS, TAPES, VIDEOS,
AND WEB SITES ABOUT DREAMING 297

INDEX 303

Thank you, Rick Moss, for your loving support; Jan Edelstein, for your jump-start coaching and labors; Richard McWilliams, for your on-call emergency computer-wizard and friend-in-need missions.

Thank you, dear Bill Delaney, for your consistent good cheer and fatherly caretaking.

Thank you, Erik Craig, for your comments and assistance in a field so dear to both of us and for bringing me to Santa Fe to your dream center, where my dreams found new inspiration.

INTRODUCTION TO
MY DREAM WORLDVIEW

As you will see in the pages that follow, I am neither a Jungian nor a Freudian, although I owe much to these pioneers. My education as an American female of my generation has led me to question authority, and to ask questions about the usefulness of elaborate psychological theories. My theory of dreaming is as simple and as unassuming as I can make it.

In developing my Dream Interview Method, I have tried to keep my theoretical assumptions to a minimum. In my opinion there is not yet sufficient evidence, nor are there sufficiently convincing arguments, to answer the following questions:

* Where do dreams come from?

* Why do we dream?

* Why don't we dream in plain English?

* What part does the mind play and what part the brain in creating the dreams we remember? How much of dreaming is psychological, and how much is physiological?[1]

Strictly speaking, we have yet to develop scientific procedures sensitive enough to issues of meaning and feeling that are capable of proving or disproving the theory that a dream "has" a message, or that it intends to mean something. We still don't know why or how dreams are made into picture stories. And we don't know exactly where they come from—the unconscious? God? neuronal discharges? What most practitioners *do* say is that when the dreamer sees and grasps a metaphor in a dream, she usually understands more clearly a basic truth about herself or her relationships, or about a problem she has been trying to solve.

I will not enter what would be a lengthy review of the arguments here. I want to make a point: one does not need to finally decide these matters in order to take advantage of the insights and creative ideas provided by a careful exploration of a dream, however that dream is created, and for however many purposes. My focus is neither to find the cause of a dream nor to decide its purpose. Rather, I ask my dreamers, "To what uses can you put the insights you have gained by noting the metaphors in your dream that relate to your waking life?"

A theoretical assumption can open up possibilities for good work, or it can close them off. I have abandoned a number of assumptions (which are often presented as facts) because they close more doors than they open and because they have not been validated in my twenty-five years of working with the dreams of healthy people. Therefore, I have rejected the following assumptions:

Most dreams are nonsense. There is significant research that demonstrates that dreams reflect our waking concerns and are helpful in coping with conflict, solving problems, and generating new ideas. Almost anyone who works at understanding dreams as metaphors for even a few weeks will not fail to recognize the meaningfulness of at least some dreams.

Most dreams are the expressions of unconscious wishes. Dreams show us in metaphorical form the dynamics of our important relationships, how we honestly feel and think about things and about ourselves. They help us see our hopes, fears, talents, weaknesses, and heaven knows what else. Some dreams certainly do express wishes of which we are mostly unaware while awake; others express very conscious wishes, as when a hungry dieter dreams of dining at a sumptuous banquet.

Dreams speak in a language meant to camouflage the truth. Dreams certainly don't speak our waking language, but to say that their natural language of visual imagery is a camouflage is like saying the Chinese speak Chinese in order to keep secrets from the rest of us. If we want to understand what the Chinese are saying, we have to learn their language. Individuals seem to dream more direct or transparent dreams at times of emotional openness or emotional emergency, and to dream more obscure dreams when they are generally more defensive or when dealing with issues that are new or unfamiliar to them. I would rather describe this as a readiness for or resistance to straightforward dreaming, rather than suggest that the language of the dream is a disguise.

The male and female psyches are fundamentally different, and therefore the dreams of men and women must be interpreted differently. Throughout history, the differences between men and women have been vastly exaggerated and often fabricated. It will be many generations, if ever, before we can separate the effects of our social training from any inherent psychological differences between men and women. In the meantime, why not leave each person free from premature categorization? Too many dreams are inadequately explored and badly interpreted because the interpreter jumps to conclusions about certain images. These conclusions are often based on severely biased opinions about the natures of the male and female psyches.

Intuition plays a large part in good interpretation. If you carefully elicit the relevant information from the dreamer, you should be able to point to the very responses that led you to form a given interpretive hypothesis or that led you to ask a particular question. What analysts Erika Fromm and Thomas French call an "act of intuitive imagination" in their interpretive work is usually a guess based on theoretical presuppositions, common sense, and experience.[2] *Intuition* is a word often misused as a long, dark cloak to hide a multitude of sins. The sins usually have to do with the interpreter's imposing his own preconceptions, associations, and personal projections. Beware the interpreter who depends on his "intuition"! A well-trained dream interviewer explores and assesses the elements of the dream in light of the dreamer's associations and bridges. He makes certain deductions from this information, which he uses to formulate further questions and hypotheses. The questions are based on theoretical hypotheses concerning the nature of dreaming, upon the facts or information from the dream interview, and upon an appreciation of the dramatic structure of the dream. It is through acts of critical judgment, not intuition, that the interviewer chooses his questions and forms interpretive hypotheses.

There can be many good, divergent interpretations of the same dream. When the interviewer accepts that many conflicting interpretations are true, or that interpretations that depart from each other in confusing ways are all true, he has usually failed to explore the dream adequately and to verify that the interpretations are consistent with the dramatic structure of the dream. There may be many levels of meaning in a dream, and many ramifications of an interpretation, but they all will follow the general thrust and dramatic structure of the dream.

It is impossible for an interviewer to have no presuppositions, and it is important for the interviewer to recognize exactly what presuppositions he or she does have. I have found the following theoretical hypotheses or assumptions to be helpful in conducting dream interviews that yield insights and creative ideas.[3]

Most dreams easily yield metaphorical expressions of feelings, thoughts, and ideas that, when understood, can help the dreamer to adapt to changes in life, and to recognize, assess, and solve personal and professional problems. I would dare to say that this is at least one of the reasons why we dream. It seems that, at least to some degree, some dreams have these effects without being understood or even recalled. However, in most cases the dreamer must arrive at a conscious understanding of the meaning of the dream, of how it relates to waking life, if it is to have any significant impact. Researchers Louis Breger, Ian Hunter, and Ron Lane studied the impact of dream work with people in highly stressful circumstances, and wrote:

> Without work directed at integrating the dreams—at breaking down the dissociations that are present both in the dreaming and the reporting—the subjects do not learn anything about themselves. Just as one must work hard in the real world to transform a creative inspiration into a poem, a painting, or a piece of music or literature, so one must work hard at making individual sense of one's dreams if they are to be more than fleeting, uninformative glimpses of what is within.[4]

Dreams seem to have a point, and metaphorical reflections on them offer new or unappreciated pieces of information that can be grasped and used for the benefit of the dreamer. Dreams rarely seem to present old news unless the dreamer is stuck in a destructive pattern. We generally consider an interview incomplete if it has not uncovered new information, or a new understanding of familiar issues.[5] Jung takes this position,[6] but Medard Boss and others do not, saying that we cannot prove any intent on the part of the dream or on the part of the dreaming person. I would suggest that a careful reading of the dream yields to the waking dreamer metaphors that shed new light on, or at least timely reminders about, his life concerns. Whether or not the dream "intends" this is of secondary importance.

We use the term *interpretation* because it is defined as "finding meaning and making sense of something." Dream *reading, reflection,* and *appreciation* are other terms that have been suggested by writers who want to distinguish their work from associations with rigid, fixed-symbol substitution forms of interpretation. Interpretation does not necessarily use fixed symbols, nor does it necessarily presuppose that the dream has a hidden meaning.

Whereas Boss describes the dreaming mode of existence as more dimmed and restricted than the waking mode, which he says is more open and capable of abstraction and conceptualization, we would describe dreaming as a highly focused state of awareness. The intense focus of dreaming allows the dreamer to experience things vividly, and often with intense feelings that are usually warded off while she is awake. Dream focusing carries with it a narrowing of attention, but not, in our opinion, a dimming or impoverishment of experience relative to waking. The ability to take a close look at something in a dream can be a highly enriching experience in itself. If the waking dreamer then employs her conceptual powers of abstraction to make bridges or metaphors from dreaming to waking, the world of the dream becomes a valuable resource for insight and creativity.

The dreamer, upon awaking, has all the information he needs to understand the dream, although some of it may be out of his immediate awareness. If the dreamer lacks the skills to tap this information, he will need to learn them, or ask the assistance of an interviewer.

Freud, Jung, Mary Ann Mattoon, and many contemporary dream workers not only make interpretations based on systems of thought external to the dream, but feel justified in explaining the whole or parts of the dream to the dreamer. Freud insisted that symbolic substitution was a necessary, if auxiliary, method—to be used with his method of free association.

Jung and his followers claim that the interpreter must be well versed in mythology, the history of religion, and alchemy, among other things, in order to properly amplify certain dream images and help the dreamer see their deeper meanings. This can easily lead to the analyst's usurping the private experience of the dream and of its meaning—all in the name of broadening its scope to the universal, archetypal level. All too often such hijackings of the dreamer's attention by references to mythological, religious, or psychological systems of belief render impossible a recognition of the dream itself and of its highly personal, highly relevant, connection to the individual dreamer.

Mini-lectures to the dreamer about myths that are someone else's dreams, or about how the male or female psyches work, can mislead the dreamer and distract him from an immediate experience of his unique dream. More importantly, as Boss points out, a dependence on external explanations often seduces the dreamer to "take refuge from the personal and the concrete, in something distant and alien which does not oblige the patient in any way to become more responsible for the concrete ways of living his day-to-day life."[7] The interpreter, feeling pressure to solve the dream puzzle, is often tempted, out of her own anxiety, to take refuge in a prefabricated formulation of the dreamer's experience. I do not believe that adding to the dreamer's associations the "truths" of explanatory systems adds anything to the immediacy or depth of the dreamer's appreciation of the dream. Quite the contrary. Erik Erikson, in warning his fellow psychoanalysts against too hurriedly dismissing the manifest dream in favor of attending to what they thought might be hidden behind it, said, "So many in . . . [this] field mistake attention to surface for superficiality, a concern with form for lack of depth."[8]

As Boss wrote, if one learns to ask effective questions rather than give interpretations, "both the nature of the dream and its therapeutic message will emerge, contrary to the Jungian viewpoint, without any support from mythology or folklore, without any knowledge of primitive psychology or comparative religion, without any aid at all from psychology. In fact, no doctrine of the psyche is required."[9]

References to archetypal situations, and to mythological character types, can indeed be skillfully employed by therapists in their work with patients, and it always makes fascinating reading for academics and laypeople. I would simply ask that these references be kept out of the interview while one is trying to help a dreamer understand his or her own dream.

Since the dream interviewer cannot work without any assumptions, the ones he does work from should, it seems to me, be rather reasonable and modest, and require much smaller leaps of faith than do the assumptions of some schools of interpretation.

* * *

Those of you who have followed my work over the years may note that I have become more outspoken, less polite, about dream practice that I find nonproductive or misleading. That is because I am more impatient than ever with both prejudicial ignorance on the one hand, and naive gullibility on the other. The skeptics who refuse to inform themselves are no less troubling than the gullible followers who believe anything and test nothing. I hope to encourage you to do your own research into what skills you can use to make sense out of your dreams. I hope to encourage you not to give in to the lure of following a prefabricated belief system that short-circuits your developing your own understanding of yourself. My twenty-five years of study have convinced me that dreams are a call to reality and to living life coura-geously. Most of us live lives of quiet intimidation—in the big things, and especially in the little ones. When we listen to our dreams, which show us how we really feel and what we really think, when we let them nudge us to act on our insights, our lives get very interesting. I can think of no more exciting way to live, nor of one less suited to a passive acceptance of old formulas of interpretation or indeed of living.

In this book I want to give you a look at what I find most interesting and useful about dreaming. I have been studying and writing about dreams for a long time and have developed a strong preference for the practical, insight-giving, problem-solving aspects of dream work. In the following pages, I present a history chapter to point out the roots of much of our superstition and romanticizing about dreams, and to give you a feel for the great distance we have traveled in understanding them as a reflection of our thoughts, feelings, and lives. Plus, it's just plain fascinating to read the words of people who have grappled with the subject over the centuries in different cultures.

After then considering the contributions and problems in the work of Freud, Jung, and Boss, the architects of modern dream work, I present an outline of six ways people interpret dreams. Some of this material will surprise you, because I shall be talking about what people actually *do*, rather than about particular theories of interpretation.

The next chapters will teach you how to interpret your dreams using my Dream Interview Method. Then, in a chapter that I hope will give new meaning to the idea of "dream dictionary," you will have a chance to apply this method to your dreams about common themes and images. Here you will learn how to ask yourself the right questions at the right time instead of plastering your dream over with silly, fixed interpretations.

Then you will read about how to direct your dreams by incubating them to solve a particular problem on a particular night; by using lucid dreams to experiment with, play in, and explore your dreams; and by learning to conquer recurring nightmares.

After all that, I shall, I hope, give you new inspiration by telling you of the many practical ways in which businesspeople, artists, scientists, writers, musicians, engineers, and health professionals have used and are using their dreams.

Then I shall give you tips for developing your dream skills via individual, pair, and group study. You will find in the "Resources" section suggestions for good books, good classes, and good Web sites aimed at making you your own dream analyst. For that is my goal. We were not born with an analyst for each person, yet we all dream. I think it perfectly reasonable to expect that with sufficient information and practice, most if not all of us can learn to understand most of our dreams when we wake up in the morning.

 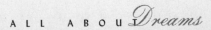

One

HOW OTHERS HAVE INFLUENCED
WHAT YOU THINK ABOUT DREAMS

ow have people in different times and in different cultures regarded their dreams—as illusions or realities? What are the causes and purposes that have been assigned to dreams? What have different people said one should do with and about a dream? Who should interpret dreams, and by what authority? What is the relative balance of power between the dreamer and the interpreter? And finally, what difference does it make if the dreamer is a man or a woman?

The way you interpret your dreams today depends upon which traditions you have accepted from the past and upon the quality of those traditions. And of course your ability to understand your dreams depends upon your ability to modernize the best of these traditions so that they fit the reality of your current life. Many of us have accepted old beliefs of dubious quality, and need to reconsider their validity if we are to understand our dreams and make them a part of our problem-solving strategy for living a good life. Knowing how the history of dream interpretation has shaped our current beliefs about our own dreams enables us to shed the straitjacket of superstition and to choose our own path with greater discrimination.

My brave editors told me that we would be taking a chance by leading off with a serious history chapter, but we decided that readers deserve a better look at the forces that have formed so many of our opinions about dreaming. Personally, I've had enough of those vague, dull five-page histories on dreaming. I want to give you a feel for how dreams were worked with in other times and places, and so have included descriptions that take you back in the principals' own words. We have included note references so that you can go into more depth on your own if you are curious about specific areas. If you are not in the mood to read about the often surprising dream practices of the past, you can skip this chapter and go right to chapter 2 or 3 and begin there. But reading this chapter will, I hope, fascinate you. Here we go on our quick global tour of the history of dreams.

How Real Are Dream Images?

It has often been said that people in primal societies are unable to distinguish between dreaming and reality. Barbara Tedlock, a psychological anthropologist with a special interest in dreaming, cites Edward B. Tylor, a nineteenth-century anthropologist, as an example of someone with the ethnocentric attitude that limited the perceptions of many Western observers of these cultures.[1] Tylor said, "The entire life of primitives was nothing but a long dream," adding, "The savage or barbarian has never learned to make the rigid distinction between imagination and reality, to enforce which is one of the main results of scientific education."[2] Tedlock concurs with anthropologist Irving Hallowell that "such notions are absurd, given that humans could not have evolved without making some sort of distinction between dream experiences and those of the waking physical world."[3]

What Tedlock has appreciated and so many of her predecessors have not[4] is that people in primal cultures as well as in other cultures often consider the world seen in dreams to be as real as, or more real than, the waking world. At the same time they distinguish clearly between waking and dreaming realities. What is considered real and unreal in any given society is determined by that society's religious and scientific beliefs.

Our own Western culture's dim view of the reality of dreaming has been greatly influenced by Aristotle, Francis Bacon, and the later empiricists. In the

ALL ABOU*Dreams*

fourth century B.C.E., Aristotle, the greatest theoretical scientist of the ancient world, launched an effective campaign to deny the reality of dream images by explaining dreaming as a secondary function of our apparatus of sense perception.[5] Aristotle believed that the movement of blood in our sense organs, which continues day and night but of which we are generally unaware during waking, causes certain images to arise in dreams. Aristotle wrote that the first subtle symptoms of an impending illness might make themselves known to the dreamer through this mechanism. He said that the emotions and reason of the dreamer would determine the final shape of these images, which he compared to waking illusions.

Aristotle allowed that clairvoyant dreams are worth interpreting. He theorized that the dreamers of such dreams received "movements" (we might say *vibrations*) caused by an event, and the consequent sense perceptions of which sleepers are exquisitely aware produce dream images of varying degrees of clarity.[6] So at best, according to Aristotle, dreams could reflect the real world, including the state of the physical body, but they themselves were only visual images that most dreamers mistake for reality.[7]

Aristotle has been described as having foreshadowed the empiricist's way of thinking, which was later articulated by Francis Bacon (1561–1626), who brought to the forefront of Western thought the belief that systematic, empirical evidence was the only key to obtaining reliable knowledge about what is and is not fact.[8] As methods of empirical inquiry developed, phenomena like the images in dreams that apparently could not be isolated, quantified, experimented upon, and interpersonally verified were consigned to the realm of the unreal.[9] In the West, the reality of the experience of dreaming was not denied, but the images of dreams certainly did not qualify to be considered as a meaningful part of the real world. But let us take a broad overview of how different people have judged the reality and meaningfulness of dreaming before we look more closely at our Western tradition.

Dreams Around the World

As we look around the globe, it becomes clear that our Western ideas of what is real and what is unreal are not shared by people whose philosophical traditions define reality in different ways. Clearly, the way a culture values dreams, and its methods of interpreting them, will be profoundly influenced by its beliefs about the nature of the reality of dream imagery.

In primal societies, people believe that in dreams one enters another real world, the world of power and spirit. This world may be seen as equally real as, or more real than, the waking world; it is certainly seen as a more powerful world. One calls on tribal elders, matriarchs, patriarchs, priests, and shamans to act as interpreters of dreams. Shamans are especially skilled with dreams, it is believed, because they are able to enter the dream world through trance states, or through their own dreams, and recover lost souls, fight evil spirits, contact ancestors, and discover meaning on behalf of the dreamer.[10]

The historian Donald Hughes has located the account of an early-twentieth-century explorer's description of the dream work of a shaman among the Siberian Chuckchee. According to this account, "The shaman's search for the soul was formerly effected in a shamanistic trance which nowadays is replaced by the usual sleep over night since dreams are considered by the Chuckchee one of the best means of communicating with spirits. When the search is successful the shaman returns bringing the soul."[11] In the words of Geza Roheim, "The spirits start communicating with the future shaman in dreams."[12]

Among American Plains Indian tribes, it was a common practice for young men at puberty to fast and to sleep in a special place, or in the wilderness, and to pray for a dream or vision that would reveal to them their role or mission in the tribe. These dreams would generally be reported in terms of images and symbols common in the lore of the tribe. Robert Van de Castle reports that "among the Oglala Sioux, a difficult choice confronted a male youth if he were to dream [for his puberty dream] of the moon as having two hands, one holding a bow and arrows and the other a burden strap of a woman. The moon would bid the dreamer to take his choice and would sometimes try to confuse him by crossing its hands. Should he become the possessor of the burden strap, he would be doomed [sic] to live the remainder of his life as a woman. He would be required to dress as a woman, marry another man, and undertake woman's work. Such a person was known as a *berdache* and suicide was his only recourse to avoid the fate meted out to him in his dream."[13]

I have never read that similar practices of evoking or incubating dreams existed for the women of the Plains tribes. Frequently when we read about the dream beliefs and practices of different cultures, we are reading about the theories and practices of the men in the culture as they pertain to the dreams of their male dreamers. Obviously the women of all cultures dreamt, but what they dreamt, how their dreams were regarded and interpreted, and what contributions they may have made to dream practices and beliefs are matters often left to conjecture.

The elders and the shamans of North American and Siberian tribes were invested with the power to determine the meaning of dreams and to take or prescribe remedial action regarding unfavorable ones. The authority of these interpreters derived from their experience with dreams and tribal lore. In the case of the shaman, who claimed the power to effect cures through dreams, his authority came from his personal experience as a wounded healer who knew the ways of the spirit world, to which his own initiatory illness or dream had introduced him. The dreamer was not expected to be of any help at all in the discovery of the meaning of his own dream. That ability was thought to rest with the authorities of the tribe.

The Yolngu, aboriginal Australians of Arnhem Land, are among the more traditional of their race and have retained many of their original cultural attributes.[14] Like those in most or all primal societies, like many in early civilizations, and like some in contemporary Eastern and Western societies, the Yolngu believe that a part of the dreamer, the soul or the shadow, leaves the physical body in dreams. The soul is believed to travel to real places in the physical or spiritual world, where during some dreams it meets with other people's shadows. John Cawte, a professor in New South Wales, writes: "[The] Yolngu contend that in a dream a person's shadow, or 'mali,' leaves the body during sleep to go on excursions during which it may engage with other people's mali. Sleeping persons are invariably softly and slowly awakened, when it is necessary to do so at all, in order to give their mali, which could be dreaming outside the body, time to return to it."[15]

Cawte's interviews with a number of the Yolngu revealed that they interpret their own dreams without the aid of any tribal authority figure. They may tell their dreams to their spouses, or discuss them with members of their group, and interpret them along traditional cultural principles and formulas. The dreams Cawte was told were interpreted variously as prophetic, as meaningless, as visits from dead souls, as giving permission to break taboos, as warnings, as direct healing, and as experiences in the newly introduced Christian religion. The Yolngu dreams that Cawte recorded covered a "wide range of subjects comparable with those of Westerners' dreams, though with the expected different cultural emphasis. Intrinsic dream factors such as the frequency, length, detail, substitution, derailments, and recall seem essentially like those dream-features familiar to Westerners. From these observations there is no reason to believe that Aboriginal dreams are different in psychophysiological kind [from contemporary Westerners' dreams]."[16]

Judging from Cawte's interviews, the Yolngu distinguish between false dreams and true, prophetic ones. If the dreamer has been thinking or worrying about a subject the day before dreaming about it, the dream will not be prophetic. It is prophetic only if the subject of the dream has not been on the dreamer's mind the previous day. Yolngu women tell and interpret their dreams. For example, one wife told her husband a dream that they both interpreted as a literal warning for another member of the tribe not to fish until the rainy season was over because otherwise he might be bitten, as he was in the dream, by a shark. The husband then related the dream and the warning to the man who had appeared in the dream.

Yolngu healers, unlike Native American shamans, do not use dreams to diagnose and heal the sick, and apparently are not regularly consulted to interpret dreams. This may or may not have much to do with the arrival of Christian missionaries in 1946. A Christian Yolngu interprets some of his dreams as reflections of happy times in the past and of ones to come. Cawte also reports his informant having told him that "if he thinks and prays a lot about Jesus, he is filled with joy and is likely to have a true and happy dream. God has given people something special in their brain to let them dream in order to learn more than they can while wide awake."[17]

Egyptian Dream Traditions

The Chester Beatty papyrus, named after the man who donated it to the British Museum, was written around 1350 B.C.E. and was found in Thebes. This papyrus, which may be a copy of one written in 2000 B.C.E., is probably the oldest surviving dream book in existence.[18]

The Beatty papyrus, like most dream books, lists images and gives fixed interpretations based on contraries (the interpretation of a dream image as meaning its opposite) and verbal and visual puns, and on cultural associations that are often surprising to modern readers. As you might expect, the papyrus lists several incantations and magical rituals aimed at warding off the effects of bad dreams. The god Bes "was believed to protect sleepers against the demons of the night and send them pleasant and good dreams. Appeals to Bes took the form of rituals and magic spells involving strange ingredients. One papyrus declared that the ink for a petition must be made from the blood of a white dove, mulberry juice, cinnabar, rainwater, and myrrh."[19] Bes was the favorite of several Egyptian gods of dreams: "Headrests, carved of wood or stone, often had a figure of Bes as the support, as if to guarantee propitious dreams."[20] Formulas are also given for insuring that a friend or enemy is sent a special dream. Apparently, stuffing the formula into the mouth of a dead cat increases the chances of timely delivery of the dream![21]

The Egyptians believed that some dreams were omens from the spirit world, but unlike the Australians, Africans, Indians, Asians, and Mesopotamians, they did not seem to believe that a person's soul could leave the body and travel while the body slept. Dreams played an important part in the religious beliefs and magical practices of the country and in the government, as the Old Testament story of Joseph and the pharaoh indicates.[22]

The Egyptians apparently were less preoccupied with demonology than many, and focused their accounts on dreams in which gods appeared demanding the execution of a pious act; giving unsolicited warnings, predictions, or revelations; or responding to a question or request made by the dreamer before sleep.

Most recorded dreams were seen as the recall of real events on a spiritual plane. When the future King Thutmose IV (1450 B.C.E.) slept by the great sphinx at Giza, he dreamt that the god Hormakhu promised him a successful rule over Egypt if he would sweep away the sands that covered the holy sphinx. Thutmose inscribed the story of his dream on a stone plaque placed before the sphinx after he complied with the god's wish.

Many political predictive dreams are recorded, and we are left to wonder about their authenticity, but not their expediency. Take the dream of Tanutamon, the Ethiopian who conquered Egypt in the seventh century B.C.E. Tanutamon is said to have dreamt that he saw a serpent to his left, and another to his right. The interpretation? That he would rule the two Egypts, upper and lower.[23]

According to Donald Hughes, dream interpreters in Egypt were well educated, and of high status. They were special temple priests called "Masters of the Secret Things" or "Scribes of the Double House of Life" or "Learned Ones of the Magic Library." Hughes writes: "As the names indicate, they were in charge of collections of papyri containing knowledge about omens, dream images, and the gods who had particular ability to interpret dreams and send good ones."[24]

The Book of the Dead, one of the most influential books in all history, was Egypt's most important body of religious authority for three thousand years. Maspero, an Egyptologist, suggests that much of the material in the book, written down soon after writing was invented in 3100 B.C.E., was already old in 5000 B.C.E.[25] This book was used in temples for the living on a daily basis. Some of its chapters provide prayers for the banishment of nightmare spirits, and others "can be read as instructions for the incubation ritual."[26]

Incubation is the term historically used to describe a variety of practices, carried out before sleep, aimed at causing a person to dream about a particular topic. The incubation of dreams was a popular and elaborately developed art in Egypt from early times well into the Roman era. The "Masters of the Secret Things" practiced their rituals and interpretations at special temples to which people would come to incubate dreams. The temple at Memphis, dedicated to Imhotep, the god of healing, was the most important of these. Imhotep, before he became a god, was a noted architect, astrologer, and medical man, and lived around 2980–2950 B.C.E. Norman MacKenzie, in his book *Dreams and Dreaming*, writes that

> after his death [Imhotep] was gradually elevated to the status of a deity, and his temple became the center of a healing cult whose beliefs have persisted almost to modern times. . . . The priests at Memphis, like those in the sanctuary of Isis at Philae, and at the oracles of Khimunu and Thebes, practiced "incubation." This simply meant that sick persons were brought to sleep in the temple, where they fasted, or took potions, to induce beneficial dreams.

> Like many of the Egyptian attitudes to dreams, the idea of incubation was passed on to later civilizations [the Greeks especially borrowed heavily, taking over gods, magic learning, and medicine from the Egyptian traditions].

> The later Egyptian forms of dream interpretation, possibly even the cult of incubation, resemble earlier practices in Mesopotamia [and significantly differ from the main Egyptian tradition] closely enough to suggest that the Egyptians had grafted Assyrian ideas and methods on to their own concepts—as they certainly did with astrology.[27]

Most of the dreams in the Old Testament are literal message dreams that come from God or his angels and needed no interpretation. In these biblical dreams, the dreamer is given divine warnings, orders, or promises. In a story about Abraham,

it is not Abraham, but his host Avimelech, who received a clear order, a warning from the Lord, the god of his guest. Abraham had told Avimelech that Sarah, his wife, was his sister, . . . [fearing he would be killed by the king who desired his wife, and failing to mention that Sarah was only his half-sister] (Gen. 20). So "Avimelech king of Gerar sent, and took Sarah (Gen. 20:2). But God came to Avimelech in a dream by night, and said to him: 'Behold, you are but a dead man because of the woman whom you have taken; for she is a man's wife' (Gen. 20:3)." And since Avimelech had not had relations with her, the situation could be unraveled without hostility.[28]

In Jacob's dream, God appears, identifies himself, and promises:

The land whereon thou liest, to thee will I give it, and to thy seed; and thy seed shall be as the dust of the earth, and thou shalt spread abroad to the west, and to the east, and to the north, and to the south; and in thee and in thy seed shall all the families of the earth be blessed. I am with thee, and will keep thee in all places whither thou goest, and will bring thee again into this land; for I will not leave thee, until I have done that which I have spoken of.[29]

JEWISH DREAM INCUBATION

The practice of incubation appears in at least two instances in the Old Testament. Abraham had a vision that may have been a dream (the distinction is often not made in the Bible) in which he asks God if he must die childless. God responds with the promise that Abraham will have a son and numerous seed. Following God's instructions received in a vision, Abraham prepares a burnt offering and sleeps in a high place. As he sleeps, God says, "Know of a surety that thy seed shall be a stranger in a land that is not theirs, and shall serve them; and they shall afflict them four hundred years. . . . And also that nation, whom they shall serve, will I judge: and afterward shall they come out with great substance."[30]

Marielene Putscher points out that Solomon, upon becoming king, incubated his famous dream in 1 Kings 3:1–15:

There is not yet a temple in Jerusalem, and "the people were sacrificing in high places" (3:2), as did Solomon (3:3). But once he "went to Gibeon to sacrifice there, for that was the great high place; Solomon would offer a thousand burnt offerings [i.e., a very great offering] upon that altar" (3:4). As we have seen sacrifice is the beginning of the ritual. It is followed by sleep and dreaming in the sanctuary, where God appears and inquires into the sleeper's desires. This is what happened to the young king: (3:5) . . . "the Lord appeared to Solomon in a dream by night; and God said, 'Ask what I shall give you.'" And then, this motive of so many fairy tales is followed in Solomon's moving words (3:6–9): "I am but a little child . . ." (3:7), "Give thy servant therefore an understanding mind to judge thy people, that I may discern between good and evil . . ." (3:9). And the speech "pleased the Lord" (3:10) and he answers him gracefully. "And Solomon awoke and, behold, it was a dream. And he came to Jerusalem . . . and offered up burnt offerings, and peace offerings, and made a feast to all his servants" (3:15). We may add to all this that the offerings of thanks and a banquet are always the last stage of an incubation ritual and are an integral part of the ceremony [in this period, 961 B.C.E.].[31]

While for centuries many Jews probably consulted local dream interpreters who claimed to read the future from dreams, the practice of necromancy was officially frowned upon—with the exception, of course, of the two biblical interpreters, Joseph and Daniel. Besides the spontaneous and incubated direct message dreams that appear in the Old Testament, a few symbolic dreams appear that are easily understood, like Joseph's dream in which the sun, the moon, and eleven stars all bowed down to him. In a practice common in the Near East, the dreamer's father interpreted the dream as the expression of Joseph's wish that his mother, father, and eleven brothers would all bow down to him, the little brother.

Here we see an often overlooked example of the Hebrews' recognition of the psychological nature of some dreams. It may be that since dreams of spiritual encounters with God make such exciting, convincing, and educational reading for a large audience, the more personal, psychological dream work that may have been common was not included in most holy scriptures.

Some symbolic dreams required greater interpretive expertise, and this was obtained through God's inspiration when Daniel interpreted Nebuchadnezzar's dream, and when Joseph interpreted the butler's, the baker's, and the pharaoh's dreams. Actually, the interpretations of these dreams could perhaps have been made on the basis of the Near Eastern and Egyptian dream books and practices of the period without divine inspiration. The fact that the pharaoh elevated a former prisoner to such a high rank in his household reminds us of the high regard the Egyptians had for dream interpreters who could predict the future.[32]

Whereas the Old Testament suggested that the loss of dream recall was a punishment from God (I Sam. 28:6), later writings were often contradictory regarding the value of dreaming. Philo (c. 30 B.C.E.–c. 40 A.D.) was the most important Jewish philosopher of Hellenic Judaism. Among his many works, this Alexandrian scholar wrote a trilogy on dreams *(De Somniis)*.[33]

Philo categorizes dreams as:

1. "Those [dreams] in which God originates the movement and invisibly suggests things obscure to us but patent to himself" (*Somn.* 2.2; cf. *Somn.* 1.1)

2. "Dreams . . . in which our own mind, moving out of itself together with the Mind of the Universe, seems to be possessed and God inspired, and so capable of receiving some foretaste and foreknowledge of things to come" (*Somn.* 1.2; cf. *Somn.* 2.2)

3. "Dreams that arise 'whenever the soul in sleep, setting itself in motion and agitation of its own accord, becomes frenzied, and with the prescient power due to such inspiration foretells the future'" (*Somn.* 2.1)[34]

The first type of dream has probably been known to humans forever. Gudea's 2100 B.C.E. dream of the god who told him to build a temple in Mesopotamia is probably the first recorded example. Philo cites Jacob's dream as an example of the second category of dreams, one that contains hints of a mystical union with the deity such as the Hindus and Tantric Buddhists described.

The third type of dream is, according to Jouette M. Bassler, "self-activated . . . , not divinely motivated, and the soul is asleep, not moving in concert with a divine principle."[35] Philo lists Joseph's dreams and those of the butler and the baker in this category; he rates these dreams lowly because they are associated with the irrational, feminine, sensual, and vainglorious side of human nature. Philo's conception of this psychological makeup of man is better understood when we appreciate his belief in the masculine nature of reason that enlists masculine self-control. The enemy of holy reason is "the effeminate softness of those ruled by passions . . . and vain opinions."[36] No wonder women's dreams are not recorded in the Bible!

THE BABYLONIAN TALMUD

The Babylonian Talmud is a collection of writings compiled by scholars and rabbis between 200 B.C.E. and about 300 A.D., paralleling in time the Graeco-Roman period.[37] Much is said in these writings about dreams that reflects not only Hebrew, but Egyptian, Babylonian, Greek, and Roman influence. Here again we read that there is a part of the soul that travels away from the body in dreams and has experiences that are pictured in dreams. The writers of the Talmud express conflicting opinions about dreams, ranging from expressions of disdain for dreams to discourses on good and bad dreams and how to make the best of them.

In the Babylonian Talmud we read:

> Rab Hisda said: [There is no reality in] any dream without a fast. An uninterpreted dream is like an unread letter. . . . A bad dream is preferable to a good dream. When a dream is bad, the pain it causes is sufficient [to prevent its fulfillment], and when the dream is good, the joy it brings is sufficient.[38]

Here we learn that fasting, a form of incubation, is considered helpful, even necessary, to obtain a dream that is real, or tells about the future. Prayer is also a form of incubation that is suggested to elicit good dreams and mitigate the influence of bad dreams. Dreams are described also as omens or prognoses of one's illness. Elsewhere we learn that dreams are never fulfilled in every detail, that all dreams contain inaccurate or superfluous details, and that evil spirits can be blamed for dreams that speak falsely. In this text we find a clear statement that dream interpretations must take into account the specific dream if they are to be good. Apparently, some rabbis were well aware of the limitations of using dream books that decoded dream images in isolation from the context of the whole dream.[39]

According to Sandor Lorand, a psychoanalyst who studied 217 references to dreams in the Babylonian Talmud, dream interpreters were also encouraged to take into account the dreamer's personality, occupation, life circumstances, and mood at the time of the dream.[40] This respect for the individualized nature of dreams signals a giant leap in thinking about dreams, one the ancient Egyptians, who so influenced the Jewish dream tradition, never made.

A reference to the psychological and emotional nature of dreaming comes from Rabbi Nahmani, who said in the name of Jonathan: "A man is only shown [in a dream what emanates] from the thoughts of his heart. As it is said, 'As for thee, O King, thy thoughts come into thy mind upon thy bed'" (Dan. 2:29).[41]

Several techniques of interpretation are described. M. Caquot classifies them as follows:

1. Literal application of a verse in the Bible to the object seen in the dream: "He who dreams of olive trees will have many children, for it is written: 'Thy children [shall be] like olive plants round about thy table'" (Ps. 128:3).

2. Application of the verse in the Bible by a play on words: "From him who dreams of barley (se'Orim) his iniquity shall be taken away, for it is said: 'Thine iniquity is taken away *(sar awoneka)*'" (Isa. 6:7).

3. A play on words pure and simple: "He who dreams of a palm tree *(lulab)* has only one heart *(eyn laella leb ekhad)* for his heavenly father."

4. Transparent allegory: "He who climbs on to a roof in a dream will rise to greatness; he who descends from a roof will fall from greatness."[42]

Associations to and word plays on holy writings were thus added to general plays on words and allegorical metaphor as potential tools of the interpreter. As Raymond De Becker points out, the Muslims highly valued dreams and borrowed from the Jewish dream tradition these basic means of applying sacred texts—in their case, the Koran—to dreams in order to assign interpretations.[43]

In modern Israel, large numbers of Moroccan Jews make yearly pilgrimages to the sanctuaries of various Jewish saints and often have dream visitations from the saints in connection with the pilgrimage, either while sleeping in the sanctuary, or while at home before making the pilgrimage. The saints were charismatic, erudite, pious men who were believed to have had a special spiritual force in life. In 1983 over 150,000 devotees visited the sanctuary of Rabbi Shimeon Bar-Yohai, "a charismatic mystical figure of the second century [who] is the alleged author of the most sacred text in Jewish mysticism [Kabbalah], the Book of Splendor [Zohar]."[44] The pilgrims expected the saint, in return for their faithful devotion, to heal them of physical, economic, and emotional problems through his blessings or in a dream.

Yoram Bilu, at the Hebrew University of Jerusalem, and Henry Abramovitch, at Tel Aviv University, collected one hundred dreams from pilgrims to Rabbi Shimeon's sanctuary in Meiron near the town of Safed during the annual pilgrimages on three consecutive years between 1980 and 1982. They note that "more than 80 percent of the dreams in our sample were supplied by females, who, being more profoundly involved with the saints in general, were overrepresented in the pilgrimages. . . . It seems certain that for women, who have only limited access to the more institutionalized religious life such as synagogue prayer, hagiolatry [the veneration of saints] has been an alternative religious channel."[45]

Some of the dreams in which the rabbi appears in person or in symbolic guise, the ones dreamt during the pilgrimage or at the sanctuary, or those asked or hoped for by the dreamer at home, could be considered as incubated dreams. Others occur spontaneously in the life of the devotee. Bilu and Abramovitch report that for these visitational dreams, the help of a professional dream interpreter is never sought. One interprets the dream either oneself or with the help of friends and family who are familiar with the traditional interpretive lore. The researchers were struck by the fact that these visitation dreams regularly and obviously reflected the life problems of the devotees, were devoid of bizarre and exotic content, and appear as an extension of waking reality.

Bilu and Abramovitch write that "the therapeutic assets inherent in the bridging . . . [between past events and expected future outcomes in these dreams], generally manifested in the heightened morale of the devotees following their dream experiences, may in some cases culminate in dramatic symptom relief."[46] Here is the dream of a fifty-year-old ailing woman who, like many others, claimed to have been healed by Rabbi Shimeon the night she slept in the saint's sanctuary.

The *saddiq* [saint] came to me in a dream dressed in white and in his hands were mint leaves. He came near to the house and said "Shalom. Arise! Arise!" [in an authoritative voice]. I cried and said to him, "How can I get up? I have headaches, tears from my eyes for over 2 months, from so much crying. No one helps me. Not the doctor. Nobody." He said to me, "Get up. Enough! You came to me [i.e., to my tomb] and cried so much, I came to help you. Get up." He gave me his hand and raised me up. On the next day, the pains were gone, thank God. There certainly is a God and also saints in the world. He said to me, "Arise! Enough! You have cried so much, it hurts my heart."[47]

Bilu and Abramovitch report that "the mint leaves . . . which the *saddiq* holds are a traditional Moroccan symbol for blessing, fertility and good health."[48] Thus the dreamers are guided in their interpretations and perhaps even in their unconscious choice of dream images by the traditional beliefs they are taught from childhood.

In recent years, I have met several rabbis who take dreams very seriously and use them in counseling. In addition to their scriptural heritage, they use modern psychological approaches to dreaming. Rabbi Sky at temple Beth El in Maine is reportedly sought out by psychoanalysts, ministers, teachers, psychologists, and social workers because he works so well with dreams. He advises, "Listen to your dreams; keep a journal. If you write down whatever comes to you, you will discover how you fit into the eternal quest all of us are involved in. I believe there's a divine spark in all of us and the ultimate is to link up with the other sparks."[49]

Hindu Dream Traditions in India

The dreaming state has always been of great interest to the simplest as well as to the most sophisticated people of India. They have lavished a great deal of reflection upon the subject. The earliest Indian beliefs about dreaming told of dreams that were caused by disease, by foods eaten in the evening, by waking wishes, and by clairvoyant perceptions. Again the belief that the spirit leaves the body in dreams and has encounters with other spirits is common from earliest times. The greatest written authority on orthodox Hinduism, the Vedas, are the oldest scriptures of India, and come from an oral tradition that dates from the fifteenth to fifth centuries B.C.E.[50]

In the *Treatise on Dreams* in the Atharva Veda, we are presented with long lists of favorable and unfavorable dreams. The reasons for many of these interpretations seem arbitrary to us now, but there are some patterns that stand out. Images of aggressiveness, power, violence, and blood, including most amputations, were good omens. Images of loss of hair, nails, and teeth were seen as bad omens. Interpretation of an image by its opposite is common in the *Treatise on Dreams,* as it was and still is in many traditions around the world where fixed meanings for each symbol are applied. For example, sorrow meant happiness, seeing oneself dead meant happiness, and a man who dreamt that his head, foot, or penis was cut off was thought to have had a lucky dream.[51] The *Treatise* tells us that only the last dream remembered in the night should be interpreted, and that unrecalled dreams have no consequences. Methods for canceling the effects of bad-omen dreams include rites of purification, sacrifice, and gifts to the Brahmans.[52]

As Raymond De Becker points out in his wonderfully informative book *The Understanding of Dreams,* the *Treatise* contains nothing like a modern method of dream analysis, which focuses on the unique history and psychological structure of each individual. But, "it does contain a remarkable attempt to interpret images with reference to the personality, or at least the temperament, of the dreamer."[53] The Indians at the time recognized three temperaments: the bilious, the phlegmatic, and the sanguine. The *Treatise* taught that these types could be recognized by their dream imagery. The imagery of a particular type could, in part, be predicted by the type of dreamer. According to De Becker, this is the first systematic effort to relate dream images to the physiological roots, thus ridding dreams of some of their magical trappings.[54] Here we have perhaps the earliest expression of the belief in the physiological causes of dreams, which we shall refer to as the *physiological reality* of dreams. Because the conception of temperaments was not entirely physiological, but was considered a description of personality type as well, this may also be the earliest written account of the belief in the *psychological reality* of dreams as they pertained to the individual dreamer's personality type, not just to his future.

The Upanishads, written between perhaps 1000 and 300 B.C.E., are to Indian Brahmans (Hindus) what the New Testament is to Christians.[55] The first recorded Hindu attempts at systematic philosophizing, the Upanishads (upon which the later philosophical schools of Vedanta are based) are considered a development of the highest wisdom of the earlier Vedas. One hundred twelve Upanishads have been preserved, and in a good number of them we can find significant attention to dreams. In these writings the psychological reality of dreaming is developed as many dreams are described as mental impressions of objects and emotions carried forth from the dreamer's waking life.

The Upanishads identify three states of consciousness.

The first is the waking state, characterized by the awareness of things external to the body, sensual enjoyment of gross objects, and conviction as to the identity of consciousness and the physical body. . . .

The second is the dreaming state. When in this a man . . . is aware of internal phenomena and enjoys mental impressions. This is a condition intermediate between waking and deep sleep. The mind is now active, though independently of the sense organs, and is without consciousness of the gross body. In this state a man is a purely mental being.

The third state is that of deep sleep. When in this a man . . . is entirely unaware of the external world, and also of the internal world. As when the darkness of night covers the day, and with the day the objects before us seem to disappear, similarly the gloom of ignorance in deep sleep covers up consciousness, and thoughts and knowledge apparently vanish.[56]

What follows the third state in one's spiritual evolution is Pure Consciousness, which transcends all states and is called simply, the Fourth. The Fourth is the supreme mystic experience of pure unitary consciousness. The Upanishads teach how one may use dreaming as a stepping-stone to recognizing the illusory nature of waking and dreaming so that one may enter dreamless sleep, free of desire, thoughts, and images, and maintain consciousness at the same time in order to experience the Fourth. It is easy to see how in this tradition the Hindu version of reality, together with the belief in the illusory nature of dream images, directs dream practices.

In the Brihad-Aranyka Upanishad we read:

When one goes to sleep, he takes along the material . . . of this all-containing world, himself tears it apart, himself builds it up, and dreams by his own brightness, by his own light. Then this person becomes self-illuminated.

. . . There are no chariots there, no spans, no roads. But he projects from himself chariots, spans, roads. There are no blisses there, no pleasures, no delights. But he projects from himself blisses, pleasures, delights. There are no tanks there, no lotus-pools, no streams. But he projects from himself tanks, lotus-pools, streams. For he is a creator.[57]

On the subject of the soul in deep, dreamless sleep:

As a falcon, or an eagle, having flown around here in space, becomes weary, folds its wings, and is borne down to its nest, just so this person hastens to that state where, asleep, he desires no desires and sees no dream. . . .

. . . He is not followed by good, he is not followed by evil, for then he has passed beyond all sorrows of the heart.[58]

On attaining the Fourth:

An ocean, a seer alone without duality, becomes he whose world is Brahma, "O King!"—Thus Yajñavalkya instructed him. "This is a man's highest path. This is his highest achievement. . . . This is his highest bliss . . ."[59]

The Advaita Vedanta school of Hinduism de-emphasizes the function of dreams as good and evil omens of the future, and focuses on describing dreams as mental creations, and as memories and reflections of past experiences.[60]

The flux of everyday states of consciousness [like waking, dream, and deep sleep] is said to point to the advaitin's basic philosophical conviction, that there is a single, eternally self-luminous substratum of existence *[atman/brahman]* beyond ever-changing states and the "everyday" world *[vyavahara, maya]*. Advaitins aim for *moksa*, liberation from bondage to appearances, reaching immediate awareness of nondual Brahman.[61]

Clearly, in Hindu India, waking is not the yardstick by which reality is measured; rather, it is considered a prime example, along with dreaming, of the illusions that keep us from seeing the eternal, nondual reality of Brahman. One of the main paths to liberation from the bondage of the mind and senses to illusion is described in the practice of Yoga, which guides the aspirant to transcendental knowledge of the unity of all being. The revered Yogi Aurobindo expressed a minority view on dreaming.

Aurobindo called attention to the benefits of understanding the apparently trivial dreams so often disregarded in the yogic tradition. He writes:

> They can indicate things with which the subconscient is burdened and from which it has to be freed, binding memories of the vital and of the cells which have to be dismissed, forms, embedded notions, tendencies, habitual movements which it is no longer good to harbour, seeds of the past which have to be pulled out so that these undesirable fruit may no longer recur. . . . These things have to be got rid of if we are not to be bound to our past selves, if there is to be a true and complete liberation and transformation of the external being. If one can learn to detect and understand the indications of these dreams when they come up, and act upon what they show us to be still there in the obscure bed of our nature, it can be a great help for the successful change of what seems to be the most obscure and trivial and yet the most sticky and intractable part of the nature.[62]

Aurobindo reaffirms that in dreams one can meet with the dead and the living, but cautions that in dreams where symbolism is evident, the people are most likely to be just symbolic representations of the lower vital world of forms, social and domestic feelings, and so forth. As you may have noticed, this view of reality is an extremely hierarchical one; waking consciousness is considered petty and lower; the illusion free consciousness, eternal and higher. Although Aurobindo takes the time to interpret dreams using metaphor and fixed symbols,[63] he expresses his greatest interest in the following lines:

> In the waking state you are conscious only of a certain limited field of action of your nature. In sleep you can become vividly aware of things beyond this field—a larger mental or vital nature behind the waking state or else a subtle physical or a subconscient nature which contains much that is there in you but not distinguishably active in the waking state. All these obscure tracts have to be cleared or else there can be no change of Prakriti [the changing world]. You should not allow yourself to be disturbed by the press of vital or subconscient dreams—for these two make up the larger part of dream-experiences—but aspire to get rid of these things and of the activities they

indicate, to be conscious and reject all but the divine Truth; the more you get that Truth and cling to it in the waking state, rejecting all else, the more all this inferior dream-stuff will get clear.[64]

Dream Traditions of China

Chinese historical documents contain many references to dreams as they were understood and used by different segments of society in different social, literary, religious, and political periods. There are, however, very few works devoted directly to the subject of dreams.[65] Michel Strickmann, a Sinologist with a strong interest in Chinese dream beliefs, emphasizes the importance of remembering that the meaning the Chinese attributed to dreams "is always determined by context—above all, by the social function of the interpreter."[66] For example, medical texts show that doctors interpret dreams along psychophysiological lines, and religious authorities interpret them in terms of their ultimate goal of transcendence.[67]

According to Strickmann, Chinese works of history and fiction link dreams "with the overriding concern of the genre and its intended audience: the attainment of official position, power, and prestige."[68] Historians and poets for many centuries assumed that their audience understood that the superior part of the soul *(hun)* left the body in dreams and was free to meet distant or departed loved ones and holy beings. It was also understood that waking desires could create dream events, just as indigestion could cause strange dreams.[69]

The literature that pertains to the religious and psychophysiological aspects of dreams shows that the Chinese saw dreams as a means of communication with external beings and gods as well as a means of contacting inner, corporeal demons and spirits. The mind and body were inextricably linked, and Strickmann tells us that "nowhere are dreams viewed as a purely psychological phenomenon."[70] Of course, most dreams were viewed as omens and were seen as being of neither a psychological nor a physiological nature.

One of the earliest Chinese references to dreams was reportedly made by Confucius in the fifth century B.C.E: "'It's just too much,' he lamented near the end of his life, 'I am declining. It has been a long time since I have seen the Duke of

Chou in my dreams.'"[71] The duke of Chou had been the brother of one king and regent for another, and was the official ancestor of the state of Lou, which was the homeland of Confucius. He was also Confucius's mentor; he appeared in his disciple's dreams and exhorted him to the virtuous life.[72]

Early traces of a concern common among most people in China were provided by the spells used to ward off nightmares found in a third-century-B.C.E. tomb in Hupeh. Today, many Americans hang circular webs called dream catchers above their beds in a half-serious effort to catch nightmares before they get to the dreamer. This tradition comes from various Native American practices, and reminds us that superstition has an ever appealing allure.

The tradition of miraculous birth is well and early represented in dreams. From the second century B.C.E. on, dreams of miraculous births became common clichés. In these dreams, "the mother of a future emperor or prince dreams of a sun or a moon of a great light, or of a dragon, . . . which enters her body, or illumines her, or surrounds her and she conceives."[73]

In the mid–second century A.D., Wang Fu wrote *Essays by a Hidden Man*, which contained a treatise on dream types and their interpretation. Wang Fu identified ten types of dreams, which include dreams of a spiritual, physiological, psychological, and problem-solving nature:

1. Direct

2. Symbolic

3. "Concentrated" or essential dreams, apparently dreams produced by the dreamer's "concentrated sincerity," as when, to resolve a problem, he "earnestly seeks" a dream

4. Thought dreams—that is, dreams recalling one's [waking?] thoughts

5. Dreams whose meaning varies with the status of the dreamer

6. Dreams produced by the environment

7. Dreams corresponding to the season

8. Antithetical dreams

9. Dreams indicating physical disorders and imbalances

10. Dreams whose meaning varies according to the dreamer's temperament—that is, taking into account the dreamer's personal likes and dislikes.[74]

From a very early date, high officials in the Chinese court were responsible for the interpretation of dreams and for the management of divinatory practices. Perhaps due to this centralization of authority over dreams, many Chinese dream books go beyond the familiar mechanical, fixed-symbol substitution approach to dream images and emphasize certain principles of interpretation. One book, the *Chou Li*, dates from the fourth century B.C.E. and teaches that astrological and geomantic factors must be taken into account in the interpretation of dreams.[75]

A Taoist dream book, the *Lie-Tseu*, provides a coherent theory of dreaming, and looks more specifically into the causes of dreams, teaching that waking wishes, illness, or environmentally caused somatic discomfort can cause dreams.[76] The *Lie-Tseu* teaches that understanding of the causes of a dream will destroy the fear of the dream, if not its effects. This idea, later espoused by Freud, was probably not recognized by many interpreters, but "it was inherent in the Taoist philosophy, which held that mental troubles, whether of the day or the night, could be reduced by knowing their causes."[77] The scholar Michel Soymié notes that this idea certainly did not affect the point of view of the dream interpreters "in the field," and that the *Lie-Tseu* does not seem to leave much of a role for the professional interpreter.[78]

The *Lie-Tseu* dealt with such physiological and psychological causes of dreams not because it held the realms of the physiological and the psychological to be real, but because focusing on dreams inhibited one's ability to see the truth that transcends them. Recognizing the causes of dreams would help the individual to recognize their illusory nature and free him to go beyond them:

The master Lie-tseu says: a mental encounter produces a dream. A bodily contact produces an event. That is why the thoughts of the day and the dreams of the night are what the mind and the body encounter. That is why for the man whose mind is "coagulated" [highly focused?], thoughts and dreams stop of themselves. He does not speak of the realities of the day. Dreams, which are also real things, he does not try to understand. For they are only phases of the coming and going of the metamorphosis. The sages of antiquity, when they were awake, were unmindful of themselves. When they slept, they did not dream. Why should they have spoken emptily?[79]

In Ch'ing times, Wei Hsiang-shu described how dreams reflect the state of the dreamer's mind: "If our mind is at ease, so will be our speech and action. If our speech and action are at ease, so will be our dream soul. And if our dream soul is at ease, so will be our life and our death. If however, one is ill at ease in life and in death, the reason is to be found in one's mind."[80]

Wei Hsiang-shu did not share the common belief that demons and gods visited humans in dreams, but saw the dreamer's mind as the source of such images:

The moment our mind thinks of evil, a demon is present therein to beguile and play upon it, so that during the day it appears in discernible shape and at night in our dreams, and [this demon] won't rest until damage has been done. Hence an evil mind is the demon itself. . . . The moment our mind is righteous, a god is found therein to protect and keep watch over it, and [this god] won't rest until both our parents and our offspring have earned its blessing. Therefore a righteous mind is itself a god.[81]

A method for expelling evil spirits and for counteracting their effects that dates from the eighth century A.D. is still practiced in twentieth-century China. The picture of Zhong Kui, a scholar who lived in the eighth century, is hung in homes on the fifth day of the fifth moon, considered to be the most poisonous day of the year, when all the evil vapors gather together. Legend tells us that because of his extraordinarily ugly physical features, Zhong Kui

was unjustly deprived of his rightful honors in one of the civil service examinations. He committed suicide on the steps of the Imperial Palace. Nevertheless, when Emperor Minghuang (712–756), the same emperor who caused his death, was having a nightmare, Zhong Kui appeared and chased the ghosts away. In gratitude, the emperor restored full honors to Zhong Kui and bestowed on him the title of "Demon-queller"; since then, copies of Zhong Kui's portrait became talismans for the whole country.[82]

The Chinese and the Japanese have a number of gods who eat up bad dreams, and one can find netsuke and other representations of these dream-devouring gods that are worn as talismans against evil spirits and bad dreams. As you can see, the universal desire to deal with bad dreams and uncomfortable feelings by magically banishing them has a long history in superstitious practices. The effort to try to make such dreams disappear through magic or manipulation leads to repression, but not any long-term solutions. Later in this book, you will see how you can learn from bad dreams and thereby heal the conflicts and fears that give birth to them. Wishing away bad dreams is like taking sleeping pills: the more you do it, the more you will have to do it and the less effective your potions will become.

Interpretive Traditions Among the Greeks, Romans, Christians, and Muslims

The Greeks inherited many of their beliefs about dreams from the Egyptians, and many of their rituals and legends followed Egyptian models. However, the Greeks went beyond imitation. The historian Donald Hughes writes that

of all ancient peoples, the Greeks had most to say about dreams. . . .

The Greeks as a nation respected their dreams, believing that they were messages from the gods, that they foretell the future, that they are means of curing illnesses, and that they enable one to speak with the dead and witness events taking place at great distances. These beliefs were also typical of the neighboring ancient civilizations, but the Greeks, more consistently than others, also tried to give a rational account of dreams and a scientific approach to their interpretation.[83]

In Homer's *Odyssey* and *Iliad*, dreams are generally direct messages sent by a god in the form of a ghost or a deity who "stands above the head" of the dreamer and delivers a message.[84] True dreams are said to leave the Palace of Dreams by the Gate of Horn and false dreams by the Gate of Ivory. In the *Odyssey*, Penelope tells Odysseus a symbolic dream that is correctly interpreted by the figure of the eagle in the dream before the dream ends. Homer also refers to dream interpreters who can not only see the future in dreams, but help mortals to understand the actions of the gods.[85]

The use of dreams as a literary device continued to be popular throughout the early history of Greek literature. Pindar, Aeschylus, Euripides, and Plutarch were among the many who in their dramatic, poetic, and biographic works used dreams as predictors of the future and as communications with the gods. Aeschylus, in *Prometheus Bound,* writes that "it was the hero Prometheus who taught human beings the art of interpreting dreams, so that they might discover the intentions of the gods."[86]

Greek historians such as Herodotus and Xenophon recounted dreams as important turning points in military and political history due to the warnings and predictions they provided to important men at crucial and decisive moments. Donald Hughes notes that Thucydides, who never mentioned dreams in his histories, was one of the few skeptics of dreams in ancient times.[87]

Incubation temples dedicated to the cults of Serapis, Trophonius, Amphiaraus, Isis, and Asclepius among others flourished among the Greeks, who, even more than the Egyptians, turned to the gods to heal them through dreams. The cult of the mythical doctor Asclepius, later raised to the status of a god, was the most popular, and the rituals at the approximately 420 Asclepian shrines were the most elaborate.[88]

For example, imagine that you are ill and have journeyed to the Asklepieon at Epidaurus. You have walked on the *via sacra* for five miles from the port into a place of exquisite beauty. The temple buildings, which include a theater and a rotunda, are world famous for their beauty. As you approach the entrance, you read on the stone stelae the inscriptions of the famous cures Asclepius has granted to other pilgrims. Harmless snakes, symbols of the god, move about freely. You enter the sacred precinct, bathe, and perform purification rituals and preliminary sacrifices before going to sleep in a special place in the temple. If Asclepius appears as himself or as a dog or a snake in a dream or vision, you will be cured. You can stay at Epidaurus for as long as it takes to have the necessary dream. Finally Asclepius appears in your dream and touches the sick part of your body and disappears. If the tradition holds true, you awaken healed, pay fees to the priests, and make offerings of thanks.[89] From now on you will have a deep belief in the god of your dream, and this just might help prolong the effects of your cure.

The cult of Asclepius was well established at Epidaurus by the sixth century B.C.E., and by the early fourth century B.C.E. the temple there was a Mecca for healing; its national importance continued into the early third century.[90] Classical historian Robert Rousselle notes that the cures ascribed to Asclepius at Epidaurus were those of maladies related to neurotic and hysterical conditions, which could well be cured in one night: "Despite the scepticism of the moderns, ancient Greek scientists concurred on the efficacy of dreams."[91] Two renowned doctors, Rufus in the first century A.D. and Galen in the second, reported Asclepian cures, and along with Hippocrates they valued highly the importance of the patient's attitude toward life and toward his or her illness.

In the later periods of the cult, it appears that the positive suggestion and anxiety reduction of the incubated dreams were augmented by a team of priests who became physicians and dream interpreters who prescribed treatment.[92] Were the priests trying to treat a broader spectrum of ailments, were they helping a failing god, or were they expanding their influence and power?

According to historian Donald Hughes, the first discussion of dreams from the standpoint of medical science is to be found in a book from the golden age of Greece, the fifth century B.C.E., attributed to Hippocrates and titled *On Dreams*.[93] Hippocrates, the founder of modern medicine, whose famous oath opens with the line "I swear by Apollo the physician, and Aesculapius, and Health, and All-heal . . . ," considered dreams a potent diagnostic tool in ascertaining the patient's state of physical and mental health. The mind, freed from waking tasks and concerns, could better perceive the subtle cues indicating the physical state of the body and express through dream imagery the condition of the body and the mind, and give early warnings of illness.[94] Here we find an explicit description of the image-making function of the mind unaided by a divine force.[95] The Hindus had already described this function, but saw it as a distraction of illusion, whereas Hippocrates valued it for its diagnostic worth. As Hughes points out, Hippocrates clearly recognized the value of dreams in indicating the general state of the psyche and in diagnosing mental disturbances. A number of authors have missed this point, saying that Hippocrates was interested only in physical illness. But as Hughes says, "The underlying assumption here, as in most Hippocratic thought, is that mind and body are interdependent parts of the human totality, and that a physician gains a much improved chance of healing the mind-body organism if the aid of both parts is enlisted."[96]

Hippocrates wrote that some dreams might be sent by the gods and augur the future. But Hughes notes that "this admission is made to preserve the more general and conventional Greek opinion about dreams, and perhaps to save [Hippocrates] the trouble of answering charges of impiety."[97] The common dream interpreters of the day could be employed to discover the meanings of these predictive dreams, but they were incapable of understanding dreams dealing with medical matters (the only kind that interested Hippocrates) since they were not educated in the subject. Hippocrates insisted that the dream interpreter's prescriptions of prayer were inadequate to the task of diagnosis and healing, and said, "Prayer is indeed good, but while calling on the gods a man should himself lend a hand."[98] Although Hippocrates did not see illnesses as caused by the gods, he did appreciate the positive effects of prayer for a dreamer who believed in the healing power of the gods.

Dreams of natural, normal, salutary actions indicate good health, but dreams that contradict the natural order of things or that portray conflict and struggle indicate a disturbance in the body or mind due to some excess or deficiency. Hippocrates usually prescribed changes in diet, emetics, massage, and various exercises, including voice exercises. A dreamer who dreamt of wandering stars would be diagnosed as having a "disturbance of the soul arising from anxiety" and would be instructed to contemplate things that would make him happy and full of good humor.[99] The fact that Hippocrates recognized that mental illness is not caused by the gods or by evil spirits, and that through an understanding of their imagistic metaphors dreams can indicate the state of health or illness of the mind, is very noteworthy. This marks him as the first, and perhaps the only, writer on the subject to have understood these two important points before Freud, who was not to write on the subject until another twenty-four hundred years had passed.

Plato and Aristotle accepted Hippocrates' teachings about the use of dreams as medical diagnostic tools, as did the ancient medical scientists Herophilus of Alexandria and Galen of Pergamon.[100] Galen, a celebrated physician of the second century A.D. and the founder of the science of experimental physiology, owed his choice of a profession to a dream in which Apollo appeared to him twice and ordered him to give himself to the study of medicine from that time forth.[101] He believed in the Hippocratic notion that one could diagnose the mental and physical state of the dreamer through a recognition of the analogies that dream images offer to the basic human humors, but he also clearly believed in the divine influence in certain dreams. He thus synthesized the beliefs in divine and psychophysical causes of dreams. Galen, who of course adhered to the Hippocratic oath, claimed to have been cured himself at an Asclepian temple. According to MacKenzie, modern versions of these temples exist in Greece today. A picture of Saint Luke, said to have been discovered by a series of dreams and believed to have healing powers, hangs in a church at Tenos. The faithful still come to sleep in the church in search of healing.

Greek philosophers were fascinated by dreams and offered many explanations of their causes and functions.[102] The most important philosophers to write about dreams were Plato and his student Aristotle. Plato noted that "even in good men, there is a lawless wild-beast nature, which peers out in sleep."[103] Like many before him, Plato acknowledged that some dreams fulfill repressed wishes, and like the Hindus and the Buddhists he encouraged people to attain a certain state of mind before sleep in order to have dreams of truth and insight. In one of his dialogues, Plato writes:

Certain of the unnecessary pleasures and appetites I conceive to be unlawful; every one appears to have them, but in some persons they are controlled by the laws and by reason, and the better desires prevail over them—either they are wholly banished or they become few and weak; while in the case of others they are stronger, and there are more of them.

Which appetites do you mean?

I mean those which are awake when the reasoning and human and ruling power is asleep; then the wild beast within us, gorged with meat or drink, starts up and having shaken off sleep, goes forth to satisfy his desires; and there is no conceivable folly or crime—not excepting incest or any other unnatural union, or parricide, or the eating of forbidden food—which at such a time, when he has parted company with all shame and sense, a man may not be ready to commit.

Most true, he said.

But when a man's pulse is healthy and temperate, and when before going to sleep he has awakened his rational powers, and fed them on noble thoughts and enquiries, collecting himself in meditation; after having first indulged his appetites neither too much nor too little, but just enough to lay them to sleep, and prevent them and their enjoyments and pains from interfering with the higher principle—which he leaves in the solitude of pure abstraction, free to contemplate and aspire to the knowledge of the unknown, whether in past, present, or future: when again he has allayed the passionate element, if he has a quarrel against anyone—I say, when, after pacifying the two irrational principles, he rouses up the third, which is reason, before he takes his rest, then, as you know, he attains truth most nearly, and is least likely to be the sport of fantastic and lawless visions.[104]

Plato clearly understood that some dreams are the direct expression of repressed instinctual wishes: while reason sleeps, the wild beast in every one of us wakes, and "goes forth to satisfy his desires."[105] Plato saw dreams, whether true or false, as irrational, and in need of interpretation that applied reason in order to understand their prophetic, diagnostic, or revelatory significance.[106] His understanding that one's state of mind preceding sleep deeply affects the nature of that night's dreams may be exaggerated, but it is reminiscent of the Hindu and later Buddhist practices of using meditation to clear the sleeping mind. It is my opinion that those of us who are not aiming at dreamless sleep, nor even at avoiding instructive if unpleasant dreams, would do well to experiment with a presleep period of meditation, of allaying the passionate element, or of immersion in something that fills our minds with beauty and calm pleasure. Comparing such dream nights with those in which we go to sleep right after viewing an upsetting war film, engaging in an argument with a spouse, or harboring resentments toward a friend or enemy would make an interesting experiment.

As noted at the beginning of this chapter, Aristotle reduced dreams to sensory afterimages of perceptions made while waking or by movements of blood in the sensory organs that go on all the time, but of which we are more aware while sleeping. These dream images are to varying degrees distorted by the dreamer's emotions, full stomach, or state of health and/or intoxication.[107] Aristotle flatly denied that God sends dreams to man: "For, in addition to its further unreasonableness, it is absurd to combine the idea that the sender of such [divinatory] dreams should be God with the fact that those to whom he sends them are not the best and wisest, but merely commonplace persons."[108] Apparently, prophetic dreams are most often coincidences.

But, Aristotle reasoned, since even animals dream, then "dreams are natural; since nature is divinely planned, there is a certain divine aspect to dreams, and this could include their being prophecies."[109] Some may seem to predict the future because just as daytime events are the starting points of some dreams, so "it must happen that the movements set up first in sleep should also prove to be starting-points of actions to be performed in the daytime."[110] Without admitting to the existence of clairvoyant dreams, Aristotle does provide explanations of how they might occur based on his theories of "movements" or "waves," which, emanating from events and other people's psyches, may be picked up by the sleeper's sense organs and translated into dreams.

In rejecting much of the superstition that surrounded dreaming in his time, Aristotle seems to have thrown the baby out with the bathwater. In his extreme reductionism, he makes no attempt to discover or to recount the history of the instructive truths dreams might offer of an emotional, problem-solving, or creative nature. Donald Hughes has written an interesting paper about the dreams of Aristotle's most famous student, Alexander the Great, whom he tutored for three years, but who nevertheless continued to believe in dreams as supernatural oracles.[111]

THE ROMAN EMPIRE

The Roman attitudes toward dreaming were largely inherited from those of the Greeks and, with at least one exception, covered much the same ground between extreme skepticism and superstitiousness. The literature of the period is replete with references to dreams. Virgil writes that King Latinus consulted a dream oracle,[112] and Plutarch includes dreams as turning points in his biographies of famous people. Plutarch commented that "unclear or wrong ideas might lead to bad dreams; those who do not know how to value the gods correctly fear the revelations . . . of sleep."[113] Aristotle's writings had not extinguished the exploration of the mental and emotional aspects of dreaming.

In the midst of a highly superstitious civilization addicted to divination of all kinds, we see incubation temples take on the names of local gods, but some retained their Egyptian flavor—such as the Isiacs of imperial Rome, where Isis and Osiris appeared in incubants' dreams. As late as the fifth century, Claudian still recalls these *aegyptia somnia*.[114]

According to MacKenzie, "The emperor Augustus who succeeded Julius Caesar took dreams so seriously that he made a law that anyone who dreamed about the commonwealth must proclaim it in the market place."[115] At that time, it was the fashion that important events, births, and deaths be announced by "prophetic" dreams, which, like the official dreams of other cultures, gave divine honor and authority to those holding temporal power. Three hundred years later, in the first part of the fourth century A.D., Emperor Constantine, who was struggling to achieve his military ambitions, had recently and falsely claimed that the title of emperor was his by hereditary right. He had probably already decided that it would be expedient to proclaim Christianity the official religion of the realm, and therefore announced that he had had a dream instructing him to convert Rome to Christianity.[116] It is worth noting that throughout history, leaders, politicians, and generals have claimed that God in a dream had instructed them to go to war or make other important governmental decisions. A good dose of skepticism regarding such divine inspiration is a healthy response to such stories, which might owe more to self-interest than to God.

A few voices in Rome fought against the common superstitious beliefs. One of Nero's advisers, Petronius, wrote: "It is neither the gods nor divine commandments that send the dreams down from the heavens, . . . but each of us makes them for himself."[117] Titus Lucretius wrote in the first century before Christ: "Men dream about the activities and circumstances which occupy them in waking life . . . repeat in their dreams the acts, emotions, and passions of life."[118] Galen came to Rome in the second century and became physician to Marcus Aurelius and many other eminent people in the city. He taught his more enlightened approach to medicine—and, we may suppose, to dreams—to the most important of Rome's citizens and earned great honor and fame.

But these voices were drowned out by the roar of those who looked to dreams for divination alone. In his essay *On Divination*, Cicero roared back, insisting that "obscure dreams are not at all consistent with the majesty of the gods"[119] and that it is foolish to prophesy with a rare coincidence that occasionally makes one dream come true when most never do at all. He even discounts a dream of his own that he had while in exile. "In it he heard the ex-consul Marius, bearing a token of victory, tell him to be of good cheer. Marius conducted him to his own memorial temple. Later, Cicero heard that the decree for his recall from exile had been enacted in the Temple of Marius."[120] Cicero calls this dream a mere coincidence, saying, "In the time of my banishment Marius was often in my mind as I recalled with what great fortitude and courage he had borne his own heavy misfortunes, and this is the reason why I dreamed about him."[121]

Cicero points to imagination and desire as the cause of dreams: "All things, then, which we desire to be so, can be known to us, for there is nothing of which we cannot think. Therefore, no images steal in upon the sleeper from without; nor indeed are such eternal images flowing about at all: and I never knew anyone who talked nonsense with greater authority."[122] It is too bad that Cicero did not explore *why* the imagination presents particular images in particular dramatic contexts. But he was fighting an important battle against the forces of blind superstition and corrupt dream practitioners. Complaining that several dream interpreters will provide several different interpretations, he cries, "How delusive, then, is this conjectural art of those interpreters! Or do these stories [interpretations] that I have recited . . . prove anything else but the subtlety of men, who, from certain imaginary analogies of things arrive at all sorts of opposite conclusions?"[123] As we shall see later (chapters 4 and 5), it is exactly when contemporary interpreters work from imaginary analogies not derived from the dreamer's world experience that they devise conflicting interpretations of the same dream.

After rejecting the possibility of ever being able to conduct meaningful experiments on the interpretation of dreams, and saying that "dreams are not entitled to any credit or respect whatever," Cicero writes: "Let us reject, therefore, this divination for dreams, as well as all other kinds. For, to speak truly, that superstition has extended itself through all notions, and has oppressed the intellectual energies of all men, and has betrayed them into endless imbecilities."[124]

If only we could rid dream work of the many superstitions that have led to so many imbecilities, we could then get on with the work of meaningful research and practical applications of dreaming.

About two hundred years after Cicero, Artemidorus wrote the most complete and famous dream-interpretation manual to survive from ancient times. *Oneirocritica: The Interpretation of Dreams* in five books summarizes Graeco-Roman dream theory from the late fifth century B.C.E. to about 140 A.D. Artemidorus was a Greek who traveled widely during the height of the Roman Empire. Having devoted his life to the study and interpretation of dreams, Artemidorus wrote his dream books based on a wide reading of past masters, and on his extensive experience. He leaves undecided the question of divine delivery of dreams: "For the god—or whatever it is that causes a person to dream—presents to the dreamer's mind, which is, by its very nature, prophetic, dreams that correspond to future events."[125] In criticizing the lack of common sense and the sheer nonsense of incubated dreams that are reported to reveal a god's medical prescription, Artemidorus ridicules such prescriptions as the "brain of a monster" or the "broth of sea-nymphs." He writes that such dreams must have been invented in waking states since he has never seen such dreams in his practice. He adds, "I believe that the gods themselves, to whom they attribute this nonsense, would be angry, as one might expect, with those who fabricate these stories, since they make the gods appear tasteless, malicious, and stupid."[126]

Artemidorus was interested only in dreams that predicted the future. He was not, as some modern analysts have suggested, interested in, and perhaps hardly aware of, what dreams have to say about the personality and internal conflicts of the dreamer.[127] The author of *Oneirocritica* clearly defines two types of dreams and his interest in them:

A dream that has no meaning and predicts nothing, one that is active only while one sleeps and that has arisen from an irrational desire, an extraordinary fear, or from a surfeit or lack of food is called an *enhypnion*. But a dream that operates after sleep and that comes true either for good or for bad is called an *oneiros*. . . .

You must bear in mind, moreover, that men who live an upright, moral life do not have meaningless dreams *(enhypnia)* or any other irrational fantasies but rather dreams that are by all means meaningful *(oneiroi)* and which generally fall into the theorematic [direct, almost literal predictive dreams that come true almost immediately] category. For their minds are not muddled by fears or by expectations but, indeed, they control the desires of their bodies. In short, *enhypnia* and other irrational fantasies do not appear to a serious man.[128]

Though Artemidorus recognized that some dreams serve the functions of wish or fear fulfillment, or of reflecting the physical condition of the dreamer, and that they can reflect the level of uprightness of a dreamer's life, he considered these dreams to be without interest, and meaningless. Like most of the people of his time, and like most of the people since the beginning of civilization, Artemidorus focused his attention and his method of interpretation on discovering the future through dreams that were in the form of predictive allegories. The closest he came to a personality theory (which would not be developed until many centuries after his death) was to describe certain social dynamics. Following the basic principle that "things that always and inevitably follow certain things in real life must necessarily follow one another in dreams also," Artemidorus cites the case of a painter who dreamt that he had intercourse with his stepmother. It was easy to predict the outcome: the dreamer would antagonize his father, "for jealousy and enmity follow every act of adultery."[129]

Artemidorus, like Galen, and unlike most of his fellow interpreters, was greatly influenced by the empiricist theory of medical knowledge. He studied tradition *(historia)* in his wide reading and travels; he depended greatly on his extensive experience *(peira* or *teresis)*, which allowed him to reject certain earlier pronouncements; and he worked by a method of analogy *(metabasis tou homoiou)*.[130] It is his emphasis on recognizing the metaphoric nature of dream images and of entire dreams, and his willingness to adapt meanings to a dreamer's circumstances, that distinguish Artemidorus from most dream interpreters active long before and after him. Here, for example, are his interpretations for a dream of detention and imprisonment:

> Being forcibly detained and guarded by someone foretells hindrances in affairs, delays, the postponement of appointments, and the intensification of one's illnesses. But it means salvation for those who are in extreme danger. For while we call life a keeper, and overseer, and a preserver of being, the opposite of these, dissolution and destruction, is death. Entering a prison or a barracoon willingly or being thrown in forcibly by other men foretells a serious illness or great pain. Public executioners and jailers are symbols of delay and pain. They indicate fetters to criminals and they also signify that secrets will be revealed. For they come into contact with those who have been apprehended and caught red-handed.[131]

Artemidorus insisted that an interpreter learn the local customs and beliefs of the dreamer as well as his or her identity, occupation, birth, financial status, state of health, and age in order that the interpreter be able to draw relevant analogies to the images and actions in the dream.[132] Seventeen hundred years later, Freud was to comment that his method, like that of Artemidorus, was based on observation and experience but differed from this ancient method in one essential respect: "It imposes the task of interpretation upon the dreamer himself. It is not concerned with what occurs to the *interpreter* in connection with a particular element of the dream, but with what occurs to the *dreamer*."[133] Artemidorus was using his own associations based on his studies of local customs and his wide reading in many fields including medicine—associations that were not personal, but cultural and mythological. This would have been a big problem had he been trying to discover the psychological meaning of dreams. But since he was interested only in the predictive, he did not notice that his assumptions about a particular dream image may often have had little to do with the dreamer's personal perception of its nature.

It should be pointed out that Artemidorus's interest in the dreamer's status, profession, state of health, economic circumstances, social customs and beliefs, and mood before sleep was aimed at helping the interpreter formulate an analogy or metaphoric bridge between the dream images and a prediction of the future. It was not aimed at assessing the developmental or personality characteristics of the dreamer, nor at eliciting anything like personal associations. Nor was it aimed at helping the dreamer to better understand his or her personal dynamics. A number of writers have succumbed to the temptation to read modern conceptions of personality assessment and exploration into Artemidorus's work, and into the Talmudic instructions to investigate some of the characteristics and circumstances of the dreamer. Such modern ideas simply did not concern these people, who looked to dreams mainly for divine guidance. The fact that these traditions, later to include that of Islam, recognized that an interpretation must take into account the situation of the dreamer rather than give only one fixed interpretation of a given dream was an important contribution to the development of interpretive method.

Artemidorus, unlike most authors of dream books, did not limit himself to interpreting single images out of the context of the dream: "In this way, then, one should interpret all complicated dreams, collecting and combining each of the main points into a complete whole. In judging a dream, therefore, one must imitate the diviners. For they know how each individual sign fits into the whole and base their judgments as much on the total sum of the signs as on each individual sign."[134] Artemidorus is, to my knowledge, the first to encourage, however slightly, a cooperative effort between dreamer and interpreter. Up to this time, the dreamer would be asked for little more than his name, rank, and serial number, if that, and the interpreter would depend upon his magic, his associations, his intuition based on traditional lore, and his perception of the dreamer's circumstances. Artemidorus suggests that when unsure of the proper interpretation, the interpreter should offer two plausible ones and let the dreamer decide. Before Artemidorus, we have no written records of any interpreter who was willing to enlist the opinion and aid of the dreamer. And we shall have to wait until 1900, for Freud, before we see a significantly greater appreciation for the information that the dreamer can provide.

Artemidorus did, however, seem to have a richer appreciation for metaphor than did Freud. Whereas Freud tended to relate all dream imagery to a rather narrow group of meanings contained in his psychosexual theory, Artemidorus was more heedful of the modifying effect on meaning exerted by the context of the dream and the context of the dreamer's life. Take for example Artemidorus's treatment of dreams in which the male dreamer has sex with his mother:

> The case of one's mother is both complex and manifold and admits of many different interpretations—a thing not all dream interpreters have realized. The fact is that the mere act of intercourse by itself is not enough to show what is portended. Rather, the manner of the embraces and the various positions of the bodies indicate different outcomes.
>
> First, then, we will discuss face-to-face intercourse between a dreamer and his living mother, since a mother who is alive does not have the same meaning as a mother who is dead. Therefore, if anyone possesses his mother through face-to-face intercourse, which some also call the "natural" method, if she is still alive and his father is in good health, it means that he and his father will become enemies because of the jealousy that generally arises between rivals [which would be greater in their case]. But if his father is sick, he will die, since the dreamer will take care of his mother both as a son and as a husband.
>
> But it is lucky for every craftsman and laborer. For we ordinarily call a person's trade his "mother." And what else would having intercourse with her mean if not to be occupied with and earn one's living from one's art?
>
> It is also lucky for every demagogue and public figure. For a mother signifies one's native country. And just as a man who follows the precepts of Aphrodite when he makes love completely governs the body of his obedient and willing partner, the dreamer will control all the affairs of the city.

And if the dreamer is estranged from his mother, they will become friends again because of the sexual intercourse. For sexual intercourse is also called "friendship." ... But frequently this dream has indicated that people who live apart will be brought together into the same place and will live together. It also signifies, therefore, that a son will return from a foreign country to his own land, if his mother lives there. If she does not, the dream signifies that he will journey to wherever she lives. If the dreamer is a poor man who is lacking the necessities of life but one whose mother is rich, he will receive from her whatever he wishes or she will die shortly afterwards and leave him as her heir and, in this way, he will take pleasure in his mother. ...

But the meaning will not be the same in the case of a sick man, if his mother is dead. For then the dreamer will himself die very soon afterwards, since the anatomical structure of a corpse is broken down into the material from which it has been formed and composed. And, since bodies are generally made from earth, they are changed into their proper substance. Furthermore, we speak of "Mother Earth," and what else would intercourse with a dead mother signify to a sick man if not that he will have intercourse with the earth?

But for a man who is involved in a lawsuit over land rights, for a man who wants to purchase land, and for a man who would like to farm land, it is good to have intercourse with one's dead mother. Some people say that it indicates bad luck only for farmers. For they will cast their seeds down into, as it were, dead land. That is, it will bear no fruit. In my opinion, this does not seem to be the case at all unless, of course, the person dreams that he repents or is distressed by the intercourse. [Artemidorus continues with many more variations on this theme and provides as many more interpretations.][135]

Once you accept that Artemidorus turns all his interpretations into predictions of future events, it is easier to appreciate his finely tuned valuation of metaphor as it is expressed in the specific details and the general context of the dream and the dreamer's life. In the example of the dream of sexual intercourse with one's mother, Artemidorus demonstrates how he takes into account the dreamer's occupation, location, and economic, social, and financial status, as well as the dreamer's waking relationship to the dream mother, before announcing his metaphoric interpretation. He even considers the dreamer's emotional response to the dream action, noting that if the dreamer, while dreaming, is distressed by the intercourse, the meaning will be different than if he is not distressed by it. This is a very important recognition of the fact that *the dreamer's feelings and judgments about the dream action while dreaming are vital indications regarding the meaning of the dream.* This point has been insufficiently noted by many contemporary interpreters.

In *Oneirocritica* there is a fair amount of superstition related to a method of anagrammatical transposition in dream interpretation, and this has offended many a modern reader. But listen to what Artemidorus says about this in a latter part of the book, meant for his son's eyes only:

> As for anagrammatical transposition, something perfectly ridiculous has happened in regard to Aristander, who was the best dream interpreter, and some other early writers. For in their introductions, they define anagrammatical transposition, but it appears that they have made absolutely no use of the principle anywhere, either by transposing syllables or by omitting or adding letters. I have already mentioned anagrammatical transposition at the beginning of this treatise and now I advise you to use the principle whenever you are interpreting dreams for someone else and wish to appear more qualified than some other person. But whenever you are interpreting dreams for your own benefit, you should not use it at all, since you will be misled.[136]

Artemidorus encouraged his son to use his intuition, but always to provide some reason for his interpretation, even if he had to pull one out of the hat of his general knowledge and learning: "You must make an attempt to investigate the causes of all things and to provide a reason and some plausible arguments for each thing. For even though you are saying something that is perfectly true, if you give only a bare, simple explanation, you will appear to be less experienced."[137] Here we can see that antiquity's premier dream scholar was also well schooled in the politics of the transmission of knowledge.

Artemidorus's, and perhaps imperial Rome's, greatest contribution to the interpretation of dreams is explicitly stated in the *Oneirocritica:* not only should dream images be looked at metaphorically, they should also be considered in the context of the dramatic structure of the *entire dream;* the metaphorical interpretation is not fixed but *must be modified to fit the circumstances of the dreamer.*

This contribution, however, seems to have been little appreciated by a reading audience whose main interest was in finding in this book a simple formula for predicting the future through dreams. And who constituted this reading audience? Many people through many centuries. The historian S. R. F. Price describes the availability and influence of *Oneirocritica* as follows:

> Our earliest extant manuscript of Artemidorus dates from the eleventh century, and interest in him was sufficient for his language to be "corrected" to a purer standard. Along with the Latin translation of Achmet, Artemidorus was the main (but unacknowledged) source for a Latin dream book composed in Constantinople in 1165. This Latin text, of which five manuscripts survive, may have helped to transmit Artemidorus' ideas to the Latin-speaking world. Artemidorus was also translated into Arabic in the ninth or tenth century, as a practical guide to dream interpretation, and had a considerable influence on Arabic oneiromancy.
>
> The development of printing allowed Artemidorus to reach a wider audience: in the sixteenth century there appeared translations into Latin, Italian, French, English, and German. (The popularity of the English translation was such that it reached a twenty-fourth edition by 1740.) Artemidorus was also cited in new dream books. For example, both sixteenth- and seventeenth-century German dream books and the *Universal Dream Dictionary*, first published in America in 1795, treat him as a major authority.[138]

The popularity of *Oneirocritica* and of less sophisticated dream books that followed much later suggests that predictive dream interpretation, although often officially scorned by the major institutions of many societies, was consistently practiced by members of all levels of these societies. Indeed, this is true even today among many all over the world who hope that their dreams can tell them their future and that such dreams can be interpreted by fixed, formulaic, symbolic substitution.

Dreams in the Christian Church

Inheritors of the dream traditions of the Old Testament, the early Christians continued the Jewish beliefs in dreams as sources of inspiration, insight, and prophecy from God. The New Testament describes the four dreams of Joseph, the dream the three wise men shared warning them not to return to Herod after locating Jesus, the dream of Pilate's wife, and the dreams of the apostle Paul, which told him to change the direction of his missionary plans from Asia to Macedonia and the West.[139]

Virtually all of the major writers and church fathers in the first three centuries after Christ believed in the revelatory power of dreams, and the stories of the martyrs' and saints' lives are punctuated with dreams that foretold the future and provided meaningful encounters with God or his angels. Dreams were seen to portray real events, or at least to predict them. Even dreams that were seen to be sent by demons could predict the future correctly in order to tempt the dreamer into greater contact with the devil.

"Now, who is such a stranger to human experience as not some-times to have perceived some truth in dreams?" asks the influential church father Tertullian in the early third century.[140] He was referring to famous historical examples of predictive dreams. Tertullian, whose writings later greatly influenced Cyprian and Augustine, and through them became a major foundation of Christian theology,[141] made a simple but highly influential classification of dreams, which distinguished clearly dreams emanating from demons from those emanating from God, but which left very vague two categories of dreams: those arising from the soul, and those from the ecstatic state that accompanies sleep. Of the first two and most important categories he writes:

We declare, then, that dreams are inflicted on us mainly by demons, although they sometimes turn out true and favorable to us. When, however, with the deliberate aim after evil, of which we have just spoken, they assume a flattering and captivating style, they show themselves proportionately vain, and deceitful, and obscure, and wanton, and impure. And no wonder that the images partake of the character of the realities. But from God—who has promised, indeed, "to pour out the grace of the Holy Spirit upon all flesh, and has ordained that His servants and His handmaids should see visions as well as utter prophecies"—must all those visions be regarded as emanating, which may be compared to the actual grace of God, as being honest, holy, prophetic, inspired, instructive, inviting to virtue, the bountiful nature of which causes them to overflow even to the profane, since God, with grand impartiality, "sends His showers and sunshine on the just and on the unjust." It was indeed by an inspiration from God that Nebuchadnezzar dreamt his dreams; and almost the greater part of mankind get their knowledge of God from dreams. Thus it is that, as the mercy of God super-abounds to the heathen, so the temptation of the evil one encounters the saints, from whom he never withdraws his malignant efforts to steal over them as best he may in their very sleep, if unable to assault them when they are awake.[142]

This telling passage describes the major concerns of the Christian church regarding dreams. Yes, God speaks to men and women through dreams, but one must be ever vigilant in order not to fall prey to dreams from the evil one.

Whereas Plato saw sexual dreams as a distraction from and an impediment to clear dreams of truth, and Artemidorus dealt with sexual dreams as good or bad portents in a very matter-of-fact way, the Church was now redefining such dreams as the devil's doing. As Plato and others noted, passions denied in waking would always surface in dreams. The Church's condemnation of most human passions as sinful assured an inexhaustible crop of dreams that would be labeled demonic by many Christians well into the twentieth century. Tertullian's assurance that "we shall no more be condemned for visionary acts of sin [in dreams], than we shall be crowned for imaginary martyrdom,"[143] and John Chrysostom's and others' later pronouncements that we are not morally responsible for dream thoughts and deeds, were unevenly absorbed into the ruling opinions about dreams that reigned with Church authorities in different periods.

One need only consult the writings of Justin Martyr, Irenaeus, Clement of Alexandria, Origen, Athanasius, Augustine, Saint John Chrysostom, Anthony, Basil the Great, Gregory of Nazianzen, Gregory of Nyssa, Ambrose, and Gregory the Great to see how firmly established in the early church was the belief that God speaks with mortals in dreams: "Cyprian, bishop of Carthage in 250 A.D., one of the founders of the Latin Church, asserted that the very councils of the Church were guided by God through dreams and 'many and manifest visions.'"[144]

In the fifth century, Synesius of Cyrene wrote a book that Morton Kelsey describes as representing the "culmination of early Christian thinking on the subject."[145] As late as the fourteenth century, this book of the bishop of Ptolemaïs in Egypt was held in high esteem by the Eastern Church. Synesius taught that dreams reveal bodily illness and cures. He believed that God teaches man in dreams, that God reveals his truth and the future in dreams, that dreams turn the soul toward God and develop a deeper love for him, and that dreams give the great and indispensable gift of hope to humankind.[146]

Of his own experiences with dreams, Synesius wrote:

I have not yet stated my own indebtedness to dreams. And yet it is to the minds given to Philosophy that dreams especially come, to enlighten them in their difficulties and researches, so as to bring them during sleep the solutions which escape them when awake. We seem in sleeping at one time to apprehend, at another to find, through our own reflection. As for me, how often dreams have come to my assistance in the composition of my writings! Often have they aided me to put my ideas in order and my style in harmony with my ideas; they have made me expunge certain expressions, and choose others. . . . At other times, in the hunting season, I invented, after a dream, traps to catch the swiftest animals and the most skillful in hiding. If, discouraged from too long waiting, I was preparing to return to my home, dreams would give me courage, by announcing to me, for such or such a day, better result: I then patiently watched some nights more; many animals would fall in my nets or under my arrows. . . . But then again divination has been singularly useful to me: it has preserved me from ambushes that certain magicians laid for me, revealed their sorceries and saved me from all danger.

That natural necessity [to sleep] becomes a source of enjoyment and we do not sleep merely to live, but to learn to live well. . . .

Then let us all deliver ourselves to the interpretation of dreams, men and women, young and old, rich and poor, private citizens and magistrates, inhabitants of the town and of the county, artisans and orators. There is not any privileged, neither by sex, neither by age, nor fortune or profession. Sleep offers itself to all.[147]

Synesius suggests that the "essential nature [of dreams] is personal, and [that] they must be understood by the dreamer in terms of his own life."[148] He encourages anyone who would understand his dreams to keep a dream journal and to constantly check dreams with experience.[149] His method of interpretation is apparently that of finding metaphors and analogies. Donald Hughes says, "His principle seems to be that like follows like, that is, that a dream foretells similar events in the waking world."[150] In noting the connection between myths and dreams, Synesius expressed the belief that myths are based on dreams, and that a familiarity with mythology would help in the understanding of dreams.[151] In this, Synesius, whose work was of almost no influence in the West, foreshadowed by fifteen hundred years Carl Jung's use of myths to explain dreams.

A contemporary of Synesius and also a bishop in Roman Africa, Augustine (A.D. 354–430) was to have a profound effect on the development of the Western Church. Considered the greatest thinker of antiquity, Augustine developed a religious philosophy of predestination that was to reappear in a modified form in Thomas Aquinas and virtually unchanged in the reform of Calvin. Augustine had a mystical experience of God as the "Changeless Light," which he believed to be at once immanent and transcendent, and the sole source of man's ability to perceive or do good. Humankind—hopelessly sinful, corrupt, prey to sexual lusts—was entirely dependent on God's grace, not human effort, to find truth.[152]

Augustine denied Plato's idea that the soul in sleep was able learn the future through its own natural powers and insisted that on its own, the soul contemplates in sleep only *phantasmata,* or memories of bodily sensation constructed by the lowly imagination without correspondence to any reality.[153] It was in visions, initiated by God—not the body, memory, or imagination of the sleeper—and which could occur in waking or in sleep, that God would make himself known to man. Augustine believed that God and his angels, as well as demons, send messages of truth and delusion to people in dreams.

In his *Confessions* Augustine beautifully describes a dream that came to his Christian mother, in which she was reassured of her son's eventual conversion. But Augustine's preoccupation with his own sexual passions led him to emphasize the diabolical dangers of dreams. Augustine's analysis of memory, to which he said dreams give access, was a sophisticated one that anticipates later concepts of the unconscious and in another intellectual climate might have led him to different conclusions about dreams.[154] But Augustine's dark view of humankind, cursed with the original sexual sin of Adam and Eve, together with the political/religious climate of the time, led Aquinas to counter the earlier Church's emphasis on personal freedom and self-control with a picture of humans as utterly incapable of good on their own account. The political/religious complex of ruling powers, then in a struggle to the death with invading barbarians and competing heretics, seized upon Augustine's writings to justify greatly increasing institutional control.[155]

It was in the early twelfth century with the rediscovery of Aristotle's science and Greek medicine, and the translation of the writings of the Arab physician and philosopher Avecenna, that "the physiology of the 'new science' stimulated a shift in the interests of dream theorists. No longer are the modes of divine communication of primary concern, but the mechanism of sleep and image presentation."[156]

Writers such as William of Conches appropriated these "new" scientific ideas and put forward creative physiological explanations of both the insignificant dreams brought about by bodily and psychological causes, and the way certain physiological factors can allow the soul to receive revelations from God.[157]

In the thirteenth century, the eclecticism of the new dream theories was extended to include physiological explanations of prognostication in dreams. As dream theory reentered the secular domain, the writings of Aristotle, Galen, and Avecenna provided source material for theories in which dreaming was classified as one of the powers of the soul.[158]

The Dream in Islam

The religion of Islam was begun by Muhammad in the seventh century. This movement soon shook the Sassanid Empire in Persia and in 1453 overran the Byzantine Empire and created a new civilization based on the religious beliefs and rules for social organization described in the Koran. Islamic Arabs ruled Moorish Spain from the eighth to the eleventh centuries and created a center of learning and culture in that country that greatly enriched medieval European culture. Islam is practiced today by about one-seventh of the world's population.[159]

Toufy Fahd, the author of one of the most authoritative works on the interpretation of dreams in Islam,[160] writes that

> oneirocritic literature represents for Islam the most authentic cultural heritage of its Semitic past. In it, we can find a great many ideas, symbols, images . . . , all reproducing the prototypes of ancient thought. . . .
>
> Enriched by a Greek element working within like ferment, Arab-Muslim oneirocriticism reached heights no other civilization seems to have known.[161]

Dreams as a means of divination and spiritual communication were of considerable importance even in pre-Islamic Arab antiquity. Many Islamic dream traditions can be traced back to similar ones followed in the fifth and even fourth centuries A.D.[162] According to one tradition, Muhammad's initial revelation and his recognition of his mission in life came in a dream.[163] The first portion of the Koran was made known to him in a dream.[164] In Muhammad's time, the seventh century, "dreams, poetry, and religious inspiration were already linked in the popular consciousness of ancient Arabia, and this trinity was apt to be judged rather negatively. Doubting Meccans, therefore, rejected the results of Muhammad's ecstasies as 'a tangle of dreams, trickery, words of a poet' (Koran 21.5)."[165]

But Muhammad's appeal to a very deeply rooted popular belief in the ability of dreams to provide divine revelation was tremendously successful. In the Koran, which is believed to contain the revealed word of God, the objective reality and the prophetic nature of dreams are guaranteed by God himself. G. E. von Grunebaum, a professor of Near Eastern history, provides us with a translation of the writings of a fourteenth-century Islamic scholar, Nabulusi. These writings on dreams give us a flavor of Islamic writings on the matter while at the same time illustrating similarities to the writings of other cultures.

"Thus your Lord will prefer you and teach you the interpretation of events,"[166] meaning the science of dreams, the prime science since the beginning of the world, which the prophets and messengers did not cease to study and act upon. . . . To invalidate the significance of dreams, some unbelievers have stated that what a man sees in his sleep is dictated by the dominant of the four humors. . . .

. . . But this constitutes only one type of dream, to which the whole range of dreams cannot be limited. For we know for certain that while the humors do dictate some dreams, some dreams are sent by the devil and some originate in the self. The latter, the truest of the three, are "confused [or: incoherent] dreams" . . . , so-called because they are mixed. . . .

It has been said that dreams are of three kinds: dreams of glad tidings from God; they are those good dreams cited in the tradition; dreams of warning from the devil; and dreams that originate in the self. Dreams of warning from the devil are false and have no interpretation [or: significance]. . . . As examples of dreams that originate in the aspirations of the self, a person sees himself with one whom he loves; or, sees something of which he is afraid, or, being hungry, sees himself eating; being replete, sees himself vomit; sleeping in the sun, sees himself burning in fire; there being pain in his members, sees himself tortured.

False dreams are divided into seven types: (1) those that originate in the self, in desire, ambition, and confusion; (2) [sexual] dreams that necessitate ablution and have no interpretation; (3) warnings from the devil—threats and nightmares—which do no damage; (4) dreams that are shown by sorcerers, both *jinni* [spirits] and human, and are just as much a burden upon dreamers as those sent by the devil; (5) falsity shown by Satan, not counted among dreams; (6) dreams shown by the humors when they are at variance and turbid; (7) "reversion," that is, when a dreamer sees himself in the present as if he were twenty years younger.[167]

Islamic dream tradition was influenced by the Jewish, Greek, and ancient Near Eastern dream beliefs and practices. Islam taught that dreams and waking visions were man's main channel to the divine, and that dreams can provide theological enlightenment and even elucidate theological doctrine.[168] The Muslims also taught that one needs to learn to distinguish true from false prophetic dreams, and divine from diabolic ones. Like the Christians, they believed that demonic forces would present "revelations" in an effort to lead mankind astray.[169] Dreams were interpreted best by good Muslims, and care was given to seeing that heresy was not promoted in any interpretation.[170]

Breaking Free of Tradition and the Birth of Contemporary Dream Interpretation

In the sixteenth century, dreams were not of serious concern to most Europeans, but changes occurred in society that would foster new developments in the study of dreams. Among religious leaders, Calvin, who clarified and organized Protestant doctrine, upheld the belief that some dreams are sent by God and some by the devil. He reminded his readers that dreams arise from different causes including our daily thoughts and that it would be ridiculous to think all dreams come from God. Calvin held that even God-sent dreams come in obscure, difficult-to-understand language, and Calvin offered no assistance in their interpretation.[171] To my knowledge, no new major movement in the understanding of dreams is to be found in the rest of the history of Christianity, Judaism, Islam, Hinduism, or Buddhism.

From the middle of the thirteenth century through the seventeenth, a series of devastating plagues swept through Byzantium, North Africa, Europe, and England, decimating the populations and upsetting the religious, economic, and social status quo. Formerly accepted authorities began to lose their hold over European populations. As labor became scarce, serfs began to leave their masters for those who would offer higher pay. The Christian Church, which continued to blame the plague on sin, was unable to save anyone, and even the most repentant flagellants died. The Church was seen to be corrupt by many who saw priests desert their flocks and run to the country to escape the personal danger of contagion. The Church was powerless to save the people, many of whom turned to folk beliefs in magic potions, witch burning, and other superstitious practices.

Many physicians and scientists questioned the authority of Aristotle and Hippocrates, who taught that illnesses proceeded from an imbalance of the humors in the body. Physicians coping with the plague developed better skills of observation and noted the many failures at finding an effective treatment based on classical teachings. Classical explanations of the world, not just of the body, were increasingly doubted and disqualified, thus opening the way for new theories based upon careful observation.

From this period on, if we want to investigate new attitudes toward dreams we must look to scientists, writers, philosophers, psychiatrists, and psychologists. It was during the Renaissance (between the fourteenth and early sixteenth centuries) that writers like William Shakespeare explored and portrayed the dynamics of the behavior and personality of individuals, and this growing awareness of human personality reflected in the arts laid the groundwork for future psychodynamic explorations of the dream. But the developing sciences were moving in another direction, one that would delay the development of the psychological study of dreams.

The new worldview that began to form in response to Francis Bacon's empiricist ideas is described by Fritjof Capra:

The terms in which Bacon advocated his new empirical method of investigation were not only passionate but often outright vicious. Nature, in his view, had to be "hounded in her wanderings," "bound into service," and made a "slave." She was to be "put in constraint," and the aim of the scientist was to "torture nature's secrets from her." Much of this violent imagery seems to have been inspired by the witch trials that were held frequently in Bacon's time. As attorney general for King James I, Bacon was intimately familiar with such prosecutions, and because nature was commonly seen as female, it is not surprising that he should carry over the metaphors used in the courtroom into his scientific writings. Indeed, his view of nature as a female whose secrets have to be tortured from her with the help of mechanical devices is strongly suggestive of the widespread torture of women in the witch trials of the early seventeenth century. Bacon's work thus represents an outstanding example of the influence of patriarchal attitudes on scientific thought.

The ancient concept of the earth as nurturing mother was radically transformed in Bacon's writings, and it disappeared completely as the Scientific Revolution proceeded to replace the organic view of nature with the metaphor of the world as a machine. This shift, which was to become of overwhelming importance for the further development of Western civilization, was initiated and completed . . . by Descartes and Newton.[172]

Medieval chivalry and the adoration of the Virgin Mary had momentarily, if largely symbolically, raised the status of women, but the witch hunts and the new truth of science, which identified itself with "male" rationalism, put females, especially females interested in dreams, in an awkward position. The interpretation of dreams fared even worse than did women in this period. Dreams had long been identified in the West with the irrational, and European civilization was trying to grow its way out of the stagnating traditions and superstitions of the past. Irrationality was the sickness, and science the antidote. Belief in dreams as a channel to God faded almost to the point of extinction, and what was left was a broad, popular belief in the demonic powers of dreams, and in their power to predict the future. These beliefs continued to be fueled by the brisk sales of dream dictionaries derived from simplistic, impoverished versions of Artemidorus. Most educated people came to identify dreams with superstition. As time went by, both devils and superstition lost their grip on the opinion setters of the day, and the nonoracular exploration of dreams was of interest only to writers and a few philosophers.

Cartesian philosophy and Newtonian science liberated society from the tyranny of the authority of tradition, but at the high cost of a growing denial of the validity and importance of feelings and subjective experience in attaining knowledge and processing it. A few famous people, like the sixteenth-century artist Benvenuto Cellini, still recounted religious dreams that changed their lives. In

Cellini's case, an angel who appeared to him while he was suffering in prison convinced him that he should not have contempt for God's handiwork and spoil it by killing himself.[173] René Descartes wrote an essay describing how three dreams he had one night in 1619 revealed to him the basis of a new philosophy and way of knowing truth that led eventually to the scientific method.[174] His dream, like Cellini's, came in the form of a divine revelation, but the effects of Descartes's dream revelation would profoundly affect the future of Western thought. It would be another three centuries before a new intellectual movement, Romanticism, would offer a serious challenge to Cartesian denials of the importance of emotional life in perceiving various aspects of reality.

Philosophers like Blaise Pascal (1623–1662) brought up the question not of the agency or the cause of the dream, but rather of the nature of the experience. He commented that "the heart has its reasons that reason does not know," and posed once again Chuang Tzu's ancient question, "Am I a man dreaming I was a butterfly, or am I now a butterfly dreaming I am a man?"[175] Gottfried Wilhelm Leibniz (1646–1716) went much further. He held that thought continues in sleep, and that it continues out of our awareness while waking as well as while sleeping. By carefully observing his own marginal states of consciousness, Leibniz noted the operation of an unconscious censor and the solution of problems in sleep and dreams. As the historian Leroy Loemker points out, Leibniz hypothesized that "the conscious aspect of life . . . is but the higher level of a complex spiritual process of responsive perceptions, appetitive acts, and reasonings, most of which are too minute and pass too quickly for our self-observation."[176] Blending God and science, Leibniz the natural scientist and mathematician wrote:

> For not to mention the wonders of dreams in which we invent, without effort but also without will, things which we should have to think a long time to discover when awake, our soul is architectonic also in its voluntary actions and in discovering the sciences according to which God has regulated things (by weight, measure, number, etc.). In its own realm and in the small world in which it is allowed to act, the soul imitates what God performs in the great world.[177]

In the next century, Leibniz's formulation of unconscious thought and reasoning helped to bring the era of rationalism to an end. After the demise of the Romantic movement, Leibniz's ideas were revived and neorationalists and neopositivists were confronted with the idea that if we think unawares, then that unconscious thinking must be out of our rational direction and control.[178] Scientific faith in absolute rationalism would never be the same.

"Leibnitz's [*sic*] [continuity] doctrine was almost universally adopted in Germany, but in other countries, notably in France and Britain, his continuity theory had little success. The neglect of Leibnitz's ideas was most probably due to the great influence of Descartes's identification of the mind with consciousness"[179] and to the influence of Diderot. In England, where Locke's ideas that "all knowledge must come through the senses, and that the only ideas are those formulated in the mind from sensory information," were dominant,[180] physiological explanations of dream phenomena like those of the most influential seventeenth-century philosopher, Thomas Hobbes, were the most popular. Hobbes's somatic theory of dreams explained how sleeping in a draft may cause a dream of being in a blizzard, and how a dream of being consumed by fire could be caused by mustard plaster on the chest.[181]

The Enlightenment

In the early eighteenth century the Enlightenment was born in France, and soon spread to England and Germany. The French philosopher, art critic, and man of letters Denis Diderot (1713–1784) was the chief editor and energetic contributor to the *Encyclopédie,* "the magnificent testament of the age of Enlightenment."[182] Diderot and his team of writers, scientists, and philosophers planned the *Encyclopédie* as a tool to further human knowledge and to further depotentiate reactionary forces in the church and state. "The *Encyclopédie* was to bring out the essential principles and applications of every art and science. The underlying philosophy was rationalism and faith in the progress of the human mind."[183] In his other writings, Diderot developed the ideas of Descartes and heralded a new approach to science; he "developed his materialist philosophy, foreshadowing the evolutionary doctrine and evolving the first modern theory of the cellular structure of matter."[184] In 1749, Diderot suggested that the blind be taught to read through the sense of touch and, in the same essay, "[presented] the first step in his evolutionary theory of survival by superior adaptation."[185] But Diderot, like many a

European of the time, was not just a rationalist. As a playwright, art critic, and essayist he showed a deep fascination for human personality, and for the meaning and message of artistic expression.

Diderot affirmed the heuristic value of dreams, contradicting the prevailing belief that dreams can contain only transformed waking thoughts and memories. He treated the dream as a magic mirror that revealed connections and meanings not visible to the waking mind. Because in dreaming one has access to experience that is more intense than in waking, Diderot saw in dreams a pathway to the sublime. He believed that the head ruled the waking state, and that physical organs ruled the dream state. Yet Diderot the artist did not fail to appreciate some of what the passions could offer to waking reason.[186]

François Marie Arouet, also known as Voltaire (1694–1778), was a contributor to the *Encyclopédie* and a highly influential man of letters whose works energetically attacked "persecuting and privileged orthodoxy" and fueled the French Revolution. His plays, poems, tales, histories, criticism, and miscellaneous writings had enormous impact upon his own time, the Enlightenment. Regarding dreaming, Voltaire noted that although one in one hundred dreams seems to come true when it pictures a common event like death, most fail to come true. He laments, "How constructed are we for the reception of error! Day and night unite to deceive us!"[187] Believing that "our thoughts proceed not from ourselves" in waking or in sleeping, but from nature, Voltaire writes:

> The laborer who has waked without chagrin, and fed without excess, sleeps sound and tranquil, and dreams disturb him not. . . . Every dream of a forcible nature is produced by some excess, either in the passions of the soul, or the nourishment of the body; it seems as if nature intended to punish us for them, by suggesting ideas, and making us think in spite of ourselves.[188]

Yet Voltaire allowed that the souls of the dead can appear in the dreams of the living, and considers it common and natural for one to dream at night of the things that concern the dreamer in the daytime. He goes so far as to write:

> I have known advocates who have pleaded in dreams, mathematicians who have sought to solve problems; and poets who have composed verses. I have made some myself, which are very passable. It is therefore incontestable that constructive ideas

occur in sleep, as well as when we are awake, which ideas as certainly come in spite of us. We think while sleeping, as we move in our beds, without our will having anything to do either in the motive or the thought.[189]

Voltaire also noted that "it is most certain, however, . . . that uneasy and horrible dreams denote pain either of body or mind; a body overcharged with ailment; or a mind occupied with melancholy ideas when awake."[190] Like a number of writers, artists, and philosophers who embraced the Enlightenment, Voltaire did not subscribe to the belief that in dreams reason always sleeps and useless irrationality reigns.

In the mid 1700s the influential English physician David Hartley wrote *Observations on Man,* in which he described his view on dreams, which was to dominate "most English writing on the subject for over a hundred years."[191] Perfectly expressing the dominant Enlightenment attitude toward dreams, which persists in some circles to the present day, Hartley wrote:

> Dreams are nothing but the imaginations, fancies, or reveries of a sleeping man, and . . . are deducible from three causes, *viz.:* First, the impressions and ideas lately received, and particularly those of the preceding day. Secondly, the state of the body, particularly of the stomach and the brain. And thirdly, association. . . . A person may form a judgment of the state of his bodily health, and of his temperance, by the general pleasantness or unpleasantness of his dreams. There are also many hints relating to the strength of our passions deducible from them.[192]

Thus Hartley engages in the typically English interest in explaining the *cause* of dreams. He ventures to explain the *role* dreams play in the human mind only so far to say:

> The wildness of our dreams seems to be of singular use to us by interrupting and breaking the course of our associations. For, if we were always awake, some accidental associations would be so much cemented by continuance, as that nothing could afterward disjoin them; which would be madness."[193]

In ascribing this function to dreams, Hartley anticipates the late-nineteenth-century theory of W. Robert, who saw the function of dreams to be that of excreting worthless, incomplete, un-worked-out, and superficial impressions, which if not dreamt out would lead to derangement.[194] Hartley also anticipates another theory true to the positivist spirit of the Enlightenment, the 1983 theory of Francis Crick and Graeme Mitchison. This theory hypothesizes that dreams are best forgotten because they contain useless and potentially parasitic patterns of thought that the brain tries to clean out and forget via the dream.[195]

In an intellectual environment that discouraged introspection and the exploration of feelings, the Scottish physician John Abercrombie (1780–1844), in his *Inquiries Concerning the Intellectual Powers, and the Investigation of Truth,* proposed that buried memories appeared in dreams via the mechanism of the association of ideas. Like his contemporaries, he was interested in the physiological and environmental causes of dreams. He hypothesized that some form of reasoning or intuition might function in sleep and thus explain how dreamers are able to locate lost objects, solve difficult problems, and generate new scientific and artistic ideas in dreams. Abercrombie also suggested that in dreams the dreamer may become aware of traits in others to which he or she was blind in the waking state. Therefore a dream that appears to be prophetic is often only prognostic in that it plays out the likely result based upon the unconsciously perceived information.[196]

In France, the hypnotic treatments of various maladies, especially hysteria, developed and popularized by Franz Mesmer and the Marquis de Puységur, had led by 1803 to formulations of dipsychism and polypsychism. The concept of dipsychism dealt with the "new and often more brilliant" personality that would appear in hypnotized subjects and that was thought to be composed of forgotten memories and impressions only fleetingly perceived by the conscious mind. Polypsychism postulated that under hypnosis the conscious ego was pushed aside and various sub-egos would surface with their own consciousness, memories, and psychic operations. By 1803, J. Reil had related the phenomenon of dissociated personalities to normal dreams in which the dreamer identifies with only one actor in the dream, but in which all the other actors represent subpersonalities that may be more knowledgeable than the dreamer's main ego. The psychiatrist and scholar Henri F. Ellenberger writes: "One cannot overemphasize the influence that these two models of the mind, dipsychism and polypsychism . . . [had] (on Janet, Freud, and Jung)."[197]

Emphasizing the more general, psychodynamic aspects of dreaming, Heinrich von Schubert Gotthilf (1780–1860), in his book *The Symbolism of Dreams,* wrote of dreams as a form of thinking in picture language *(Traumbildsprache).* He described dreams as using a universal language of symbols that are the same for all people in all times and places. He described the way one symbol can condense many ideas or concepts into one image, but stopped short of explaining how or why. He also subscribed to the theory that an image can represent its opposite and that although one might dream of future events, most dreams have a demonic character because they reflect "the neglected, repressed, and strangled . . . aspects of the personality."[198]

According to Ellenberger, the first presentation of a complete and objective theory on unconscious psychological life was presented by the painter and physician Carl Gustav Carus in 1846. Given the Enlightenment's hold on science, it is not surprising that it was a German physician and artist who wrote, "The key to the knowledge of the nature of the soul's conscious life lies in the realm of the unconscious."[199] Carus described the science of psychology as the study of the soul's development from the unconscious to the conscious: "Consciousness arises gradually, but it always remains under the influence of the unconscious and the individual periodically returns to it in his sleep."[200] Although Carus (like Jung in the next century) saw the unconscious as a compensatory, autonomous, and creative force, he failed to interpret dreams as a channel to that resource.

It was not until the last decade of his life that Arthur Schopenhauer's (1788–1860) work began to meet with recognition and success, which would peak in the 1880s. This philosopher's ideas were to profoundly influence Wagner, Nietzsche, and Freud. Schopenhauer described humans as basically irrational beings motivated by powerful sexual instincts and other unconscious forces of which they are scarcely aware. He identified the mechanism of repression in describing the will's opposition to recognizing anything that might interfere with our wishes, injure our pride, or interfere with our interest.[201] Schopenhauer apparently also believed in the ability of dreams to indicate possible futures. On New Year's Eve in 1830 he dreamt that he would die in the coming year. He wrote that this dream greatly contributed to his decision to leave Berlin as soon as cholera broke out there in 1831.[202]

Early psychotherapy was practiced by a few scattered physicians of the Romantic period. Some considered the influence of the sexual instinct and its frustrations to be the key to mental illness, while others identified feelings of sin or guilt, or anxiety, as the most important factors. Therapeutic methods included art therapy, shock therapy, work therapy, and even a form of psychodrama.[203]

You can see why Ellenberger goes so far as to say, "There is hardly a single concept of Freud or Jung that had not been anticipated by the philosophy of nature and Romantic medicine."[204] The way was now prepared for someone to get the bright idea to use dreams therapeutically to explore and resolve conflicts and to assist in the growth and maturation of the individual.

Positivism

Just as circumstances looked favorable for a development of a psychodynamic understanding of the dream, a new movement arose. The philosophy of positivism, an offshoot of the Enlightenment and traceable to the French encyclopedists, surged over Europe. Ellenberger says, "Positivism's basic principle was the cult of facts; the positivists did not search for the unknowable, the thing in itself, the absolute, but for the kind of certitude afforded by experimental science and for constant laws such as laws of physics."[205] A series of events combined to shift public interest to the applied sciences: the revolutions of 1848, the publication of the Communist Manifesto in the same year, the rise of socialism, and the spread of the Industrial Revolution. In addition, Darwin's ideas were deformed into "social Darwinism," which claimed the theory of the survival of the fittest to be a confirmed law and was used to excuse the worst of industrialism's excesses. Theoretical and introspective explorations of phenomena like the unconscious and dreams gave way to organic and physiological studies of the mind.[206]

Although most educated people held the opinion that dreams were meaningless artifacts of random activity in the sleeping brain and were not worthy of study, two men at the Collège de France experimentally induced them and manipulated at will their content.

In 1861, Alfred Maury published *Sleep and Dreams,* in which he described his careful recording and observations of his own dreams. He also experimented with a variety of external sensory stimuli to determine their effects on the content of his dreams. He found, for example, that on the night that his assistant caused him to smell perfume while sleeping, he dreamt of being in a perfume shop in Cairo. Maury noticed that many dream images were not so much creative as reflective of forgotten memories that might go as far back as childhood.[207]

A scholar of Oriental studies, the Marquis Hervey de Saint-Denys (1823–1892) gave a vivid account of his efforts to become the master of his dreams in his book *Dreams and How to Guide Them*. Hervey's goal was to remain conscious in his dreams and to direct their action. He developed a technique to attain these goals and found that he could at least fleetingly control his dream imagery. His method, however, was so difficult that few could duplicate his results.[208]

More interested in the psychodynamic-meaning level of dreams, but less in tune with the positivist times and far less popular, was the work of Karl Scherner. Scherner's book *The Life of the Dream* presented a phenomenology of dreams and distinguished between the regressive and more positive manifestations of the dream. Scherner's interpretation of the symbolic language of dreams was of a metaphoric nature, and he emphasized the images elicited by sensations in the bodily organs and described symbols such as towers, pipes, knives, and pointed weapons as representing sexual organs.[209]

Sound familiar? It is out of this period that Sigmund Freud emerged and triggered the modern conception of dreams as a potentially powerful tool for the recognition and resolution of personal conflict. Let's take a look now at the architects of modern dream work.

Two

THE ARCHITECTS OF TWENTIETH-CENTURY

DREAM INTERPRETATION

If you have a good understanding of the work of Sigmund Freud, Carl Jung, and Medard Boss, you will be able to make sense of any modern interpretive method. The work of these men forms the three main currents of the psychodynamic understanding of dreams, and every contemporary method of interpretation uses some combination and development of the ideas and practices of these three European psychiatrists.

The social and intellectual world of the second half of the nineteenth and the first half of the twentieth centuries in which Sigmund Freud (1856–1939), Carl Jung (1875–1961), and Medard Boss (1903–1990) spent their formative years was heir to a rich development in thinking about human personality, dreams, and the unconscious. But it was Freud who opened the door to psychotherapy and the understanding of dreams as we think of them today.

Sigmund Freud and the Psychoanalysis of Dreams

Unlike the more authoritarian hypnosis and suggestion therapies used in the previous century, Freud's therapy would answer the call for a psychotherapy that "would keep personal liberty intact, explain to the patient what is going on in his mind, and guarantee 'that all the methods employed act only through his own psyche.'"[1] By today's standards, Freud's methods may look rather authoritarian, but at the time the idea of consulting with the patient in a collaborative exploration of personal history, symptoms, and dreams was simply revolutionary. His method of free association allowed for an unprecedented opportunity for input from the patient. No less revolutionary was Freud's therapeutic use of dreams to uncover truths about the dreamer and use these truths to foster insight, resolve conflict, and alleviate symptoms.

In developing his theory and practice of dream interpretation, Freud drew upon prior explorations of the unconscious. He drew especially upon the work of Friedrich Nietzsche. From him Freud took and developed the concepts of "the self-deception of consciousness by the unconscious and by emotional thinking, the vicissitudes of instincts . . . the self-destructive drives in man, the origin of conscience and morals . . . , [and] the origin of civilization in the repression of instincts."[2]

Unfortunately, in my opinion, Freud did not develop one of Nietzsche's most attractive ideas, that of vitalism, of personal growth. Nietzsche envisioned the possibility that man could learn about himself, unmask himself, and be the better for it—that man could flourish. Robert McGinn, a philosopher at Stanford University, describes Nietzsche as having promoted a "thrival" as opposed to Freud's "survival" worldview. McGinn points to the greater influence of Hegel's ideas of dialectical growth and change on Nietzsche in contrast to the influence of Darwin's survivalist ideas on Freud.[3]

Freud's interpretive method of free association consisted of having the patient lie on a couch and describe whatever thoughts and feelings came to mind, including dreams, no matter how senseless, irrational, shocking, offensive, or embarrassing they might seem. When a dream was told, the patient would make associations to the images and feelings in the dream. Freud believed that through a process he called "dream-work," an internal censor created the dream to disguise the true meaning of the latent or hidden dream thoughts and wishes. The free-association method was aimed at going behind the facade of the manifest dream and thus undoing the deception created by the dream-work. If the associations led far away from the manifest dream, that was just part of the path to discovering the latent meaning that Freud was sure was *not* in the manifest dream.[4] These beliefs, to which Freud fanatically clung, resulted in his treating the dreamer and the dream as criminals who camouflaged the truth, and allowed the good doctor to impute to them all manner of motives derived from his pet theories.

Freud believed that the dream was but a distortion of repressed wishes: "A dream is a [disguised] fulfillment of a [suppressed or repressed] wish."[5] This led him to some very strange and autocratic interpretations. Freud engaged in stunning theoretical and interpretive acrobatics in order to justify his original proposition that almost all dreams are the fulfillment of a wish. For example, reviving the ancient practice of interpreting by opposites (which, unfortunately, is *still* not extinct), Freud wrote:

> Incidentally, reversal, or turning a thing into its opposite, is one of the means of representation most favoured by the dream-work and one which is capable of employment in the most diverse direction. It serves in the first place to give expression to the fulfilment [*sic*] of a wish in reference to some particular element of the dream-thoughts. . . . Again, reversal is of quite special use as a help to the censorship, for it produces a mass of distortion in the material which is to be represented, and this has a positively paralysing effect . . . on any attempt at understanding the dream. For that reason, if a dream obstinately declines to reveal its meaning, it is always worth while to see the effect of reversing some particular elements in its manifest content, after which the whole situation often becomes immediately clear.[6]

Freud went even further with the method of reversal, applying it to the chronological structure of the dream events:

> And, apart from the reversal of subject-matter, *chronological* reversal must not be overlooked. Quite a common technique of dream-distortion consists in representing the outcome of an event or the conclusion of a train of thought at the beginning of a dream and of placing at its end the premises on which the conclusion was based or the causes which led to the event. Anyone who fails to bear in mind this technical method adopted by dream-distortion will be quite at a loss when confronted with the task of interpreting a dream.[7]

Believing that "in some instances, indeed, it is only possible to arrive at the meaning of a dream after one has carried out quite a number of reversals of its content in various respects,"[8] Freud felt that he was able to "discover" hidden wishes in the most unlikely places. In so doing Freud, I think, took liberties with dreams that were tantamount to the rape of a dream and that demonstrated his failure to appreciate the meaningfulness of the manifest content and structure in dreaming.

Freud believed that, given enough time to overcome his or her resistances, the dreamer, through free association aided by well-timed interpretations from the doctor, would come to the identification of the hidden wish that lay behind every dream. These wishes were, according to Freud, of an infantile, sexual, or aggressive nature and were unacceptable to patients, who unconsciously used the deceptive, camouflaging dream imagery to achieve a symbolic gratification of their repressed needs. Freud recognized that internal and environmental sensory stimuli, and especially events of the day preceding the dream—"day residue"—could trigger a dream, but that these stimuli neither caused the dream nor explained it. He believed that they would be incorporated into a dream in the service of the "dream-work," which was the process by which the dream camouflaged the latent wish in an effort to harmlessly and symbolically gratify that wish.

The epitome of Freud's extraordinary efforts to force the facts to fit his theory is exemplified by the case of a woman who presented him with a dream that she believed to contain no disguised wish, nor any repetition of a traumatic event (the only exception Freud allowed to his theory of wish fulfillment). In exploring the dream, Freud concurred that he too was unable to find support for his most cherished theory. Not easily daunted, Freud, on the spot, came up with a solution to his problem. He pronounced that the dream was in fact after all the fulfillment of a wish—namely, the dreamer's wish to prove him wrong![9]

The goal of Freud's dream interpretation was to help the dreamer to sufficiently overcome various defense mechanisms in order to bring to consciousness those repressed memories and wishes that Freud insisted were the driving force in every dream. Since repression used up valuable psychic energy, and often led to the formation of neurotic symptoms, Freud encouraged the dreamer to recognize consciously his or her repressed infantile wishes, which some current life conflict had triggered. This conscious recognition or insight was thought to have a curative effect on the patient by freeing up energy previously invested in repression and symptom formation. Freud believed that the survival of individuals and of civilized society depends upon the individual's ability to sublimate unacceptable instinctual drives in order to meet the demands of society.

Freud thought that behind the manifest dream lay a hidden or latent meaning related most often to repressed infantile wishes of a sexual nature.[10] In order to uncover or unmask this meaning, the father of psychoanalysis developed a systematic method of interpretation. His method called for the therapist to intervene at appropriate moments with interpretations based on one or two sources of information. In most cases, Freud insisted upon making use of the dreamer's associations as well as using "dream symbolism" in which Freud substituted the meaning he ascribed to a particular image or common dream action for the literal images in the dream. Thus Freud interpreted staircases as representing the sexual act, for one mounts and descends them rhythmically.[11]

Freud's treatment of flying dreams illustrates how he used both his patients' associations and his own ideas derived from his understanding of dream symbolism:

> Dreams of flying or floating in the air (as a rule, pleasurably toned) require the most various interpretations; with some people these interpretations have to be of an individual character, whereas with others they may even be of a typical kind. One of my women patients used very often to dream that she was floating at a certain height over the street without touching the ground. She was very short, and she dreaded the contamination involved in contact with other people. Her floating dream fulfilled her two wishes, by raising her feet from the ground and lifting her head into a higher stratum of air. In other women I have found that flying dreams expressed a desire "to be like a bird"; while other dreamers became angels during the night because they had not been called angels during the day. The close connection of flying with the idea of birds explains how it is that in men flying dreams usually have a grossly sensual meaning; and we shall not be surprised when we hear that some dreamer or other is very proud of his powers of flight.[12]

Regarding dreams of falling, Freud is less open to a variety of possible meanings, at least for women: "Dreams of falling, on the other hand, are more often characterized by anxiety. Their interpretation offers no difficulty in the case of women, who almost always accept the symbolic use of falling as a way of describing a surrender to an erotic temptation."[13]

Freud would not only pronounce interpretations, but actually argue with some of his patients who resisted his interpretations. While defending his use of symbolic substitution, Freud nevertheless cautioned that there was some danger in putting too much trust in symbol systems external to the dreamer's associations:

I shall . . . [show] how impossible it becomes to arrive at the interpretation of a dream if one excludes dream-symbolism, and how irresistibly one is driven to accept it in many cases. At the same time, however, I should like to utter an express warning against over-estimating the importance of symbols in dream-interpretation, against restricting the work of translating dreams merely to translating symbols and against abandoning the technique of making use of the dreamer's associations. The two techniques of dream-interpretation must be complementary to each other; but both in practice and in theory the first place continues to be held by the procedure which I began by describing and which attributes a decisive significance to the comments made by the dreamer, while the translation of symbols, as I have explained it, is also at our disposal as an auxiliary method.[14]

Yet just a few pages later Freud writes: "The failure of the dreamer's associations gave us a right to attempt an interpretation by symbolic substitution."[15] When the dreamer failed to give a sufficient number or quality of associations, both Freud and Jung chose not to find new ways to free up the associative process, but to insert their own associations, which they thought of as their knowledge of dream symbolism. Reading Freud's and Jung's writings, one sees that they both made liberal use of this method of interpretation.

In describing his understanding of Artemidorus's method of "decoding" in which each image can be translated according to a fixed key, Freud writes that Artemidorus modifies and "to some extent corrects the purely mechanical character of . . . [this] method . . . [by taking] into account not only the content of the dream but also the character and circumstances of the dreamer."[16]

Freud then comments:

The principle of . . . [Artemidorus's] art, according to Gomperz, is identical with magic, the principle of association. A thing means what it calls to mind—to the dream-interpreter's mind, it need hardly be said. An insuperable source of arbitrariness and uncertainty arises from the fact that the dream-element may recall *various* things to the interpreter's mind and may recall something different to different interpreters. The technique which I describe . . . differs in one essential respect from the ancient method: it imposes the task of interpretation upon the dreamer himself. It is not concerned with what occurs to the *interpreter* in connection with a particular element of the dream, but with what occurs to the *dreamer*.[17]

In reading these lines I often imagine Freud to be saying what my ice-skating teacher, Harry Stafford, would periodically bellow across the ice: "Do as I say, not as I do!" For again and again Freud violates his own rules, as when he writes:

In some dreams of landscapes or other localities emphasis is laid in the dream itself on a convinced feeling of having been there once before. . . . These places are invariably the genitals of the dreamer's mother; there is indeed no other place about which one can assert with such conviction that one has been there once before.[18]

Because Freud was unswervingly committed to the conviction that "the more one is concerned with the solution of dreams, the more one is driven to recognize that the majority of the dreams of adults deal with sexual material and give expression to erotic wishes," he was bound to turn all his formulations about how dreams work to the confirmation of this belief.[19]

Not surprisingly, Freud's dream interpretations were also concordant with his beliefs about the male and female psyches. As Ellenberger notes, "Freud seems to have taken the natural inferiority of woman for granted, since, in one of his early writings, he assumed that the stronger sexual repression in woman is the cause of her intellectual inferiority. Later, he came to speak of the natural masochism of woman."[20]

Freud recognized the problem solving function that dreams could serve:

Reports of numerous cases as well as the collection of instances made by Chabaneïx (1897) seem to put it beyond dispute that dreams can carry on the intellectual work of daytime and bring it to conclusions which had not been reached during the day, and that they can resolve doubts and problems and be the source of new inspiration for poets and musical composers. But though the *fact* may be beyond dispute, its implications are open to many doubts, which raise matters of principle.[21]

These implications and matters of principle had to do with Freud's belief that the waking problems taken up in a dream sometimes would be solved only if they connected with an infantile or repressed wish, which was the indispensable motivating force behind every dream.[22]

A detailed description of Freud's work on dreams is beyond the scope of this chapter. If you would like to read more about Freud's work, why not begin with his landmark book, *The Interpretation of Dreams*? Reading *The Interpretation of Dreams* is a great adventure, and absolutely necessary for any serious student of the dream. There you will see how Freud addresses almost every important question concerning the subject, and how ingeniously he works to find the alleged wish behind every dream. His synthesis of concepts of dream causation and formation as well as of interpretation ignited an explosion of interest in discovering the psychological meaning of dreams. Everyone who writes seriously about dreams after Freud is either restating him or reacting against him, and one must have read Freud himself in order to fully appreciate the work of his descendants. That our dreams reveal the truth about how we feel, providing a dynamic and developmental assessment of our emotional life from which we can gain insights that help us live more conscious, enlightened lives, is a concept we owe in very large measure to Sigmund Freud.

Carl Gustav Jung: Dream Analysis in Analytical Psychology

Although both Freud and Jung reflected Romanticism's desire to temper the Enlightenment's worship of rationalism with the recognition of the importance of emotional feelings, their respective psychological schools were profoundly different. Freud's psychoanalysis was greatly influenced by positivism, scientism, and Darwinism, and Jung's analytic psychology embraced the philosophy of nature and other neo-Romantic developments.[23]

Jung developed the "thrivalist" strain in Nietzsche, and built on the ideas of personal growth through a reorientation of the personality from the narrow ego to the inner, central Self of Troxler and Schleiermacher. He stated that the goal of life was progression in the process of individuation—a view reminiscent of Nietzsche's belief that once basic survival needs are met, the uniquely human need to thrive and to flourish comes to the fore. Jung wrote that the natural human process of individuation involved the unification of the personality through the recognition and withdrawal of unconscious projections of aspects of the Self onto others, basing this

ALL ABOU *Dreams*

conviction on the belief that recognition and integration of denied or undiscovered parts of oneself, and the recognition of the Self—or innermost psychic center, which manifests the integration of the conscious with the unconscious—are the goal of individuation.

Jung was greatly inspired by Freud, and for several years was his favorite disciple. But Jung could not accept Freud's concept of the sexual nature of psychic energy or libido, nor his belief in the centrality of the Oedipus complex. Whereas Freud was most interested in finding the *cause* of a dream, Jung was most interested in finding its *purpose*. Jung saw life as a series of transformations leading the individual out of unconscious identification with the world and into a more conscious appreciation of his conscious and unconscious being. Freud held that the individual moved through several stages of psychosexual development "culminating with the Oedipus situation, then a phase of latency, followed by a second awakening of the sexual instinct at puberty leading into maturity, and from then a period of no substantial change."[24] For both Freud and Jung, the purpose of therapy was to unblock obstacles to what was seen as normal development by admitting into consciousness material that was repressed and, in the case of Jung, yet undiscovered. Both used dreams as a primary road to the exploration of unconscious material.

To Jung the unconscious contained not only repressed feelings, instincts, and forgotten personal memories, but also a wealth of knowledge and wisdom in the form of tendencies that function to compensate for the imbalances and one-sidedness of conscious attitudes, and to complement the development of the individual. The unconscious was also universal. It was the source of primordial blueprints of human nature, called archetypes. These archetypes expressed themselves in dream and fantasy images throughout history and became central to Jungian work with dreams. Jung believed that they signaled the patient's progress in therapy on the road to individuation. The major archetypes are:

The *persona*, or the mask of personality traits one shows to the world

The *shadow*, or the personal traits and attitudes one hides from oneself and thinks one hides from the world, and which, though unacceptable to the individual, may be of great potential value

The *anima* or *animus,* or the contrasexual female or male attributes of the human soul

The *old wise man* or *great mother,* or archetype of the spirit that leads the dreamer into a deeper appreciation of inner spiritual realities

The *Self,* or true center of being and wisdom

Jung emphasized that therapy and dream work must aim at strengthening the dreamer's grasp of waking reality and that insights gained must always be translated by the patient into a better adjustment to the conditions of daily life. Jung would often give his patients homework assignments to read certain materials as well as to take concrete steps to actualize insights gained in dream work. Thus Jung tried to discourage a passive collaborative attitude on the part of the patient and encourage an active one. Borrowing from Alfred Adler, another of Freud's former disciples, Jung did not put his patients on the couch but had them sit in a chair facing him. Jung's insistence that inner work should be anchored by and enrich one's participation in social, professional, and civic life has not received the attention it merits.

Jung saw the expression of wishes as only one among many functions of dreams, which could express any drive, quality, or potential of the dreamer. Above all, the dream portrayed the current situation in the unconscious, and was triggered by current inner or outer life events. Dreams might also warn, scold, congratulate, or revitalize the dreamer as well as supply parapsychological information and provide him or her with profound spiritual experiences. Jung wrote: "A dream, like every element in the psychic structure, is a product of the total psyche. Hence we may expect to find in dreams everything that has ever been of significance in the life of humanity."[25]

Jung rejected Freud's belief that the dream was the result of an inner censor's efforts to disguise some latent meaning, and insisted that the manifest dream was the natural, not pathological, expression of the contents of the unconscious. The dream reveals; it does not conceal. Jung wrote: "The dream describes the inner situation of the dreamer, but the conscious mind denies its truth and reality, or admits it only grudgingly. . . . It shows the inner truth and reality of the patient as it really is: not as

I conjecture it to be, and not as he would like it to be, but *as it is*."[26] Jung believed, for example, that a dream about a church should not be construed as a devious camouflage for the womb of the dreamer's mother, but should be explored to discover what feelings and concerns the dreamer had about his religious life. It follows that Jung also rejected the ancient belief adopted by Freud that dreams might be interpreted by opposites or symbolic or chronological reversal. Jung also emphasized that working with a series of the same patient's dreams afforded the analyst and the analysand the opportunity to clarify and correct interpretations of a particular dream. An important contribution of Jung's is his insistence that any given interpretation should be considered a hypothesis, to be confirmed or corrected by later dreams and other developments in the patient's therapy and daily life.

Another crucial advance in dream interpretation made by both Jung and Herbert Silberer was the recognition that dream images can be interpreted subjectively as well as objectively.[27] Interpreted on the objective level, a given dream image is seen as representing the person or thing itself literally, or someone or something in the dreamer's life that shares the highlighted characteristics of the dream image. Interpreted on the subjective level, an image is seen as highlighting characteristics that the dreamer shares with those of the image; in other words, the image is seen as representing an aspect of the dreamer.

The subjective interpretation of dream images has been adopted to some extent by most contemporary practitioners of the art. But it should be noted that Jung warned about getting carried away with an overemphasis on the subjective level and ignoring the objective level, which helps the dreamer to relate to the external interpersonal world: "Enlightening as interpretation on the subjective level may be . . . , it may be entirely worthless when a vitally important relationship is the content and cause of the conflict."[28] The tendency of a few Jungian therapists to overemphasize the subjective level of dream interpretation and of life in general should not make us forget Jung's exhortations to attend to the practical, interpersonal level of dreams and waking life. In fact, Jung had a very demanding expectation of the dream: that it have a message or point, the understanding of which would enrich the dreamer's inner as well as outer life.

Part of Jung's theory of dreams includes the belief that dreams act to compensate for the one-sided attitudes of waking life. Jung does not suggest that dreams display the simple opposite of conscious attitudes, but that the message or the point of a dream can serve to show the dreamer what his waking attitude is missing or ignoring, and that this compensates for his exaggerated, or incomplete, one-sidedness while waking. In order to interpret a dream, Jung believed that the therapist needs

> a thorough knowledge of the conscious situation . . . [in the dreamer's life at the time of the dream], because the dream contains its unconscious complement, that is, the material which the conscious situation has constellated in the unconscious. Without this knowledge it is impossible to interpret a dream correctly, except by a lucky fluke.[29]

Apparently confident that the therapist could form an accurate picture of the conscious situation or waking-life context of the dreamer through the dreamer's reports, Jung proceeded to use this picture to determine how the dream might be understood to compensate for some situation or attitude in the dreamer's life.[30]

Jung's method of dream interpretation has been poorly understood. This may stem from the fact that he and his followers have not always followed it completely.[31] Part of the problem is that Jung was not entirely consistent in describing the first part of his method, which he refers to as "taking up the context."

> When we take up an obscure dream, our first task is not to understand and interpret it, but to establish the context with minute care. What I have in mind is not a boundless sweep of "free associations" . . . but a careful and conscious illumination of those chains of association that are directly connected with particular images. Many patients have first to be educated to this task, for they resemble the doctor in their urgent desire to understand and to interpret offhand. . . . They give associations in accordance with a theory; that is, they try to understand and interpret, and thus they nearly always get stuck. . . . If we associate freely to a dream, our complexes will turn up right enough, but we shall hardly ever discover the meaning of the dream. To do this, we must keep as close as possible to the dream-images themselves. When a person has dreamed of a deal table, little is accomplished by his associating it with his writing-desk which is not made of deal. The dream refers expressly to a deal table. If at this point nothing occurs to the dreamer his hesitation signifies that a particular darkness surrounds the dream-image, and this is suspicious. We would expect him to have dozens of associations to a deal table, and when he cannot find a single one, this must have a meaning. In such cases we should return again and again to the image. I say to my patients: "Suppose I had no idea what the words 'deal table' mean. Describe this object and give me its history in such a way that I cannot fail to understand what sort

of thing it is." We succeed in this way in establishing a good part of the context of that particular dream-image. When we have done this for all the images in the dream, we are ready for the venture of interpretation.[32]

I have found no examples in Jung's writings, nor in the writings or practices of Jungian analysts, of the actual implementation of this concrete, descriptive form of "taking up the context," in which, at least in cases of blocked associations, the therapist is supposed to ask the dreamer for the concrete description and history of the dream image. In a number of instances, Jung himself provides the descriptions of the images in his patients' dreams upon which he begins to build an interpretation, but we never read of an actual case in which he elicited the same from the dreamer.[33] The fact that Mary Ann Mattoon's 1978 book, *Applied Dream Analysis: A Jungian Approach*—which is, in my opinion, the clearest and most thorough presentation of Jung's method—makes no mention of a concrete, descriptive form of "taking up the context" via eliciting the descriptions from the dreamer illustrates that this idea has been sadly disregarded.[34]

Six or seven years after I had been asking dreamers to pretend I come from another planet and then give me a concrete definition and description of all dream images, and after unsuccessfully encouraging Jungian analysts and analysands to do the same, I came across the passage quoted above. It represents at least the spirit if not the practice of Jung's respect for the manifest dream image in the context of the dreamer's worldview. Jung more accurately describes his actual practice as portrayed by his written accounts of his dream work in the following passage:

I have developed a procedure which I call "taking up the context." This consists in making sure that every shade of meaning which each salient feature of the dream has for the dreamer is determined by the associations of the dreamer himself. I therefore proceed in the same way as I would in deciphering a difficult text. This method does not always produce an immediately understandable result; often the only thing that emerges, at first, is a hint that looks significant. To give an example: I was working once with a young man who mentioned in his anamnesis [life history] that he was happily engaged, and to a girl of "good" family. In his dreams she frequently appeared in very unflattering guise. The context showed that the dreamer's unconscious connected the figure of his bride with all kinds of scandalous stories from quite another source—which was incomprehensible to him and naturally also to me. But, from the constant repetition of such combinations, I had to conclude that, despite his conscious resistance, there existed in him an unconscious tendency to show his bride in this ambiguous light. He told me that if such a thing were true it would be a catastrophe. His acute neurosis had set in a short time after his engagement. Although it was something he could not bear to think about, this suspicion of his bride seemed to me a point of such capital importance that I advised him to instigate some inquiries. These showed the suspicion to be well founded, and the shock of the unpleasant discovery did not kill the patient but, on the contrary, cured him of his neurosis and also of his bride. Thus, although taking up the context resulted in an "unthinkable" meaning and hence in an apparently nonsensical interpretation, it proved correct in the light of facts which were subsequently disclosed.[35]

In practice, when Jung "took up the context," he asked the dreamer for a description of the dreamer's conscious waking situation and his or her web of personal associations, which focused on the dream image itself without going too far from it into tangential associations. Jung considered the examination of the context "a simple, almost mechanical piece of work which has only a preparatory significance" readying the therapist for the "venture of interpretation."

"Amplification" is the next major step in Jung's method. This consists of relating dream symbols to mythological, religious, historical, and psychological themes such as the archetypes and the process of individuation. Jung felt that this was such a vital aspect of dream interpretation that he wrote:

I have mentioned before that dream-interpretation requires, among other things, specialized knowledge. While I am quite ready to believe that an intelligent layman with some psychological knowledge and experience of life could, with practice, diagnose dream-compensation correctly, I consider it impossible for anyone without knowledge of mythology and folklore and without some understanding of the psychology of primitives and of comparative religion to grasp the essence of the individuation process, which, according to all we know, lies at the base of psychological compensation.[36]

Jung would amplify the dream images by drawing upon his specialized knowledge, or assist the dreamer in so doing if he or she had gained enough of this knowledge through reading and experience. Though such amplification sometimes passed for interpretation among Jung and his followers, Jung officially insisted that the dream interpretation relate the dream to the waking life of the dreamer. It seems that sometimes Jung was content to interpret the dream in terms of myths, archetypes, and the inner work of individuation, while at other times he proceeded to relate the interpretation-like amplifications to waking life.[37] In my opinion, Jung's focus on the often exaggerated archetypal dimension of dreams led him to overestimate his wisdom and to lecture, even indoctrinate, his patients, frequently missing the practical, life-related point of the dreams.

Jung often exhorted his students to "be naive," and to enter the interpretation of a dream without preconceptions. But like Freud, he sometimes depended upon his associations (specialized knowledge), even to the exclusion of those of the dreamer. In discussing the interpretation of "big" dreams of archetypal or collective significance, he writes: "It would be in vain for . . . [the dreamer] to try to understand the dream with the help of a carefully worked out context, for it expresses itself in strange mythological forms that are not familiar to him."[38] In such cases, as well as in cases where the dreamer's associations are simply inadequate, the analyst must supply the necessary amplifications and explanations of their significance.

Here, as with Freud, we find that certain circumstances (the lack of "adequate" dreamer associations) permit the return to the ancient method described by Artemidorus, that of drawing on the often extensive erudition and experience of the interpreter rather than depending upon the associations of the specific dreamer to discover the meaning of a dream. The arrogance unleashed by the belief that one has such priestly, specialized knowledge has done much damage to the development of modern dream work. Too often a cultlike belief in the theories of a wise leader has blinded interpreters from seeing the dream as an expression of the dreamer's worldview. Freud interpreted according to his model of the psyche, and Jung according to his model, which emphasized his knowledge and understanding of myths and his own system or pantheon of archetypes.

Artemidorus did not have an elaborate model of the psyche, but he did have extensive experience and knowledge of the beliefs and practices of different cultures, and he used these to come up with the metaphors and analogies by which he made his interpretation. Whereas the goals of Artemidorus were prediction and those of Freud and Jung were an understanding of what the dream was saying about the dreamer's psyche, all three sometimes used a similar method. The best presentation of Jung's actual work with dreams is to be found in the book *Dream Analysis: Notes of the Seminar Given in 1928–1930*.[39]

The role Jung ascribed to feelings in dreams is an interesting one. Jung was sure that it was vital for each individual to develop his or her ability to feel to the point where the feeling function allowed the individual to richly experience life, and he saw many of his patients' dreams as indications of the inadequacy of this function as well as indications for its development.

Whereas Freud believed that a dreamer might, through the mechanisms of reversal and disguise, express a feeling experienced in a dream that hid the dreamer's true, "latent" feelings about the person or situation in the dream, Jung took such reported feelings as indicators of the way the dreamer either consciously or unconsciously felt about the dream issue at the time of the dream.[40] However, Jung apparently did not teach his students to specifically and explicitly explore the feelings in the dream by asking the dreamer to more fully describe the reported feelings, nor, apparently, did he ask how the dreamer felt at various moments in the dream. Instead, he inferred from looking at the manifest content certain things about the feeling function or the feelings of the dreamer. He might conclude that the dreamer was dealing with the feeling function; for example, when a patient dreamt of singing, Jung noted, "Of course singing is an expression of feeling, so he is now using his inferior function."[41] Or he might infer that a particular person could represent the dreamer's feeling function,[42] as could a particular animal.[43] To date, I have been unable to locate an instance in which Jung asked the dreamer either how she felt at a given moment in a dream, or how she felt about a particular image or action in a dream. Judging from his writings, Jung did not depend upon this specific information in making his interpretations.

Medard Boss and Phenomenological Dream Analysis

Originally an analysand of Freud and a student of Jung,[44] the Swiss psychologist Medard Boss developed his phenomenological or "Daseinsanalytic" approach[45] to the understanding of dreams after having met the philosopher Martin Heidegger in 1947.[46] Profoundly influenced by Heidegger, Boss describes dreaming as a mode of human existence like waking that is "by nature a series of particular attunements and responses to the meaningful presence of phenomena that reveal themselves in one's world."[47] (Boss's style of writing makes for difficult reading, but it really is worth the effort.) Boss writes that there are two basic steps to his approach to understanding dreaming:

We must first consider exactly for what phenomena the dreamer's existence is so open that they may have entered and shone forth into its understanding light. This in turn tells us what phenomena are not accessible to the perception of his dreaming state . . . [or to what phenomena—i.e., feelings, experiences, and insights] the dreamer's existence is still closed. As a second step, we need to determine *how* the dreamer conducts himself toward whatever is revealed to him in the clearance of his dreaming world, particularly the mood that predicates this way of behaving. If both of these can be accurately described, we [will have] reached a full understanding of the dreamer's existence during the dream period.[48]

According to Boss, the dreaming state is, with few exceptions, characterized by a mode of being that is concrete, anchored to the present, "much less perceptive," and rather narrow compared to the waking state. In waking, we are able to choose our existential relationships, and can "reflect on ourselves in the attempt to gain insight into our existential state."[49] Boss describes the waking mode of being as more clear-sighted in comparison with the "dimmed" and "restricted" openness one has to the world while dreaming. It is in the waking mode that humans are able to comprehend that the experiences in dreams also characterize their relationships to their waking world.

Because Boss sees dreaming as a concrete mode of experience, almost always devoid of mental abstraction and insight, he denies that dream images are metaphoric abstractions.[50] Further, Boss refuses to postulate the existence of the unconscious, or of any unconscious knowing that reveals itself in dreaming.

Boss believed that "under the direction of a knowledgeable therapist" a patient could usually be led in the waking state to grasp the relation of significances perceived in dreaming to analogous ones in waking. He wrote:

The very peculiarity of the dreaming state . . . , that is, its limited existential range relative to the waking state, lends dreaming its great importance for therapy. While it may be said that dreaming existence is less open than its waking counterpart, often enough a person is exposed to unfamiliar significances *for the first time ever* while dreaming. Of course, significances that have never yet been countenanced in waking life tend to appear in dreaming, as every meaning does, only from alien sensory presences of entities. Yet there is some advantage in the fact that in those massive, materially visible forms, significances do not merely suggest themselves but strike the dreamer forcibly.[51]

In typical Bossian style, the vital role of the emotional impact of dreaming is recognized in the most understated manner. Actually, Boss rarely explores in an explicit fashion what the dreamer feels at various points in a dream, and this may partly explain his devaluation of the concrete, sensory, highly focused, and emotionally charged aspects of dreaming.

Boss's method of working with dreams starts with the dreamer's "explication," in which the awakened dreamer gives "an increasingly refined account of the dream sequence." But this, he says, "should be elicited only by letting the subject supplement his first sketchy remarks with more detailed statements."[52] Boss does not want to hear any "free associations," nor any interpretations as to what the dreamer thinks the dream images mean, nor does he give any mythological amplifications. He simply asks the dreamer to stay as close as possible to the dream phenomena themselves and describe them and his reactions to them as fully as possible. Boss writes that the amplification that "Jung preached generally harms the understanding of dreams and, more important, the therapeutic process itself" by "divert[ing] the dreamer from his own world and the personal existence to which he is responsible and . . . [persuading] him to savor 'interesting' accounts of distant worlds and ages instead."[53]

In order to make an interpretation, both Freud and Jung wanted to have a thorough knowledge of the dreamer's personal history, and an understanding of the dreamer's current life situation. In addition to this material, Freud generally wanted the dreamer's "free associations," which might apply to any aspect of the dreamer's life. Freud did not object if the associations led away from the dream and prevented the further discussion of the dream story. He believed that the patient's associations would lead to the issues disguised by the dream. Jung, however, was very interested in analyzing the entire dream and its every part in the context of the dream's dramatic structure. Jung elicited associations more closely focused on the images and feelings of the dream and discouraged what he considered tangential associations that strayed too far from the text. Boss, however, did not feel that one needed a life history, nor a predream description of the current life situation, nor free associations, in order to "give a phenomenological reading" of the dream:

> Thus, if we wish to see our dreamer's existential makeup, we had best dispense with "free association." Nor do we need any prior knowledge of his life history. This is true for all dreams and assumes only that the wakened dreamer describes his dreaming with enough detail about significance and context. The latter includes biographical

materials to which the dream elements themselves point—but only materials drawn from actual experience.[54]

Having elicited the material considered necessary from the dreamer, Freud would pronounce his interpretation based upon his understanding of symbolism and upon his psychosexual theory. Jung would inform the dreamer of mythological amplifications, and offer a hypothetical interpretation based upon his knowledge of mythological and common symbols and upon his theory of the male or female psyche. Boss would not offer symbolic interpretations, but would comment on the existential qualities of the dreaming experience. For example, a patient who was in an unconsummated marriage of five years described a dream to Boss:

I'm hitchhiking on a country road. A very powerfully built man, about my age, has me get in his car, and drives on. While he's at the wheel, I shoot him. I really don't know why, and I don't feel any remorse. But then I start worrying about the police. If I don't get rid of the body, they'll convict me of murder. Luckily, the body beside me turns into a burning match on its own. I'm thinking, I just have to let it burn down, then I can toss the ashes out of the window and no one will be the wiser.[55]

Boss moved right from hearing the dream to recounting it for his patient. He then "began to offer some helpful questions and hints" in the form of existential statements:

A. Now that you are awake, do you see yourself in any situation similar to that of the dreaming? Do you perhaps suspect that it was not only for a given moment that you were on a country road, but that you find yourself traveling without direction in a much more comprehensive sense, an entire human existence without origins or goals?

B. Do you not also realize more profoundly now than in your dreaming, that you are in an encompassing existential sense not standing on your own two feet and moving under your own power, but preferring instead to be carried around at other people's effort and expense?

C. While dreaming you perceive yourself murdering your driver, a vital young man, for no discernible reason. Can you now in your waking state see more clearly that the way you have been living up to now has effectively killed not some stranger, but the potential in your own existence for vital, masculine behavior?[56]

Boss eschews the traditional practice of interpreting the driver objectively as someone in the dreamer's waking life or subjectively as the dreamer himself, or any part of himself. He refuses to objectify the image and sticks to the statement that the dreamer has killed the potential for vital, masculine behavior in his existence. To some, this may seem much like a subjective interpretation in existential jargon, but to Boss the distinction is an important one that helps the therapist to avoid unprovable speculations.

One of Boss's patients dreamt "of seeing his brother's corpse lying in a coffin. The funeral is soon to take place. The brother has been killed in an auto accident on the eve of his wedding. Somehow, the dreamer has been involved in the traffic in which this accident occurred. He is extremely sad at this loss of his favorite brother, the one to whom he has always felt closest."[57] In discussing this dream, Boss provides his clearest statement of his reasons for rejecting both the objective (à la Freud) and the subjective (à la Jung) levels of interpretation.

> Current dream interpretations on the "objective level" would probably assert that this dream betrayed hidden death wishes against the brother. . . . Daseinsanalysis would have to ask how on earth such an assumption could be justified. Not the smallest feature of this dream experience actually speaks of any death wish. On the contrary, the dreamer feels genuinely sad about his brother's death. It is irresponsible arbitrariness to call this sadness a disguising transformation of aggressive death wishes into their opposite. To give such a fantastic interpretation to the patient would be a disastrous therapeutic mistake as well. . . .

> On to the so-called subjective level of dream interpretation the brother would be "identified" as the projected representation of the dreamer's own potentialities for loving, which had been killed. In his waking state this man was, in fact, on the brink of completely killing his humanity—his heart—in the "traffic" of his overwhelming, intellectual, rational, egotistical business life. He suffered from sexual impotence and emotional depersonalization. Nevertheless, all assertions that the brother of the dream

was "only" a projected symbol of psychic content are false. What actually happened in this man's world while he existed in the dreaming state was nothing but the death of a beloved brother in a traffic accident on the eve of his wedding day and the deep depression which the dreamer felt after this loss. This occurrence shows us, simply and clearly, that the patient's existence was tuned down and closed in to an extreme degree. Even in the dreaming state he was open only to a world of reckless business traffic, even in regard to that being who was closest to him and whom he had originally been capable of loving.[58]

In describing the dreamer's existence as tuned down and closed in, Boss differs dramatically from Jung, who saw dreaming as a state in which the dreamer was connected to a larger, richer, fuller sense of the self and the world. Some dream analysts, including myself, would counter Boss by describing dreaming as a state in which the dreamer's attention is highly focused, thus necessarily narrowed. But this focus enables it to take a close look at the feelings, patterns, and beliefs that vitally influence the dreamer whether or not he is aware of them.

Throughout his work, Boss focuses on two central facts about dreaming:

1. The realm of perception opened up and "occupied" by the dreaming existence of a human being permits the manifestations only of such sensory presences, and personal behavior, as he [the dreamer] himself can perceive. Dream entities neither "mean" nor are anything other than what they reveal themselves to be to the dreamer.

2. After waking up from dreaming, a person may become clear sighted enough to recognize the sensory presences of the dreaming, though in the dreaming they had nothing to do with his behavior, as being pointers to personal existential traits, whose significances are analogous to the perceived significances [of] the dreamed entities.[59]

Boss does not mention the use of incubation, or any other means of directing dreaming. He has little to say about what qualities are inherently feminine or masculine. Given his commitment not to engage in unprovable speculation, he does not define the male and female psyches, nor any architecture of psychological mechanisms in something called the psyche, which itself he sees as an unnecessary hypothetical construct.

We have traveled a long road from the superstitious to the authoritarian, to increasingly collaborative approaches to dream interpretation. Dream analysis, which for millennia meant reading the future, diagnosing illness, or determining the presence of demons or the influence of the gods, has only just been recognized as the royal road to self-knowledge thanks in large measure to Sigmund Freud. Jung's emphasis on the healthy, normal, growth-promoting functions of dreams further expanded our appreciation of this universal human experience. The phenomenological approach presented by Boss and others has only begun to significantly influence the work of contemporary dream analysts. But it has already led many to question orthodox theoretical assumptions that may be quite unnecessary and often misleading.

The work of Freud, Jung, and Boss enormously advanced the study of dreams as a scientific, therapeutic enterprise. And yet, as we have seen, their ideas were molded by their historical, intellectual, and social world.

Theirs was a world in which the white male dominated the lives of his wife, children, and fellow humans of other races who entered his sphere of influence, and achieved this with little effective resistance. Authoritarian rule was the norm in most governments and in every household. Women were poorly educated, and usually segregated when the men would engage in political, philosophical, or intellectual discussion. Only in the 1890s would a few unusual women be allowed to attend certain universities. The natural superiority of men in the physical, moral, intellectual, and creative realms was taken for granted by all but a very few. Political rights for women were almost nonexistent, and Switzerland, the country of Jung and Boss, was very slow to grant the right to vote to women. By 1971, most Swiss women were enfranchised, but as of 1989 there were still women in the inner canton of Appenzell who could not vote. All Swiss women were able to vote only as of 1990!

At the turn of the century, corporal punishment of children was considered indispensable.[60] Laws were highly repressive, and respect for authority, both governmental and patriarchal, was a nearly totalitarian command. European professors, who were of course all men, expected and usually received enormous respect and deference. Freud, Jung, and Boss were all addressed as "Herr Doctor Professor," and Freud's and Jung's theories about the male and female psyches, as well as the dream-interpretation methods of all three men, reflect their acceptance of, and their struggles against, the prevailing attitudes of their times.

The fact that we are now living in an age that is far more democratic and more sensitive to gender issues has made possible far more inclusive, nonauthoritarian approaches to dream interpretation. There is a growing emphasis among contemporary dream analysts on healthy dreamers and on their ability to learn how to interpret their own dreams. One can only hope that this will sooner or later place dream study high on the list of priorities of all those who would aspire to understand themselves and their relationships.

Three

W hen most of us think of the different ways to interpret dreams, we call to mind the various theories put forward by Sigmund Freud, Carl Jung, and others.[1] The trouble with thinking this way is that, as you've probably heard many times, if you give one dream to five different interpreters, you get five different interpretations! If this is so (and it sometimes is), then it is easy to conclude that dream interpretation is only so much nonsense coming from the preconceptions or superstitions of the interpreter and has very little if anything to do with any actual meaningfulness of the dream itself.

One reason dream interpretation has been vulnerable to such criticisms is that there has been so much confusion regarding the difference between *theories* and *methods* of interpretation. All methods of interpretation (what you actually *do* to interpret a dream) are based upon the interpreter's theory of dreams. The interpreter's theory of dreams, in turn, is based upon the interpreter's beliefs or theory of how the human mind works and why and how it creates dreams. In choosing a way to interpret your dreams, it is of the utmost importance that you learn to identify the difference between theory and method, and the degree to which a given theory determines or influences both the method of interpretation and the final interpretation itself. For example, a classical Freudian analyst is likely to interpret the images in a dream as the dreamer's disguised repressed sexual wishes. A classical

Jungian interpretation will likely find either repressed or unexpressed potential parts of the dreamer's self that are in need of a more conscious recognition.

Freud believed that the human mind uses dreams to camouflage unacceptable wishes that otherwise would wake us and disturb our sleep, and that these wishes express human sexual drives that would be unacceptable to the dreamer. His theoretical beliefs led him to use two methods of interpretation (free association and symbol substitution) in a particular way (listening for the "right" associations, and using fixed symbolic substitutions) that would yield interpretations that fulfilled his theories of the working of the human mind. Since Jung disagreed with Freud on how the human mind worked in general, and how it worked in dreams, his methods and his resulting interpretations were quite different. Jung did not believe that most dreams were the disguised expression of sexual and aggressive wishes. Rather, he believed that most dreams revealed the dreamer's effort to recognize conflict and grow beyond it by bringing to consciousness parts of the dreamer's self that had been denied or insufficiently appreciated.

Let's look at how these two pioneers dealt with the common dream of discovering new rooms in a house. Freud would interpret the dream as a disguised wish to visit a brothel, since he believed that rooms represent a woman's vagina and womb and that the dream disguises a (usually sexual) wish. Since Jung believed that dreams help us to become aware of repressed, rejected, or unexpressed parts of the larger self of the dreamer, and since he believed that houses usually represent the dreamer's self, he would interpret such a dream as opening the dreamer's eyes to new parts of herself, to a larger sense of who she is and can become. We are thus presented with different conclusions because the theoretical assumptions are so different, and because these assumptions are broad enough to act as lenses that color the dreams so strongly that the actual colors of the dream may be lost. Surprisingly, Freud's and Jung's methods were not that dissimilar, as we shall soon see. Both used a combination of asking for the dreamer's associations and offering their own associations and interpretations based upon their beliefs about what certain dream images mean, employing a method called symbol substitution.

If you want to be able to judge the accuracy and relevance of a given interpretation, you will have to be able to recognize and evaluate both the theoretical assumptions and the interpretive method of the interpreter. Are the theoretical assumptions helping you see more clearly, or are they acting like a distorting lens, letting the interpreter and dreamer see only one color? Is the method employed eliciting new and useful information, or is it simply providing the interpreter with vague material that can be used to fit any interpretation? Often the interpreter (who could be yourself) thinks she is using one method when in fact she is using another. This often leads to terrible misinterpretations.

I hope the descriptions of six ways to interpret dreams presented here will enable you to answer the following questions when you experiment with different forms of dream analysis.

1. What are the theoretical assumptions of the interpreter?

2. How do the theoretical assumptions influence or even determine the methods used and the interpretations made?

3. What exactly is the method or combination of methods actually employed?

4. What are the roles played by the interpreter and the dreamer, and can both roles be played by the same person in any given method?

Before Freud, it was almost always the interpreter who did all the interpretive work. The dreamer's role was simply to tell the dream and to accept the expert's interpretation. Freud shocked the world by saying that the interpreter should ask the dreamer to provide his or her associations to the dream images. Freud said that the interpreter should use these associations to figure out the meaning of the dream. In Freud's theoretical system, the associations were evaluated and interpreted according to his beliefs about what particular symbols meant (oblong objects were phallic symbols, etc.) and about how the dreaming mind worked. Jung used a modified version of this mix of dreamers' associations and symbol substitution based on his beliefs about how the dreamer's mind worked. Later interpreters asked dreamers to act out their dreams, describe where in their bodies they "felt" the dream, or describe in detail the dream images or feelings. Some modern interpreters take much less leading and directive roles in the interpretation process, some invite group participation, and some take on roles that are as authoritarian and as arcane as those of the soothsayers of medieval Europe.

Too often in the field of dream work we have failed to observe and take into account the paramount importance of knowing exactly what roles are assigned to the dreamer and the interpreter. In fact, many therapists are unable to describe the methods they use—that is, what they actually do to arrive at an interpretation. Often, this means that what is called dream interpretation is really just another unexamined practice of indoctrination into the interpreter's pet theories. Dreamer, beware! Frequently our own interpretations or those of our therapists owe more to a recital of theoretical catechisms than to a perceptive exploration of a specific dream. As you learn to see more clearly what actually happens in a given form of interpretation, you will be better equipped to spot sleights of hand, sloppy thinking, unfounded interpretations, and misleading, pushy interpreters. You will then have a much better chance of choosing the method or combination of methods that leads you to a clear, relevant, and useful understanding of your dreams.

The methods described in this chapter are, I think, the most frequently used by most experts and amateurs. They are often used in combination and require different, although often overlapping, behaviors on the parts of the dreamer and the interpreter. I shall have to generalize more than I like in order not to make you read a hundred pages to get to the main points. I shall call these six methods the cultural-formula method, the psychotheoretical-formula method (both are forms of the symbolic-substitution method), the associative method, the emotion-focusing method, the personal-projection method, and the phenomenological method.

1. The Cultural-Formula Method

Perhaps the oldest and most familiar approach to interpretation is the cultural-formula method. To use this approach, the interpreter should be familiar with local and/or world cultural and mythical traditions that assign certain meanings to particular dream images or themes. The interpreter then matches these consensual interpretations to the individual's dream by using the interpreter's memory of these traditions or using a dream book in which they have been recorded. The biblical account of Joseph's interpretation of the baker's and the wine steward's dreams clearly reflects the cultural formulations of the meanings of several images described in the Egyptian dream-book interpretations contained in the Chester

Beatty papyrus, which dates back at least to 2000 B.C.E. In fact, birds, which Joseph interpreted as foreboding ill for the steward, are still commonly interpreted as symbols of death in South America, among other places.

The cultural-formula method is still used today by New Age therapists and Jungian analysts who base many of their interpretations upon their understandings of myths and common symbols. The Jungians call this the *amplification method*. The principal authority to determine the correct interpretation via this method rests with the interpreter, who believes that he or she possesses specialized knowledge (regarding myths and other cultural traditions) necessary to interpret dreams—knowledge that is unavailable to the uninstructed dreamer. If dreamers study with the interpreter either as students or as analysands (patients), they can acquire some or all of this specialized knowledge and to varying degrees can learn to apply it to the interpretation of their own dreams. However, in the early stages, which could last for years, the dreamer's role is to believe that the cultural formulations of meaning for particular images or types of dreams are relevant to their inner lives and often to their daily lives as well. Interpretations derived from this method range from the most absurd predictions to very subtle, comforting, or enriching interpretations. As is true of any method, this one can be employed deftly or foolishly, to the benefit or detriment of the dreamer.

2. The Psychotheoretical-Formula Method

An important variation on the cultural-formula approach is the psychotheoretical-formula method, in which the analyst interprets dream themes and images according to meanings derived from a particular psychological theory. The most vivid example of this method is classical Freudian analysis, in which long objects are interpreted as phallic, and two pears on a windowsill are seen as the dreamer's mother's breasts. In Jungian dream analysis, certain images are interpreted as representations of particular "archetypes" or psychological landmarks defined by Jung in his theory of psychological development. Jung, who described a process of psychological growth called *individuation*, assigned certain masculine and feminine traits to particular images and interpretations based on both his cultural (mythological) and theoretical formulations. Because Jung believed that he understood the true nature of women and that of men, he interpreted dreams according to those theoretical beliefs. Some women feel Jung has helped them appreciate their femininity and also their masculinity. Others feel that Jung's perception of the sexes was severely limited by his education and Swiss culture; in 1989 (twenty-eight years after Jung's death) Switzerland still denied the right to vote to some of its female citizens. I have made no secret of the fact that I think Jung's emphasis on an archaic and inaccurate formulation of maleness and femaleness has demonstrated to all who care to look closely the hazards of thinking anyone can objectively or accurately define the ultimate nature of human beings.

The main role of the interpreter using this method is to match dream imagery to particular images and theoretical interpretations laid down by his or her school of psychology. Like the cultural-formula method, this approach requires recourse to a symbol system defined by someone other than the dreamer. In practice, it is often, but not always, combined with at least a cursory investigation of the dreamer's personal associations to the dream. I took a professional training class years ago with an unusually orthodox Freudian. He had no interest in any of the dreamer's associations. He felt he had been working with dreams long enough to know that an older man or woman in a dream represented the dreamer's mother or father and that a contemporary figure represented the dreamer's rivalrous sibling or homosexual interest! He rigidly used Freud's interpretations just like a dream dictionary, with arrogant certainty. I'm glad to say that there are very few therapists today, even among the Freudians, who are so blinded by Freud's groundbreaking but primitive interpretive rules. Needless to say, if the interpreter applies this method exclusively, the dreamer is reduced to a humble patient-supplicant who either accepts the wise doctor's wisdom or is accused of being too superficial or too resistant to the truth to accept the authoritative interpretation. If this method is used gently, in conjunction with a careful exploration of the personal nature of the dreamer's experience, the results can be very satisfying. The theory that drives the interpretations must of course seem reasonable, and be applied with tact and humility. Such interpretations, presented as hypotheses rather than authoritarian or holy pronouncements, can, even if they miss the mark, lead the dreamer to further reflection and insight.

3. The Associative Method

In the associative method, dreamers are encouraged to describe the thoughts and feelings that occur to them in connection with the dream. In Freud's groundbreaking version of this approach, the dreamers were to report any and all associations no matter how embarrassing, or how seemingly tangential or irrelevant. Because Freud employed this method of dream interpretation after he had decided how the male and female dreaming minds work, he discounted much useful information and subtly encouraged and then focused on those associations that could be connected to his psychotheoretical approach and beliefs. He wrote that although one must never completely abandon the associative method, a more efficient way to interpret dreams once one had enough experience was to principally use his psychotheoretical formula (which he called a form of symbol substitution).

Many therapists after Freud came to think that a good part of this associative material offered by the dreamer was indeed tangential and irrelevant and took up too much time. They have modified his method, and ask the dreamer for associations that are nearer to her experience or more closely related to the dream. In my own method, the dream-interview one, I ask the dreamer for experience-near associations, as well as for seemingly factual, concrete descriptions of the dream images and feelings. As you will see, these descriptions are often the dreamer's most relevant associations and projections, and lead the dreamer to a recognition of the connection between the dream and her life.

As you can imagine, the use of associations can lead to two kinds of interpretations. If the dreamer is highly influenced by a particular theoretical framework, many of the associations will be shaped by it, and others that do not fit the framework will be drowned out, or never even come to the dreamer's mind. If the interpreter or the dreamer-as-interpreter is highly influenced by a psychotheoretical belief system, associations will tend to be interpreted as symbols that trigger the application of that formula. If, on the other hand, neither the dreamer nor the analyst is brainwashed by a limiting psychotheory, the dreamer's associations can lead to a recognition of the metaphors in a dream and its potential to be seen as a parable about the dreamer's life. The range of possible metaphors in dreams is enormous. Many dream experts such as Loma Flowers, Erik Craig, Rosalind Cartwright, Harry Fiss, Stanley Krippner, Walter Bonime, and Johanna King use associations in a much more open, less restricted way than did the true-believer, slavish followers of particular psychotheories of the first seventy years of this century. Most modern, able dream analysts would never think of trying to interpret a dream without at least some exploration of the dreamer's associations. The skill with which they elicit and make use of the associations distinguishes the clumsy or the pushy from those who know how to help you find your own meanings in a dream.

4. The Emotion-Focusing Method

The best-known example of what I call the emotion-focusing method was presented by Fritz Perls. What he named the *Gestalt approach* presumes in its theory that every image in a dream is an aspect of the dreamer's personality. This method of interpretation then has the therapist encourage the dreamer to act out or role-play certain images in the dream. In group dream work the therapist may assign other members in a group to role-play some of the dreamer's dream figures and to interact with the dreamer, who plays one of the principle roles. For example, the therapist might say, "John, be the old woman in your dream, and Maria, you play the mugger who is attacking her." The therapist might assign surprising roles to the dreamer: "Jean, be the open garage door in your dream and tell us about yourself." In this way many therapists are able to help the dreamers get in touch with moderately intense to very intense feelings. These feelings may have a very direct or only a distant connection to the dream as a whole.

The feelings thus evoked may be core to the dream's emotional and dramatic thrust, or they may be tangential to it, depending upon what the therapist chooses to focus on. In Gestalt therapy, the often intense feelings are discussed in relation to the dreamer's waking life, not usually in relation to the dramatic structure of the whole dream story, which often is never explored as a whole.

In most Gestalt dream work, the dreamer is asked to role-play and to get in touch with the feelings that come from that role-playing. The therapist usually takes on the role of director, who chooses which scenes to enact and which images to act out, assigns roles, and coordinates the action. Usually the therapist resists making formulaic interpretations derived from elaborate schools of psychotheory and leaves the dreamer free to discover how the feelings evoked need to be expressed or better understood in his or her waking life. Other therapists, including Jungians, Freudians, and myself, mix the emotion-focusing method in with other methods and with small or large doses of cultural or theoretical formulations. If the therapist's framework psychological theory is too limiting and if his theoretical or cultural formulations are too rigid, the dreamer's work in connecting with his feelings can be badly interpreted. If the therapist uses his framework in an open, suggestive way, it can be helpful in assisting the dreamers to see dynamics and patterns that have been invisible to them.

One of the big pitfalls of the emotion-focusing method is that it can evoke hugely intense feelings that may or may not have much to do with the dream and can leave the dreamer suffering and confused about how to understand these feelings and what to do with them. When you work with a method that evokes strong emotions, it is all the more important that you try to elicit emotions relevant to the dream so that they can be understood in the context of the aspect of the dreamer's life portrayed in the dream. This assures that the emotions will be part of the dreamer's life that he or she was interested in and willing to present to herself in the dream.

It is easy to sit with another human being and get him or her to get angry, burst into tears, and so forth. This can be done by using words, questions, or subtle body language to threaten, insult, comfort, or explore sensitive topics. In fact, getting someone to cry has often been used as a cheap trick in countless TV talk shows and group and individual therapy sessions in order to give the spectators the impression that something important is happening. Not necessarily. We all have reservoirs of intense feelings related to a myriad of topics in our lives, which in most cases can be easily tapped by a determined or skilled person. But for this exercise to do us any good, the feelings must be relevant to our current situation, and we must know or learn how to understand and move through those feelings to new levels of awareness and integration. If your goal is to interpret a dream, you are going to be sidetracked if you focus on feelings that are tangential to the dream. This is true even if the tangential feelings are very moving. They will surely be part of the dreamer's life experience and may be worthy of exploration. But if they are not really part of the dream, they will throw you off course in seeking the interpretation of the dream at hand.

An unforgettable example of this pitfall came up at a dream conference recently. Will told a dream of getting out of a shower to find a man crouched down and about to blow his head off with a gun. The therapist who was demonstrating his method asked Will if he could remember other frightening gun-related experiences in his life. Will was visibly moved as he replied yes, but declined to describe the recalled moment. The crowd was impressed to see such a strong, manly man as Will become so sad and shaken in the space of only ten minutes. The kindly therapist encouraged Will to stay with his feelings and then after about fifteen minutes ended the demonstration session. The dreamer felt raw with his reopened memories, and asked the therapist what he was supposed to do with them. He asked whether if there had been more time the therapist would have helped him see their relevance to his dream and his current life. No, he was told, he would simply have been encouraged to keep feeling the feelings for days or longer in order to get in touch with his inner self.

Will asked me to help him out. I interviewed him about the images in his dream, and in about three minutes this is what he came up with:

GAYLE: How did you feel as you came out of the shower?

WILL: I was fresh, and I was real clean.

G: When you saw "the gunman," how did you feel?

W: Terrified.

G: What was the gunman like?

W: He was a Latino like a drug dealer I know.

G: So, is there any way in your current life that you feel fresh and real clean but are threatened by someone or something who could blow your head off and is like a Latino drug dealer?

W: Oh god, yes! This is a dream about my being clean from drugs, and feeling so good and fresh about it. The gunman is like that part of myself that is ever ready to ambush me and take me back into that deadly world of addiction. This is another one of those warning dreams that have helped me stay clean for the last five years. They come to me and scare the temptation right out of me. This had nothing to do with the episode I remembered on the stage. It's about my life right now.

As with every method, the interpreter has to learn when and how to employ it. Will benefited from connecting with the feelings of cleanliness and of terror in the dream. They provided the path to understanding his dream. But focusing on a feeling that was not in the dream, that was only tangentially related to it, took him far afield.

If you would like to read more about this method, I suggest you look at Arnold Mindell's book *The Dreambody,* listed in the "Resources" section at the end of this book. Mindell is a modern, independent-minded Jungian who shows people how to focus on feelings one feels physically in the body while reliving the dream.

The personal-projection method usually contains elements of interpretations based on cultural and sometimes psychotheoretical formulations and adds to these interpretations based on the personal associations and emotional responses of the interpreter. This method has surely been popular since the dawn of dream telling, and is often mislabeled as intuitive dream interpretation. There exist both useful and dreadfully useless forms of this method. In its worst form, it is very much like *friendly diagnoses*. We've all experienced these. Let's say you are at home nursing a terrible ache in your belly. A painter whom you have hired to paint your kitchen sees you and pronounces that he knows just what your problem is. Why, just last month he had the same thing, it was an allergy to milk. Entirely untrained in differential diagnosis or medicine, he feels no doubt in his interpretation. In fact, the less he knows about the specific nature of your symptoms, the easier and simpler. If you are suffering from ulcers or a cancer, you are out of luck. Like friendly fire, friendly diagnoses can be deadly. Anyone who interprets your dream for you without knowing the details of your particular dream and your particular life is likely simply to project onto your dream his or her personal feelings, assumptions, and conceptions. These projections are usually based upon the interpreter's dreams, personal experiences, and understanding of theoretical and cultural formulations. To call this soup *intuition* is like calling a grunt a poem.

Dreamers get into the most trouble when they see a therapist who interprets their dreams by using this method in an authoritative manner. Unfortunately, not only well-meaning if uninformed friends, but some therapists, still use personal projections in this way.

The good news is that there has been an all-important shift in dream work in the last thirty years. There has been a growing emphasis on collaborative as opposed to authoritative interpretation on the part of the majority of therapists and dream specialists. Thanks to the work of Walter Bonime, Joseph Natterson, Montague Ullman, Stanley Krippner, Ann Faraday, and others, there has been a remarkable transfer of authority away from the interpreter. The task and power of interpretation is at least shared, if not placed almost entirely in the hands of the dreamer. Things are looking up.

For example, Joseph Natterson, a psychoanalyst and the author of *The Dream in Clinical Practice,* is an extraordinarily articulate proponent of patient-therapist collaboration. He explains to his patients that he considers dream interpretation, like therapy, a collaborative enterprise. After listening carefully to his patient's associations, he carefully offers his own associations to the dreamer's images. He, like many modern dream workers, offers his associations and interpretations as hypotheses that may or may not provide an accurate interpretation, but that he hopes will trigger further fruitful reflection on the part of the dreamer. Except for a few surviving dinosaurs, gone are the psychoanalysts who dogmatically pronounce rigid interpretations.

In group dream study, Montague Ullman and Nan Zimmerman have developed a fascinating version of interpretation via personal projection. The leader of the group first makes it clear to all that only the dreamer has the authority to determine the meaning of his or her dream. Then the dream is told, and the group members are invited to ask questions clarifying the action and details of the dream as told. We hear no more from the dreamer for quite a while, no associations, descriptions, or interpretations. In fact, the dreamer sits there for the next phase and has no eye contact with the other group members as they speak. Each member of the group is then invited to state what the dream would mean if it had been his or her dream. Since the group members are not familiar with any of the dreamer's associations, descriptions, or predream life circumstances, they must draw upon their life and dream experiences, and theoretical and cultural formulations, and project them onto the Rorschach-like screen of the dreamer's dream. The hope is that their projections, humbly offered as personal responses and not as interpretations for the dreamer, will act as triggers for the dreamer's interpretive efforts. After hearing the personal projections of the group members, the group leader summarizes them and may choose to emphasize comments that he or she suspects to be the most promising. The leader then offers the dreamer the opportunity to tell the group whether or not any of the projective interpretations struck a familiar chord and helped the dreamer to better understand his or her dream.

There is no question in my mind that this approach is very useful in helping members of a group open up with each other, and, by using another person's dream as a Rorschach-like projective device, even at times discover important things about themselves. As such, it can facilitate group openness and comfort, and self-reflection. No small feat. This method is quite free of any restrictive theoretical assumptions and allows for an endless variety of projective interpretations. The dreamer is encouraged to accept only the interpretations that she finds compelling,

and she is never prodded in any direction. The method is easy to teach and easy to practice, and has great appeal among newcomers to the study of dreams.

The difficulty with this projective system is that the dreamer who hears a variety of possible interpretations in response to her dream may be tempted to adopt as her own an interpretation that is appealing, nonthreatening, or convincing for the wrong reasons. This process can thus short-circuit the dreamer's doing her own inner search for the specific connections between her life, her feelings, and her dream. Even when projective interpretations are right on the mark, they steal from the dreamer the benefits of discovering the interpretation for herself. These benefits include the thrill and satisfaction of discovery as well as a greater willingness to take responsibility for the implications of her own interpretations.

6. The Phenomenological Method

Medard Boss was the first to describe a method of working with dreams that discouraged reference to elaborate psychological theories and insisted that the interpreter play the role of coach whose job it is to help the dreamer focus on the phenomena (the images and feelings) of the dream. The dreamer is encouraged to relive and describe in great detail exactly what happened in the dream and how it felt to be there. The main goal of his method is to assist the dreamer in exploring and appreciating the fullness of the dream experience by reliving it and by describing the qualities of the manifest dream (i.e., the dream just as it is recalled). Boss wanted to rescue the dream from being distorted by restrictive theoretical presumptions, and to show dreamers that the dream images themselves, once well reexperienced, could open the dreamer to new ways of being, and to attitudes and feelings that had been out of his awareness. Medard Boss is difficult to read, but let me refer you to his book *"I Dreamt Last Night . . .",* and to a chapter by Erik Craig and Steve Walsh, titled "Phenomenological Challenges for the Clinical Use of Dreams," in a book I edited called *New Directions in Dream Interpretation.*

Loma Flowers and I have developed the Dream Interview Method of interpretation, which Erik Craig, director of the Santa Fe Center for the Study of Dreams, informed me once in 1984 is very much in harmony with the phenomenological approach. I think he is quite right, and I am indebted to him for helping me see the theoretical characteristics of my own method more clearly. In the interview method we ask the dreamer to pretend that the interviewer comes from another planet and knows little about life on earth and little about the dreamer's reality. The interviewer then asks the dreamer to describe the main images, feelings, and actions of the dream. He or she asks for both concrete and associative definitions and descriptions, seeking to know the dreamer's perceptions and to put aside his or her own perceptions and projections. The interviewer then restates the dreamer's descriptions using the dreamer's own words and asks if a particular dream element or group of elements reminds the dreamer of anyone, any part of himself, any feeling, or any situation. The interviewer, in good phenomenological form, mightily resists offering any of his or her own ideas, intuitions, projections, or associations, so that the dreamer will not be distracted by them but will be free to find the very specific connections between the dream elements and his life.

This systematic focus on asking the dreamer if a particular image reminds him of anything in his life lays much more emphasis on finding the metaphoric link between the dream and particular issues and concerns in the dreamer's life than did Boss's more general method. The Dream Interview Method is driven by a minimalist theory that rejects elaborate formulations of the nature of the human mind and the nature of maleness and femaleness. But it does posit that dreams present us with visual and emotional metaphors for situations and insights about those situations in our lives. It is aimed at helping the dreamer put descriptive words to the dream elements—words that then trigger the dreamer's recognition of the parallel between the "dashing but unavailable" movie star in her dream and, say, her habit of falling for dashing but unavailable men in her life.

As you will see in the next chapter, the dreamer can and usually does play both the role of dreamer and that of interviewer. However, I encourage dreamers (especially novices) to find a teacher, dream partner, or dream group with which to practice the roles separately until they learn the habit of asking questions and giving rich descriptions *before* attempting to make an interpretation. It is the tendency to make interpretations before we really know enough that has led to so much confusion in the field of dream work.

Four

THE DREAM INTERVIEW

D ream interpretation can be one of the most exciting and rewarding things you will ever do in your life. It can bring you thrilling new experiences, joys, and insights that will help you live and love more fully and richly than you ever imagined. The process does not have to turn into a true believer's indoctrination at the foot of a psychological guru. Rather, it can provide you all the satisfaction of learning a foreign language, one that opens new worlds to you. I developed the Dream Interview Method of interpretation because I wanted to take dream interpretation out of the fuzzy, sometimes murky world of old-fashioned theories and ill-defined and prejudicial methods.

As long as a dream is interpreted according to a given psychological doctrine, there will be almost as many interpretations as there are interpreters from different schools of thought.

If, instead, we explore a dream by following the dreamer rather than the theory of a would-be sage, and if we resist preconceived notions regarding the nature and dynamics of the male or female psyche, we will have a far better chance of hearing what the dream is really saying.

By learning to ask the dreamer (or yourself if you are conducting a self-interview) questions that explore dream images and reveal their metaphorical similarities to people and situations in the dreamer's life, you can avoid forcing the dreamer into preconceived, ill-fitting interpretations. Even in cases in which interpreters have an accurate understanding of dreamers' dreams, asking questions rather than making interpretations allows the dreamers to discover the meanings on their own. As we all know from our teen years, parents can warn, teachers can inform, but most of us have to learn life's lessons for ourselves. When someone gives me a sound interpretation without helping me to discover it myself, I can much more easily deny its uncomfortable accuracy by saying, "Well, that's one person's opinion." Or just as unfortunately, I could accept an entirely or largely inaccurate interpretation on the authority of the interpreter and thereby forfeit the opportunity to discover for myself the genuine insight the dream offers.

Still, all this having been said, wouldn't it be wonderful to find someone who could just tell us what our dreams mean? Our human desire for easy answers and for an authority who can direct our lives leads us as individuals and as world citizens to be dangerously gullible and malleable. In abandoning our responsibility and authority to others, we renounce the most important tools we have to discover the truth about ourselves and our world. The way we work with our inner images in dreams often reflects the way we see ourselves as citizens in relation to our peers and in relation to the authorities in our society. Our hierarchical, authoritarian tendencies will tempt us to ask for, accept, and give authoritative interpretations. The nonauthoritarian democrat in us will be more willing to question authority, ask the dreamers what they have to say for themselves, and finally take more responsibility for personal action or inaction either as dreamer or interviewer. As we work on developing interviewing skills, it will help to keep an eye on the struggle between our authoritarian and our democratic tendencies.

To give the dreamer an effective forum in which to speak for herself, my method involves setting up a dream interview in which the dreamer is questioned by a friend, colleague, or therapist who pretends to come from another planet. The dreamer can and most often will play both the role of the dreamer and that of the interviewer, learning to ask herself the appropriate questions. But the method will be easier to understand if in describing it I divide the roles. Learning the method is easier in pairs or small groups, but this is a luxury most of us do not have.

The would-be interpreter becomes an interviewer who will be curious to discover what life is like as seen through the waking and dreaming eyes of the dreamer. Thus the interviewer tries to set aside any personal knowledge, beliefs, opinions, and associations regarding the images in the dream. The interviewer *asks the dreamer to define and describe* the images as if she were describing them to someone who had never heard of them before. For example, someone who dreamt of Larry King would be asked, "Who is Larry, and what is he like?" The dreamer is asked for a concise, frank, and opinionated description, not for a long and often overwhelming list of associations to the man. Meanwhile, the interviewer keeps her opinions and hypotheses to herself.

Then the interviewer *restates the dreamer's description* and asks if it is accurate. In the next step, called *bridging,* the dreamer *makes the connection—or "bridges"—from dreaming to waking experience.* The initial descriptions are restated or recapitulated to the dreamer one more time as the interviewer asks if a given description reminds her of anyone, any part of herself, or any situation in her life. If the dreamer hears that she described Larry as a fabulously successful radio talk-show host who is smart, savvy, and fun, she may well realize that these are the very traits that remind her of her new boyfriend, of her boss, or of her older brother. If in the dream she is closing Larry out of her apartment because she is taking care of her former, depressed boyfriend, she will be quick to figure out her dream. In her sleep she was able to understand and portray in pictures how she is keeping her new and healthier man at a distance because she is still caught up in taking care of men like her old boyfriend. You can imagine the mess we would have if an interpreter who disliked Larry King were to impose his or her opinions and interpretations on the dreamer!

Until the dreamer takes the time to describe the dream image and then review that description, she will usually be unable to appreciate what feelings and ideas the image carries for her. After the dreamer has given a concise but feeling-rich *description* of each major element in the dream (the setting, the people, the objects, the feelings, and the major actions) and listened to a *restatement* of these descriptions, she *bridges,* or looks to see if the descriptions remind her of anything in her waking life. Then the interviewer asks her to connect all the images with their descriptions and bridges in the context of the dramatic structure of the dream. This step is called the *summary.*

The Dream Interview Method, Step-by-Step

PREPARING FOR THE INTERVIEW

The goal of the dreamer at this point is to be as open and honest as possible, and to be sure she is with an interviewer whom she trusts to be careful, gentle, respectful, and humble. The interviewer needs to be ready to use her curiosity, humility, tact, wit, empathy, and humor in the service of the dreamer.

Both partners in the interview will benefit greatly by diagramming and outlining the dream. Through the years at the Dream Center, my colleague, Loma Flowers, M.D., has demonstrated over and over again how much it helps both the dreamer and the interviewer to recognize that even the most bizarre dream indeed is composed of discrete elements for which there are specific questions that will unravel their meanings. If you take the time to diagram and outline your dream (it takes only a couple of minutes), you will find interpreting your dreams or interviewing others about theirs much easier.

DIAGRAMMING YOUR DREAM

My colleague Loma was the mother of two young boys when we started our Dream Center in 1981. In helping her sons learn to diagram sentences, she came up with the idea of teaching the students at the Dream Center how to diagram their dreams. Her idea was to help the dreamers/interviewers identify the basic categories of dream images about which they needed to ask questions. Diagramming gives the novice interviewers a helpful navigational map to follow during the interview. Look at almost any dream you have ever written down. You will notice that almost every element in your dream can be placed in one of six categories of dream elements:

Dream Elements
Settings

People

Animals

Objects

Feelings

Actions/plots

Marking these six elements is easy and will remind you not to forget key parts of the dream. Try the method we use at the center, then modify it to your tastes.

* Place a rectangle around each setting in the dream.

* Circle each person.

* Circle each animal.

* Underline each major object.

* Circle each feeling with a wavy cloud.

* Underline with an arrow the major actions.[1]

Let's look at a diagram of a short dream Norma had about Nancy Reagan.

Nancy Reagan bought a colt for her mare. I thought, "How foolish to spend money on a dumb horse when the government needs the money so badly."

As you can see, the point in diagramming is not to split hairs, but to highlight the major elements of the dream, about which the interviewer will ask specific questions and elicit relevant descriptions and associations. Although our purpose here is to demonstrate diagramming, not interpretation, I imagine that you may be curious to know how Norma understood her dream. Here is how our interview went:

GAYLE: Pretend that I come from another planet, Norma. Tell me, who is Nancy Reagan, and what is she like?

NORMA: Nancy Reagan is a very important woman, the president's wife, who does foolish things now and then.

G: What are horses?

N: They are physically beautiful and graceful. Sometimes they are useful but not in this case. Here they are status symbols that make their owners feel important.

G: What is a mare?

N: A mother horse.

G: What is a colt?

N: A male horse. Nancy bought this one to keep the mare company.

G: What is this colt like?

N: This colt is very ordinary. An extravagance. Actually, this was a dumb colt. The mare did not need him. Mares adjust to being alone. All this reminds me of my new flame. He is sort of dumb, and energy-wise, he is an extravagant drain. I guess that I am like Nancy in taking him on at this point when I need to use my energies to make a new life for myself after my divorce. Using him to make myself feel important and keep me company looks like a foolish idea now that I think about it.

OUTLINING YOUR DREAM

Another way to map a dream is to outline it. List the major actions in your dream and write them on one side of a piece of paper divided into two wide columns. Then opposite each major action ask yourself what feeling was associated with it, and write it down. Either the dreamer or the interviewer can summarize by simply repeating the major actions and linking them with their associated feelings. This procedure helps the dreamer and interviewer keep in mind the dramatic thrust or structure of the dream and sometimes enables the dreamer right away to recognize parallel situations and feelings in waking life. If we were to outline Norma's dream, we would list the following actions:

1. Nancy bought a colt for her mare.

2. I think, "How foolish!"

Now we would ask Norma to describe the major feeling associated with each action and record her responses.

1. Nancy was excited and happy to gather more status, and glad to be able to provide company for the mare.

2. I am angry at Nancy's foolishness in not knowing that mares don't need company, and at her wasting resources when the government needs them.

As you outline your dreams, remember that your purpose is to highlight the main actions and feelings. To do this you must omit all the enticing details, which you will be able to explore when you begin the interview. The more concise you are at the outlining stage, the better sense you will have for the structure or thrust of the dream—especially when working with long, complex dreams.

Diagramming and outlining are optional, but if you give it a try, I think you will enjoy it.

HIGHLIGHTING THE FEELINGS IN THE DREAM

By encouraging the dreamer to describe briefly the major feelings and moods in the dream, you will be underlining the importance of feelings and reminding the dreamer to attend to them. It may or may not be appropriate to ask the dreamer to bridge these feelings by asking if they remind her of any feelings in waking life. Sometimes the feelings in the dream are so unfamiliar or surprising to the dreamer that it is far better to wait until each feeling can be explored in depth in the context of the dream as the interview proceeds image by image. This step may not be necessary if you have already incorporated it in a dream outline.

THE FOUR STEPS OF A DREAM INTERVIEW

Step 1. Eliciting a Good Description

The interviewer from another planet asks the dreamer to define and describe each of the major elements in the dream. These elements fall into six categories: settings, people, animals, objects, feelings, and actions/plots. Later you will find specific questions for each type of dream element. These questions will allow you to execute each step of the interview.

In most cases it is better not to try to help the dreamer find words to describe his images. An impatient or overly eager interviewer who suggests words to describe the dreamer's images risks aborting the important process of discovery, which requires the dreamer to reflect and recognize certain thoughts and feelings in order to find the words to describe them. Finding the right words to describe a dream image or feeling gives the dreamer the opportunity to recognize, clarify, and express attitudes, opinions, thoughts, and feelings that he may never have been quite aware of before. The dramatically powerful effects of using waking language to describe dream language is often underestimated by those who suggest that dream imagery is distorted by verbal descriptions and that the feelings and images of dreams should not be reduced to words. On the contrary, it is precisely during the search for the right descriptive words that the dreamer forces himself to ask, "Just how *do* I feel and think about this?" In searching for the right word he must examine that which he is trying to describe. This discovery process is exciting, and it has taught more than a few dreamers how to think, feel, and express themselves to themselves and to others more clearly. So beneficial is the process of discovery precipitated by finding descriptions for someone from another planet that many of our students who are psychotherapists use it in their general non-dream-related therapy work.

By using the dream-interview questions, the interviewer avoids encouraging an avalanche of overwhelming and often tangential associations. The dreamer is encouraged to keep to the point and to describe and or define the image as it appears in the dream and as the dreamer knows it in waking life. The dreamer is reminded that he need not worry about being accurate or fair in his descriptions of the thing as it exists in waking life, only that he give a concrete description that portrays how he *thinks* and *feels* about it. For example, if the dreamer tells of a dream in which he is shot in his gallbladder, he would be asked to define and describe the functions of that organ. He should be reassured that he need not give an accurate medical-school description, just a summary of what he happens to know or think he knows about gallbladders.

When a dreamer is asked to describe his waking and dreaming images of people of a particular nationality, race, or profession, he is encouraged to give frank rather than polite descriptions. In fact, a description must be considered inadequate until the dreamer has told us how he judges or values the setting, person, animal, object, feeling, or action/plot he is describing. This approach to eliciting good descriptions is somewhat different for each dream element:

Settings: A good description of the dream setting usually leads the dreamer to a bridge that reveals the metaphor showing the area of the dreamer's life the dream explores. If your dreamer tells you of a dream set in Paris, you won't learn much if you assume you share the same impressions of the place. If, however, you ask her what Paris is *like* and what sorts of people live there, you will both gain informative material for a bridge. When the dreamer can tell you how she feels about a place and about the feelings closely associated to it, she will usually recognize a strong metaphor or bridge to an area of her waking life.

People and animals: The dreamer describes each person in the dream as if to someone who comes from another planet and has never heard of the person before. Ask the basic "Who is _____, and what is he like?" question even and especially if the character has appeared in a recent dream, is a famous public figure, or is well known to both of you. If you are asking about an animal, try questions like "What is a _____ like?" or "What is the personality of a _____ like?" Elicit a fresh, personal description that takes into account the feelings aroused by the context of the current dream and by the dreamer's current life situation. The particular words used by the dreamer are the best keys to the dream's meaning, so remember them or jot them down.

It is important never to ask that popular question "What does John [or a policeman, or a cat] mean to you?" Such a question is really asking for an interpretation before the dreamer can appreciate what she thinks and feels about an image. And it short-circuits her effort to find the descriptive words that could identify her own metaphor. We do, in fact, want to know what a given image means to the dreamer, but we know from experience that phrasing the question in that manner will greatly reduce our chances of finding out.

Objects: Ask the dreamer to define and/or describe each object generically as well as to describe it specifically as it appears in the context of the dream. Again, avoid getting bogged down in voluminous associative material by keeping the dreamer focused on the thing itself. Discourage the dreamer from making statements like "This reminds me of *X*, *Y*, or *Z*" Until he has found a good description. Then he will be much better able to be more discriminating and specific in his associative bridging.

Feelings: Ask the dreamer to describe what she feels at various moments in the dream action. Invite her to say how she feels as she discusses the dream in the present interview. Many dreamers need help in taking the time to get in touch with dream feelings, and will appreciate your patience and persistence in getting them to find words for them.

Action/plot: Ask the dreamer to describe and judge the major action in the dream. Norma's description of Nancy's actions made it easy for her to understand her dream.

Eliciting good descriptions of the various elements in a dream takes discipline and practice. It is useful to remind yourself that *you are here not to show what you know, but to find out what the dreamer knows*. I am reminded of my favorite quote from the late existentialist psychologist Paul Stern:

> What is needed more than anything else to understand the gesturing of the dream is an almost childlike, incorruptible simplicity which is not taken in by contrived complexities and is able to see, in the midst of them—the obvious. Such simplemindedness is, among clinicians, a very rare commodity.[2]

Step 2. Restating or Recapitulating the Description

After getting a good description of one or more images, repeat verbatim or in a condensed form the description the dreamer has just provided. You may have to edit the description, including the relevant and emotionally charged definitions, descriptions, and associations while omitting words that are redundant, that are less forceful than others, or that seem distractions from the thrust of the overall description. With experience, you will learn to edit out repetitive, superfluous, or tangential details without impoverishing or distorting the description. It is important to use *the dreamer's exact words* in the recapitulation in order to take advantage of their custom-tailored appropriateness as potential triggers and to avoid putting your words into the dreamer's mouth. Protecting the dreamer from your own projections is one of your most important duties.

If the dreamer has just described a person she despises, and you suspect that the dream image may reflect an aspect of the dreamer's personality or that of someone the dreamer loves, you might consider omitting the most potentially offensive descriptive words in your first recapitulation. Let the dreamer get used to the idea. Be gentle. If the dreamer has downplayed the emotional charge in her description, sometimes it helps to recapitulate using her words but adding emphasis with your voice that will amplify the emotion. The risk in adding your own emphasis rather than simply mirroring the dreamer's emphasis is, of course, that you may insinuate your own prejudice or projection, which might be inappropriate and distract the dreamer. If you recognize when you are amplifying or emphasizing certain aspects of the description, you will be able to watch the dreamer carefully for signs that you are intruding rather than assisting. When in doubt, ask the dreamer if the recapitulation feels accurate in spirit.

You may want to restate after each description, or you may find that it is more effective to string together several descriptions depending upon the nature of the descriptions, the openness of the dreamer, and your sense of timing.

Step 3. Bridging to Waking Life

Only after the dreamer has given a good description of the dream feeling or image and has listened to a recapitulation of that description is he ready to be asked or to ask himself what it reminds him of in his waking life. As with recapitulation, the timing of a potentially difficult or threatening bridge question can make the difference between hastening or retarding the making of a connection. Asking the dreamer to bridge his dream experience to some parallel waking experience is, in fact, asking him to identify the dream metaphor and note what new light it sheds on the relevant waking situation or attitude. This is the step most people recognize as the interpretation of a dream image.

If a dreamer says that a dream image reminds her of *X,* ask the dreamer to tell you how the dream situation resembles one in waking life if she does not spontaneously offer this information. We call this procedure testing the bridge. It can be initiated by the simple question "How so?" Testing gives both parties to the interview the chance to see if the image really fits the waking situation in all its important characteristics. Testing the bridge is a check against premature, inaccurate bridges that may be offered out of impatience, a need to please the interviewer, or a need to be a bright dreamer quick at getting insight. Poor, inaccurate bridges also sometimes arise out of the dreamer's desire to assign the dream image to an old, not very challenging formulation of what is going on. Testing allows both the dreamer and the interviewer a chance to see if the description of one part of the metaphor (the dream image) fits the other part (the waking person, or situation).

Now and again, an invitation to bridge is met by a blank stare. The dreamer will look disoriented and may be overwhelmed by too complex a bridge. Remember that the dreamer is usually reexperiencing the dream images as real things, not as metaphors. The dreamer is thinking concretely, thanks to your descriptive work, and now you are asking him to make a huge leap to metaphorical thinking. In these cases, step down the complexity of the bridge by being sure you are asking for only one bridge at a time. Or back off entirely and come back to the bridge after further descriptions of this or other images. Courage! Frequently a dreamer will not be able to make any bridges until the eleventh hour, after most or all of the images have been described and restated. Patience and a disciplined forbearance from inserting your own interpretive bridges will maximize your dreamer's chances of arriving at an accurate understanding of the dream.

Step 4. Summarizing the Exploration

Full summaries: After all or as many as possible of the dream's images have been explored (described, restated, and, when possible, bridged), either the interviewer or the dreamer retells the dream, linking each image to its description and bridge (if one was made). The dreamer is then asked to say how she understands the dream so far and to indicate what parts remain unclear. This allows both parties to see if the interpretive hypotheses created by the bridging are consistent with the dramatic structure of the dream as a whole. If there is a part that "doesn't fit," either the main hypothesis is inaccurate or this part needs further exploration.

In the real world of practical dream work, time is sometimes short and dreamers' defenses sometimes very powerful. In these cases it is best to let the dreamer go home with her uncertainties in the hope that further reflection will clarify things. One can almost always work with the dream again at a later date; do not succumb to forcing the dream to fit together neatly immediately.

Partial summaries: Partial summaries, executed by either the interviewer or the dreamer part way through the interview, are extremely useful. After a series of descriptions, restatements, and bridges in one scene, you can say, "Let me [or, Why don't you] summarize the dream up to this point." To avoid a dulling repetitiveness, and to keep up a lively tempo, partial summaries must be careful condensations of the salient features of the previous descriptions and bridges. As the pieces of the dream fall into place, later summaries can be more and more condensed.

Partial summaries are especially effective in leading up to a sensitive or difficult bridge because they help to reconfirm the descriptive facts and reanimate the feeling and action context of the dream that makes the bridging easier. A partial summary after a difficult bridge has been made helps to verify and reinforce the new insight.

Good summaries, full or partial, reinvolve the dreamer in the drama and assist in the correction and incorporation of new associations and insights. They give the dreamer time to digest the fruit of his varied explorations. Both the interviewer and the dreamer can use the summary to review the descriptions and connections made so far, to bring the dreamer up to speed for the next scene. Summaries also allow both participants time to listen and make further connections, recall previously forgotten images, associations, and feelings, and devise new questions.

If while a dreamer is making his own summary he strays off track by drawing conclusions or bridges that suggest a high level of denial (such as offering esoteric, hackneyed, or irrelevant bridges and conclusions), you can gently interrupt. Ask, "What led you to that conclusion?" or "How do you see that?" By doing this you test the strength of the bridge, and the two of you can look together at the process of association and understanding behind the bridging.

Here is Renata's dream, which went from apparently nonsexual imagery to a sexual issue:

I removed the red nail polish from my toes and fingernails and redid them with a pearly white polish. I smilingly showed my fingers and toes to my husband, hoping for approval and appreciation.

At the time of this dream, Renata and her husband had just started living together again after having been separated for two years. After only two interview questions, she understood her dream.

GAYLE: I come from another planet. Why do human females wear toe and nail polish?

RENATA: To look sexy and attract the opposite sex.

G: What is the difference between wearing red and pearly white polish?

R: Oh! Red is the very sexiest color, and white is not at all sexy. White is the color of purity, red, the color of passion. I remember a poem: "Oh, the red rose breathes of passion, the white rose of love" . . . meaning purity. The dream shows me forfeiting my passion in order to win the approval and love of my husband. I've given up my newfound interest in sexuality, which precipitated our separation. My husband and I just have no really sexy energy between us. Now I am wearing that ghastly white that would go best with an old-fashioned nurse's uniform. I really have wiped out my sexual passion and am trying to be good and sweet. I think I've overdone it."

Renata's dream helped her see how her efforts to be a good little wife felt like they would lead her to a pretty but bland life. Her need for approval from her husband (who disdained red nail polish) now looked like a liability to her. She eventually divorced and later married a man for whom she wore very red polish.[3]

REFLECTING ON THE DREAM AND THE DREAM INTERVIEW

The most important work the dreamer will do with a dream is in the week following a successful interpretation. Insights flow copiously from this sort of dream work, but as most therapists know, insights are soon overwhelmed by old habits of thought and feeling unless they are deepened and reinforced by reflection and review. I encourage my dreamers to reread their dreams at least twice in the week following our interview. If the dreamer has tape-recorded the interview, I suggest listening to it once and, if possible, transcribing it. These exercises give the dreamer the opportunity to correct and modify inaccurate bridges and interpretive hypotheses, to complete and elaborate incomplete bridges, and to appreciate more fully and enlarge the significance of accurate bridges and interpretations.

For dreamers receptive to additional homework, we discuss which dream images would be the best to hold in mind during the days following the interview. We often choose the most positive and the most troublesome images. For example, if the heroine in the dream were the dreamer's friend, Edith, whom the dreamer described as an especially courageous, cheerful, and uncomplaining woman who survived adversity without growing bitter, I would say, "During the week, in private moments, or in interactions with others, pretend that you are Edith. See how it feels; imagine how she would react to your life." By imagining (and, where appropriate, pretending) to be a dream character whom the dreamer has bridged to an aspect of herself, the dreamer has an opportunity to become familiar with these characteristics, to recognize the possibilities for developing the character's desirable qualities, or to recognize and modify destructive traits and behaviors portrayed by the figure. In cases where the images targeted for reflection were bridged not to the dreamer but to someone in her current life, the dreamer is encouraged to keep in mind the dream's view of that person, which may be more accurate in some respects than her waking one.

Robin dreamt of a frightened rabbit. It reminded her of a habit of thought learned from her mother's fearful attitude toward the world. Her assignment for the week was to keep a look out for every time she caught herself thinking or saying things that reminded her of her mom's fearful attitudes. By noting these occasions in her dream journal, she saw just how much of her mother's fearful worldview she had internalized and made her own. *This exercise of invoking dream images is the single most effective means I have found to insure that dream work will make a meaningful and tangible difference in the dreamer's life.*

After serious and active dream reflection, most people discover more richness and depth in reviewing their dream work and are much more likely to be able to incorporate insights into their waking lives and consolidate their gains.

In 1972, I had a cinema verité dream that unfortunately I did not take to heart until several years later. Here is how the page from my journal describing the dream read.

AUGUST 21, 1972
ZURICH

Day Notes. A peaceful, quiet day. Wrote a letter to Lynn [my oldest and best friend]. I am sick of being a second class friend to her. Whenever she has a boyfriend, she drops everything and treats me as a second-class citizen. She seems to drop everything she's doing when she has the alternative of being with even a mediocre male. Walked in the park by Zurich lake. Read Rossi's book *Dreams and the Growth of Personality.* It is great. It started me thinking of the shy child who has been showing up in my dreams lately. I have lost some of my self-confidence lately. When in my life have I felt most confident? When I was skating every day, training for competitions. It's been five years since I've done any serious skating. Rossi writes that new growth in the personality seems to manifest itself first in dreams, in the form of new and unusual dream images.

Discussion. I need and want some new awareness, some new growth in my personality to break through old habits of perception and reaction to the world. I know there is within me more creative energy than I am using, but how to let it out?

How can I release and express my deepest, most energetic creativity?

I had sent some photos to Philadelphia so that the passport people could choose the appropriate one when making up my new passport. I received my new passport in the mail and opened it to examine it. Instead of just one picture, the first four pages were filled with color pictures of myself ice-skating. Fabulous pictures I seemed to be seeing for the first time. I thought: "I didn't know I was that good after so long away from serious skating. Could I be that good?" Many pictures were vivid action shots. In one particularly my body was just right, perfect balance and form. It was exciting to see. In another picture I was about forty-five. I reached into it and examined the muscle tone of my leg. I was amazed that it was good enough for exhibition skating at that age. But this is a passport, and four pages of myself is really excessive and far too intimate and revealing. On the last page of pictures, I find my actual (present) passport picture. It is in the usual black-and-white, pleasant, calm, standard. While this should be the only picture in the passport, it was just one, an insignificantly placed one, among many. "But this can't be," thought I. "It looks as if I'm trying to show off. Why did the passport makers do it? What shall I do?" Then Lynn tells me she just received her passport with one page or so of extra pictures. Her father, a lawyer, had chemically steamed off the extra pictures. He did it very carefully so the police would not detect his tampering with the document. "My father will do it to your passport if you like," said Lynn. At first I was relieved. Then I hesitated, not wanting to tamper with my passport, for it is written on the passport itself that any alterations discovered will result in the revocation of the passport.

Commentary. I awake, thinking, "Is this my true identity expressed through skating? Did the passport people *not* make a mistake? Do they know better than I what is my true identity?" The warning printed on the passport application kept running through my head, "Passport photos must show a good likeness of the applicant, or they will not be accepted." Fully awake, I realize the impossibility of it all. I've not skated seriously for too long. I've lost too much time. I'm already twenty-three years old. Even if I were to give it another try, give up school for ice-skating, where would I find a partner? There are so few men to choose from in ice-dancing. As in the dream, I'd like to believe it possible that I could have a career in exhibition and movie ice-skating, but I cannot. The dream was so vivid, and seemed so real in a literal sense, that it is hard to see behind the metaphor. The literal-objective interpretation can't be right, so I'll try a dream interview to get to the bottom of this.

Setting. It is time for a new passport (identity). I've given the passport people a variety of self-images from which to choose the one showing the truest likeness of my identity. The passport I receive is new. The dream is surely dealing with my incubation request for new awareness of myself, and perhaps with a way to express it.

What is a passport? My favorite document. It shows one's identity and permits free access to the world. Free movement. Horrible to lose it or have it revoked. You can't see the world without it.

The black-and-white photo? The same as the one I have in my present passport. It's a good one, but it is standard. It represents my conscious self-image as a bright graduate student in psychology. It's not very exciting. My dream producer seems to be of the opinion that this is indeed a part of my identity, but not the most important part by any means.

The color photos? These represent my dream producer's idea of my true identity. It seems that I see them for the first time in the dream, or that I have been unaware of this self-image until now. These pictures showed me skating with and without a partner, in professional rather than competitive (amateur) settings, such as ice shows and movies.

The photos showed me at different ages ranging from twenty-five or so to forty-five. I was terribly pleased to see them but did not dare let myself believe they represented my true identity. Yet the photos were undeniably of me; I could even touch my future self-images as if they were three-dimensional and real.

Why would I send these off to the Philadelphia passport office, rather than the one I usually use in New York? Because Philadelphia is a more sensitive place, more aware of beauty and graceful living, than New York, which is so work oriented and pressured. I have been identifying myself with New York since I quit skating, haven't I?

Why can't I accept the passport people's choice? First, it seems impossible that I could become a really good skater again. Second, I'm afraid the photos are too ostentatious, revealing, and intimate.

How does that relate to my life? Perhaps in that I have become rather too sedate lately, in an effort to be acceptable to the intellectuals I have been surrounded by. I've somewhat repressed my flamboyance and the more free-spirited aspects of my personality because they don't seem socially acceptable in academic and professional environments. I regret this, but it seems appropriate. Perhaps I could find some outlets for my more outrageous, flamboyant characteristics. Perhaps a little skating on the side, a few times a week, would do it. Yet the dream is making a special point that my skating self is the greater, more significant part of my personality.

Who is Lynn? A good friend who is too man oriented. This has hurt me, as well as her own career. She puts herself down a lot and doesn't realize that she is dynamite as a woman, as a dancer-actor, and as a law student.

Is there a Lynn in me? I know the dream is telling me there is, but I can't believe it. Do I have more talent and "pizzazz" than I realize or have the courage to express? A little maybe. Am I too man oriented? Yes.

Who is Lynn's father, and what is he like? I like him a lot. He's sort of old world, a hardworking lawyer. He encourages Lynn to keep her nose to the academic grindstone. He likes to take car trips with Lynn. I'd rather fly. In fact, when I have traveled with my father it has always been by plane. Lynn's father, and her following in his footsteps, must represent my more conservative, cautious, security-conscious attitudes, which are capable of defacing my passport or true identity if I let them. I think Lynn has allowed these attitudes and a lack of belief in her talents to restrict the most exciting aspects of her identity.

Summary. OK. The dream is saying that my most colorful, lively, and true identity is represented by the skating pictures, and that the sedate, hardworking, nonadventurous aspects of myself, with which I now almost totally identify, belong, as does the black-and-white photo, in a subordinate position to my skating self. Just like Lynn, I tend to reject my skating self because of self-doubt, and because of an exaggerated concern for appearing respectable to people in my profession as well as to the part of myself that is like Lynn's father. As Rossi would say, Lynn's father represents my work and security-oriented attitudes, which block my realization of my true identity. These attitudes limit my personality and tend to standardize it. It is no wonder that, when I looked at myself through Lynn and her father's eyes, I felt inadequate and incapable of becoming that skater. I couldn't see the part of myself that is already like her. What does that skater represent? It seems reasonable to think that she stands for the flamboyant, risk-taking, courageous, and adventuresome part of me. Yet the sensation of skating is so real, even now, that it is hard not to take her as a literal, objective representation of my future. The fact that every one of the pictures, except for the black-and-white one, show me ice-skating and not doing something else is very interesting. It would seem to suggest that the dream is dealing with my objective professional identity rather than with a subjective metaphor for my whole identity, as that would have had to include several different representations of the other aspects of my personal identity. Perhaps I am being like Lynn now, but becoming a professional ice-skater does seem to be out of the question. Therefore, I shall interpret the dream to mean that I need to recognize, accept, and actualize the symbolic ice-skater within me—if I dare.

This dream was a harbinger of such good news on the objective level that I was tempted to place it in the category of a wish-fulfillment dream. Yet as usually happens in the course of a dream interview, it soon became clear that on the subjective level the meaning of the dream was more profound than that. Unhappily, I found both the objective interpretation (that I would skate professionally) and the subjective interpretation (that I was rejecting my flamboyant self) threatening to my current self-image and to my current professional and romantic involvements. Even after my dream interview, I decided to ignore the dream.

Finally, of course, waking and dream events conspired to convince me to take the message of this dream seriously. About a year after the dream, I began to express more and more of the symbolic skater within. Two years after the dream I put my skates on again and went to a local skating-club session. There, miracle of miracles, I met Bob Castle, a spectacular gold-medalist ice-dancer who just happened to be looking for a partner! Male ice-dancers are rare, but ones with gold medals and no partner are harder to find than water in the desert. Since Bob and I have been skating together, we have been to ice rinks in Sun Valley and Europe, and my skating is better and more fun than ever before. I never would have believed this possible in 1972. I have not turned professional, but who knows? Even that might be in the cards for me, though I still doubt it. Be that as it may, the quality of my life has improved markedly. Much more of the skater within has moved into every area of my life, and I have recaptured that sense of adventure, the longing for which had prompted me to incubate the passport dream.[4]

Now, twenty-six years after having had this dream, I continue to review it and to take inspiration from it. When I had the dream I thought forty-five years of age was ancient. I was surprised in the dream that one could have such muscle tone when so close to decrepitude. Now I am forty-nine and considering going into competition with my current partner, Dan Henry, this year in Amsterdam! At forty I took up the rather daring form of ice-skating known as pair-skating, in which your partner throws you around and, if you are lucky, catches you. I have never so enjoyed ice-skating, and I'm in pretty good shape. I'm far from a world-class skater, but the twice-weekly skating I do is enough to bring me lots of joy and satisfaction. My skating and my friends at the ice rink encourage flamboyance and playfulness, just as the dream suggested. I've tried to carry the courage and audacity of my dream images into a full-color life of Argentine tango dancing, together with regular monthlong visits to Rome, encouraging the part of myself that would like to be Italian. This dream and my keeping it in my heart have profoundly enlivened my life.

Considering Options for Action

Many insights gained in a dream interview are too new, too threatening, or too general to call for a specific action or decision to be made. For these insights, review and reflection are the most appropriate and fruitful response. However, there are often strong and clear insights reinforced by other dream work, by the dreamer's life experience, or by material the dreamer may be working with in other growth settings such as therapy or special-interest support groups such as Overeaters Anonymous or Alcoholics Anonymous. These insights call for action. At our Dream Center, in my private office, and in academic settings, I teach interviewers never to tell a dreamer what to do about a particular situation. But I do discourage the hoarding of insights for storage purposes. Some dreamers, in and out of therapy, use their dream insights the way Scrooge used money before his dream of the spirits of Christmas. They store their insights, proud of their good work, but their lives are never enriched, because the insights are never applied.

Their lives remain constricted, and their dream insights continue to repeat themselves because the dreamers stay in the same old ruts.

Therefore, when a dreamer's insights seem sound and ready for application, the interviewer may ask her if she would like to do something about the insight, and if so, what, how, and when. The dreamer is encouraged to take small rather than large steps at first so that the change will be easier to accomplish, and so that if the dreamer's decision is not an appropriate one, it can be corrected. Testing insights gives the dreamer reassurance that she is doing well and gives her the confidence to carry on.

Throughout the dream interview, there are many points that call for you to decide whether to get a fuller description or go on and attempt a bridge, whether to make a partial summary or wait till later on, and so forth. You needn't worry too much about making the perfect decision, because if you miss an important point, the dreamer, and more often the dreamer's confusion or inability to make a strong bridge, will signal you to go back and get a fuller description, slow down, or speed up. And testing the bridges will reduce the likelihood that you will go very far down the wrong path.

Five

FOLLOWING THE STEPS OF THE INTERVIEW

The most important thing to remember when you are playing the role of interviewer is that you pretend to come from another planet and therefore need to ask the dreamer questions from that perspective. Since the early 1970s I have been experimenting with various ways of phrasing a number of basic questions that are effective in eliciting from the dreamer the information necessary to understand a dream. Through the years I have revised the list of these questions several times. We call this list a *cue card* because students use it as a guide to asking their interview questions.[1] Obviously, it is impossible to list all the questions you will need in order to explore every dream image, but this cue card will supply you with enough questions to give you a good start as an interviewer. In using these questions exactly as they are worded, you will get a feel for ways to formulate your own follow-up questions when you need them.

The Dream Interviewer's Cue Card

Questions 2 through 4 are optional. They help a dreamer warm up to the feelings in the dream and can sometimes trigger a general understanding about its meaning. As you gain experience as an interviewer, or in interviewing your own dreams, you will be able to decide with confidence when to use the warm-up.

1. *Would you tell us your dream now?*

2. *What are the feelings you are most aware of in the dream?*

3. *Have you felt* [restate the feelings] *in your past or your current life?*

Sometimes, especially when interviewing people who are too quick to interpret their dreams before having carefully explored the images, it is better to omit these last two questions and wait to explore the feelings as they arise in the unfolding of the dream. All we need at this point is a highlighting of the dream feelings and an indication of whether the dreamer is aware of having experienced these exact feelings in waking life. Even if the dreamer is unable to recognize any parallel at this early stage, the questions will signal her to keep a lookout as she proceeds.

If the dreamer says that the dream feelings are familiar, ask her:

4. *When was the first or most recent time you felt this way?*

If the dreamer does not volunteer this information spontaneously, asking her to be specific will serve at least four functions. You will both be able to see whether the remembered occasion really fits the description of the dream feeling. The dreamer will become more familiar with the feeling and better able to recognize the times it has recurred in her life. You will both be better able to spot the patterns of situations that give rise to the feelings. And the dreamer will grow more comfortable discussing the feelings with you.

For each of the dream elements, there is a set of key questions that will allow you to execute the interview steps of *description, restatement, bridge,* and *summary.* Keep these questions with you as you work. In my book *The Dream Kit,* there is a set of cards listing these questions. Both the amateurs and the professionals we work with at the Dream Center have found them to be extraordinarily helpful in learning to conduct a dream interview.

1. *Describe the opening [or next] setting of the dream. What sort of place is _____?*

Name the dream setting: Texas, a restaurant, a schoolroom, an attic, Mom's house.

2. *What is* [name the place] *like in waking life?*

3. *What is* [name the place] *like in your dream?*

The way a dream modifies a setting provides clues to the particular qualities of the setting to be highlighted in the dream. For example, if the dreamer says, "I was in a prison, but now that you ask, it didn't look like a normal prison, it looked like my Uncle Willy's house," you need to get a description that blends both places. The dream prison then might be described as "a place that holds you captive in punishment for wrongdoing that looks like Uncle Willy's place, where I was dumped by my parents every summer."

This description would perhaps lead the dreamer to consider whether his feelings of being dumped included a sense of being put into prison for his wrongdoing. You could explore such possibilities by asking:

4. *How does it feel to be in this setting? or How do you feel as you stand [or sit] there?*

Questions like these will elicit the feeling or value-judgment side of a description. You could also ask, "Do you like such places?" or "How would you like to be in such a place in waking life, and why?"

5. *So this setting is* [recapitulate the description], *right?*

6. *Does this setting, which you describe as* [recapitulate the description], *remind you of anything?*

See where the dreamer goes with this question. Then, if appropriate, you can ask whether it reminds him of anything in his past or current life. Be careful throughout the interview not to focus too much on the past. This can devour all your time and energy. Use past examples sparingly to warm up to looking at the present manifestation of the issue and to consider its possible genesis. Remember to use only the dreamer's words in the recapitulation. Get a good description and a bridge (if possible) for each setting as it appears in the dream.

7. *How so?*

Test the bridge.

PEOPLE: DESCRIPTIONS AND BRIDGES

1. *Who is _____? Pretend I've never heard of _____ before.*

Ask the dreamer to tell who each character in the dream is as he makes his appearance. Remind the dreamer that you come from another planet and have never before heard of Madonna, Batman, Tom Cruise, the dreamer's sister, or policemen. If you say, "Tell me about *X*," the dreamer who is not accustomed to this method may go on and on with unfocused and redundant anecdotes and associations. If you ask, "What does *X* mean to you?" you will likely get a puzzled look from the dreamer and perhaps a premature and inaccurate interpretation. How can the dreamer really know what *X* means to him before he looks at what he feels and thinks about *X* both in waking life and as portrayed in the dream? Keep this response brief and move quickly to:

2. *What is _____ like in waking life [or in general]?*

This question usually elicits the heart of the description, in which the dreamer tells you how he thinks and feels about *X*. In twenty-five years of working exclusively with dream clients and students, I know of no other single word as powerful as the word *like*. Used at the end of a question asking for a description, it can turn a key in the dreamer's brain that unlocks the richest and most useful descriptions! Other ways to phrase this question are: "What kind of person is *X?*" and "What kind of personality does *X* have?" The dreamer will usually supply a few associations automatically as a part of the description. If you are interviewing yourself, associations will come to mind. Keep yourself or your dreamer close to the original dream image; don't let the associations go too far afield, or you will drown in irrelevant material.

Encourage the dreamer to give you his impressions of *X*'s personality in waking life and not to worry about being accurate or fair and objective. Ask questions that pull for the dreamer's gut feelings and opinions about *X,* such as "How do you *really* feel about *X?*"; "Do you like him, dislike him?"; "What are his most salient characteristics?"; "How do you feel about these?"

Some dreamers will describe *X* in terms of what he does, times they've had together, and with statements like "He's the sort of guy who . . ." Descriptions of *X*'s behavior, history, and physical appearance can be helpful in reconnecting the dreamer with his image of *X.* However, they can quickly reach the point of diminishing returns and devour precious time while they threaten to overload both parties and distract them from the dramatic thrust of the dream.

It is extremely important to help the dreamer distill these descriptions into descriptive *adjectives,* which are much easier to handle and often bring more clarity. Ask the dreamer to give you three adjectives that would describe a person who does such things, has such a history, or looks the way *X* does in the dream. This question can be very helpful in getting to the point and in eliciting a description that will be more likely to trigger a successful bridge later.

3. *What is _____ like in your dream?* and *What is _____ doing in your dream?*

By moving from the general to the particular, you can find out what specific aspects of *X* are emphasized in a given dream scene. If *X* is a major figure in the dreamer's life, such as a wife or father, the qualities of X highlighted in the dream can be used to narrow the focus of what could become an interminable description. For example: "Tell me about the part of your mom that is like the part of her portrayed in the dream." If X is a person or type of person unknown to the dreamer, you can ask, "What kind of person would you imagine X might be like, given how he looks and acts in the dream?"

4. *So _____ is* [restate the description], *right?*

5. *Does _____, whom you describe as* [recapitulate the description], *remind you of anything in your life?*

By your recapitulating the dreamer's description using the same adjectives and tone, she will often be able to bridge or to link the description to a person or a force in her life, or to an aspect of herself. By asking the dreamer if X reminds her of any*thing,* you leave her free to relate the image to some part of herself (the subjective level of interpretation) or to someone or something in her life (the objective level). Allowing the dreamer to choose the interpretive level diminishes the interviewer's possible distorting influence. If the dreamer seems to be avoiding a probable subjective interpretation by rushing to the objective level, you can always ask more pointed questions later. If X does not remind the dreamer of anything at this point, you can move on to the next image, or you can ask the more direct question that follows.

6. *Does _____, who is* [recapitulate the description], *remind you of anyone in your life; or is there some part of you that is like _____?*

By moving from asking if X reminds the dreamer of any*thing* to asking if X reminds her of any*one* or of any part of herself, you are being more direct and challenging. You may encounter strong resistance with this bridging question, especially if the dreamer has just described someone she dislikes. Though you may see some of X's characteristics in the dreamer, or in someone close to the dreamer, don't volunteer this. Keep helping the dreamer to further describe and bridge until she can see for herself the connection. Timing is all-important. An offended dreamer won't talk much. You can always leave this question and return to it (or any other question) at a time when the dreamer seems more open.

7. *How so?*

When a dreamer successfully bridges an image and says something like "Now that I hear you feed back that description, *X* reminds me of my first wife" (or "my boss," or "of the way I act when . . ."), it is important to ask the dreamer to test her bridge or explain her connection—for several reasons. Some dreamers need to take a moment to clarify and deepen the new perception, while others, upon closer inspection, find that the similarities don't really match. Perhaps they were trying too hard to make something fit that just does not fit. The dreamer's need to please can mislead both the dreamer and the interviewer. In many instances, testing leads to more questions like "You say *X* reminds you of your boss. Does *X* remind you of anyone else who is also *[recapitulate the description once more]*?" Not uncommonly, the dreamer for the first time sees similarities not only with his boss, but with his father and older brother. This question highlights important emotional and behavioral patterns.

ANIMALS: DESCRIPTIONS AND BRIDGES
1. *What is a _____ like? Pretend I've never seen one before.*

2. *How would you describe the personality of a _____?*

This may seem like an odd question, but it brings out very useful adjectives that often make it very easy for the dreamer to bridge to parts of herself or to people in her life. In fact, working this way with animal images makes animals the easiest of all images to understand. In all your efforts to elicit a right description from yourself or from another, be sure to get the dreamer to describe her feelings and judgments about the image or action. A description is not complete until you get the dreamer to verbalize her feelings about it.

3. *What is the _____ doing in your dream?*

4. *So the* _____ *is* [restate the description], *right?*

5. *Is there anyone in your life or anything or any part of yourself that is like a* _____, *which you describe as* [restate the description again]?

6. *How so?*

Test the bridge.

OBJECTS: DESCRIPTIONS AND BRIDGES

1. *What is a* _____? *Pretend I've come from another planet and have never seen such a thing before.*

Ask the dreamer to define and describe each of the major objects in the dream and to tell you what it is used for and how it works. Remind him that you come from another planet and have never even heard of such an object before. Reassure the dreamer that you are interested not in scientific accuracy but in his ideas or understanding of what a *Y* is and how it functions. Again, if you ask, "What does a *Y mean* to you?" you usually get a premature interpretation, so you need to *get a definition and a description first.* Ask questions that elicit whatever value judgments the dreamer has about a *Y.* "Do you like *Y*s?" "Do you own, eat, wear, enjoy, or hate *Y*s? Why or why not?" "What kinds of people tend to own, eat, wear a *Y?*"

2. *What is the* _____ *in your dream like?*

This question moves from the general or generic to the specific. When the dreamer describes his dream objects, he may also add some associations that you may want to explore further. With experience you will get a feeling for which trains of association are likely to be productive and which are likely to distract from the dream action and devour time. If the dream object is oddly different from the generic object, ask questions that clarify the differences, then ask questions like "How would a _____ like the one in your dream look or function differently from a normal _____?" For example, if someone dreamt of a short basketball player with four hands, you would ask, "How would a four-handed basketball player be different from a normal one?" Your dreamer might then surprise himself by saying, "Well, he would be at an obvious height disadvantage, but he might be able to make up for it with the extra hands. That makes me think that I often put myself down for being short, but my girlfriend says that I am attractive to her especially because of the way I use my hands when we make love!"

Be sure to find out how the dreamer really feels about such objects in general and about the one in the dream. If the dreamer is not forthcoming, coax him with questions like "Do you like or dislike *Ys*?"; "Do you think *Ys* are wonderful, silly, necessary, or creepy?" As soon as possible, cease suggesting words and use those that the dreamer supplies—they are the best.

3. *So the _____ in your dream is* [restate the description], *right?*

4. *Does the _____ in your dream, which you describe as* [recapitulate the description], *remind you of anything in your life?*

As when bridging from people in dreams to waking life, it may be necessary or desirable to follow this question with others like "Does the _____, which is *[recapitulate again]*, remind you of anyone or of any part of yourself?"

5. *How so?*

As with any image the dreamer has bridged, asking the dreamer to clarify and confirm by testing the bridge is vital.

FEELINGS: DESCRIPTIONS AND BRIDGES
1. *How do you feel at this moment in the dream?*

This question can be asked at any point in the interview. I especially like to ask it right at the end of the first telling of the dream, while the dreamer has been brought by the story to the last moment. Frequently the dreamer fails to spontaneously tell how she feels when, at the very last moment in the dream, the ferocious lion is shot in the chest with a bullet. The dreamer could feel relief, gratitude to the gunman, or dismay and unexpected sadness. We must know which she feels, and so must she. It is good to ask how the dreamer feels at any point in the dream where there is reason to suspect the existence of unexpressed or unappreciated feeling.

2. *Tell me more about this feeling.*

3. *Tell me about a time [or the last time] you felt this way.*

These last two invitations are useful when the dreamer is reticent or is having trouble recognizing and exploring feelings.

4. *Let me see if I understand. You are/were feeling* [recapitulate the description of the feeling], *right?*

5. *Does this feeling of* [recapitulate the description] *remind you of anything in your current life?*

By now the dreamer should be familiar with the feeling and may have bridged it already to a waking situation.

6. *How so?*

ACTION: DESCRIPTIONS AND BRIDGES
1. *Describe the major action or event in this scene.*

This is where the people and objects find their dramatic context, and bridging efforts that may have failed earlier may suddenly succeed. In order for this to happen, ask the dreamer simple questions.

2. *Why do humans do such things, and how do you feel about it?*

If the dreamer has just told you that he dreamt of dancing the tango in his in-line skates, ask, "Is this how humans usually dance the tango?" Then ask him why or why not. You will have to get a description of the skates and elicit his opinion of humans who would tango in them. You can recapitulate these answers by themselves, or you can recapitulate them as part of the following bridge question.

3. *Does* [recapitulate the description of the action] *remind you of any situation in your life?*

For example, "Is there anywhere in your life where you are dancing a sensual, intricate dance with a woman, but are also inappropriately dressed with boots you describe as ugly, unwieldy, and yet good for quick one-direction movement?" The dreamer might respond: "This reminds me of my ambivalent feelings toward my girlfriend." Then you would ask the dreamer to test the bridge with the following question.

4. *How so?*

Our dreamer might then describe more fully how he is enjoying the role of irresistible seducer and enjoying the intricate interplay with his girlfriend, but is ever ready for a quick getaway.

5. *How would you describe the central plot of this dream?*

6. *Does* [recapitulate the description] *remind you of any situation in your life?*

SUMMARY QUESTIONS
1. *Shall I summarize all the descriptions and bridges made so far, or would you like to do it?*

Either the dreamer or the interviewer strings together the descriptions and bridges in the sequential context of the dream action. If you are working alone, don't give in to the temptation to skip this step. It is amazingly useful, and may be even more so if you write out your summary. Summaries can be made at the end of the dream interview, or as you go along, scene by scene. Ask the dreamer to correct you if your summary doesn't sound just right. Sometimes the dreamer suddenly has more to say about an image in this phase of the interview.

2. *So in this part of the dream,* [recapitulate what happened], *which you [or I] described as* _____, *which reminded you [me] of* [bridge]. *Then* [recapitulate what happened next].

And so forth.

3. *Does all this remind you of anything else?*

Take your time in this phase. Even when the metaphor or analogy is obvious to you, it is important to resist the temptation to provide the dreamer with the interpretation. Dealing with these last two questions is more difficult than dealing with the preceding one, because it requires discipline and practice to accurately summarize a whole scene or the entire dream interview without slipping in your own ideas.

4. *Now, how do you understand your dream? Tell me the whole dream, adding the bridges and commenting on what you understand and what remains unclear.*

Remember to leave interpretations to the dreamer. The interviewer's job is to ask questions that will clarify or point out inconsistencies. In cases when the dreamer is unable to make important connections, suggesting to the dreamer possible hypotheses regarding possible bridges may be helpful. However, doing so is fraught with danger and should be undertaken only as a last resort. Leaving the dreamer to puzzle out for himself how it all comes together can yield better results depending upon the dreamer and the situation. Be alert during this summary phase to anything new brought up or any difference of detail. This may be significant and require reexploration.

Let's take a look now at the use of these questions in an interview with Diana. Here is a dream she had one month after meeting her boyfriend, Jeff, and two weeks before she was to marry him.

I am climbing. A woman is close beside me, exuberant but inattentive. She makes me gasp at her foolishness. My "appropriate fear" keeps me holding tight, climbing slowly. She falls. What could I have done to prevent it? Nothing. There is a gathering around her by the time I got down. Ron is taking charge. He makes a bed for her. His wife, Jill, is in the house, somewhat depressed after the arrival of their new baby, Milly. She is slim and gorgeous looking. A boredom seems to possess her. She flips listlessly through a magazine. Ron takes up the care of the baby. Although he is gentle and supportive, he is unable to reach or move Jill. He even prepares dinner. Except for Jill, we all help with dinner. Her eyes are pale blue, and a weak smile is the most excitement or emotion anyone gets out of her.

After supper, we clean up. I go out to the car to find the injured girl beside her car, offering to drive us to the movies in it. Ron insists he drive her car for her. The three of us pile in the car. She and I start speaking in French about the movie we are to see while we wait for Jill to get the baby bundled up. Then she, Mark, and Milly will get into the car too. Ron is surprised at the depth of our discussion, and soon, with great liveliness, he joins in.

GAYLE: What is this exuberant, foolish woman like?

DIANA: Well, what comes to mind is . . . moving too fast. As I
           reviewed all the dreams I recorded from the time I met Jeff,
           looking to see if my dreams had offered me any warning signals
           that I missed, I said, "Damn, here it is." Here is the foolish,
           reckless youth who doesn't pay attention to her safety, and
           goes over the edge.

G: Does the way this exuberant, foolish woman was acting remind you of any way you were acting at the time of the dream?

D: With Jeff. I was planning to marry this guy after only one month of knowing him. It was foolish, reckless, speedy movement that was not comfortable to me, but I kept doing it.

G: Does this foolish movement remind you of anything else?

D: Yes. Of the relationship I had with a younger man. I was reckless in that one too. I moved too fast.

G: What was your "reasonable fear" in the dream like? Was it reasonable?

D: Yes. There's a huge part of me that feels that when people go slowly or cautiously, they are wimps. It's a sign of weakness rather than of wisdom. So, there's always been a dichotomy between the daredevil and the wise, cautious person in me.

G: I'm still confused. In the dream, were you being wisely cautious, or were you being a cautious wimp?

D: I was being wisely cautious. But in my waking life I was acting more like the reckless woman.

G: In the dream, you say you could have done nothing to prevent her fall?

D: I don't think she would have listened. She was on the course. And that was true of me. My sister and my aunt both had expressed some trepidation about this man and I just . . .

G: Who is Ron, the one who has made the bed for the woman who has fallen?

D: Ron is the husband of a friend of mine, Jill.

G: What is Ron like?

D: Ron is . . . how shall I describe him? I've always thought he was a wimp. He's a feminine man. He's quite wealthy. He is a man who would cook or take over the baby. I mean, he is kind of attentive, and he takes full responsibility for things. He wouldn't be someone who would do something dangerous. He's cautious, contemplative, slow.

G: Does he remind you of anything or anyone?

D: No.

G: In the dream, Ron takes the responsibility of making a bed for the woman who has fallen. How do you feel about that?

D: I appreciate it.

G: What is Jill like in waking life?

D: She doesn't work. She is always searching for the thing that is going to give her some liveliness. She's not so much the mannequin as she plays in the dream, but yes, I would say that she's someone who hasn't found her place in the world.

G: Jill looks gorgeous, but . . . ?

D: Jill is . . . Maybe this has something to do with what I see as the role I would get into as a wife. I would be the mannequin woman who has the finely done nails. Soon after childbirth she has her body back, she is skinny, has her hair done. Yet there is no quality of life or loving about her. She's bored, she's listless.

G: Tell me again what Ron is like.

D: I think of feminine men and me. I rejected the feminine qualities of my father. I wanted him to be a macho man, out in the world and successful. He wasn't. My mother was. So Ron, like feminine men, and like my dad, is nurturing, and responsible, not just an aggressor, a doer in the world. My boyfriends have always been, at least on the surface, aggressive doers.

G: Does the family scene with Ron and Jill remind you of anything?

D: Again, I'm always afraid that I'll turn into the woman at home. I would lose my spark, and wouldn't have anything interesting about me. I'd be doing my nails and keeping my body thin! That is my image of married life.

G: So does the scene of the mannequin wife and the wealthy, nurturing husband bring anything else to mind?

D: Well, at the time of the dream, I thought Jeff was this big, successful millionaire with whom I could settle down and have children. He was offering me that.

G: But Jeff wasn't like a Ron, was he? [Even though at this point in the interview I suspect that Ron may be highlighting qualities of Jeff that Diana resists recognizing, I do not say so. Instead, by phrasing the question this way, I hope to elicit greater clarification.]

D: No. Although Jeff *had* offered that if I wanted to have the child I was pregnant with from my affair with the younger man, I could.

G: Not that Jeff would take care of it? [Again, I am baiting her. I take the position of her resistance, and leave her free to correct me if she wishes.]

D: But in a way he would. He promised to support me if I decided to have the baby.

G: Tell me about Ron's making the bed for the woman who had fallen.

D: He did it so that she could be attended to and taken care of. They would fix her up and make sure that she would be OK.

G: Interesting.

D: The fallen woman is myself. I had the abortion, and here comes Jeff into my life offering to make me a bed and heal me. I never ever wanted to have an abortion. What a horror that I had got myself into this situation!

G: So the first part of the dream in which the girl falls reminds you of . . . ?

D: My reckless relationship with the younger man, my abortion, and my reckless tendencies.

G: And the family scene with Ron and Jill?

D: It reminds me of Jeff, who will take care of my fallen, foolish self, and of a lifeless future as a wife who does not work.

G: What happens next?

D: We're going to the movies. I speak in French with the injured woman about the movie we are to see.

G: What sort of language is French?

D: It's a romantic language. The language of my youth. It is culture. Ron is a very cultured man.

G: What does speaking this romantic, cultured language remind you of?

D: It takes me back to my youth. To a time that I had a very good life. I lived it at my French school. My family was wealthy then. It was a time of a lot of power and juiciness in my life.

G: What do you think about the wounded woman wanting to drive her own car?

D: She was acting stronger than she was.

G: Remind you of anything?

D: Yes, I definitely was wounded by this thing with the young guy, the baby, and all that. But I was not going to allow it to get me down. I was determined to charge full speed ahead and get my life going again with Jeff.

G: Enter Ron again. He insists upon driving. What is he like? Is he Ron the Wimp, or Ron the Cultured?

D: In this dream, there is no Ron the Wimp. That's the way I used to think of Ron. I no longer thought of him as a wimp at the time of the dream.

G: OK, he's Ron the What?

D: Well, he's the caretaker.

G: The caretaker. Is he dull, exciting, interesting?

D: He's dependable. He gets interesting . . . I mean interested.

G: The caretaker gets interested. Does that remind you of any one?

D: Yes, I'd say so. When I went through the abortion, Jeff was pacing up and down. I had apparently passed out after the operation, and was taking much longer to come out than expected. He had fantasies that I was dying.

G: Did Jeff get interested in the part of you that speaks French?

D: Yes. He loved it that I was well connected in the city, and that I was cultured. At the time I thought he was very cultured. I now realize he was not.

G: Would you like to summarize the dream, or would you like me to?

D: Would you? I'd like to hear all this together. I'll let you know if you go off course.

G: It seems that in the dream you are looking at some of the ways Jeff, like Ron, is—or seemed to be—a rich caretaker who has come to save you after the abortion and the pain involved with that. Perhaps also to save the reckless woman ever in you and give her a good life. [Diana nods in agreement, so I continue.]

There is, however, a fly in the ointment, and that's Jill. And you are not sure the life of a millionaire's wife would be all that great. At the end of the dream, Ron takes the wheel much as Jeff took on the organization of your life as he became attracted to your cultured, powerful, French-speaking self?

D: That about sums it up, doesn't it?

As you can see, by answering relatively nonleading questions, the dreamer can discover for herself what her dream means. It took a few rounds of questions to bridge Ron, but in the end the connection was clear. Diana was able to use the dream to look more closely at her recklessness, her desire for a wealthy caretaker, and her fears of becoming a listless millionaire's wife. She also glimpsed the effect her mother's and father's styles had on her choice in men.

The questions from the cue card were sometimes modified to fit the tone and rhythm of the interview. I find that maintaining a normal conversational interview tone is very important in putting the dreamer at ease. The questions can be asked in various orders according to the structure of the dream and the particular interviewing strategy you are using at any given moment.

Basic Dream-Interview Strategies

If you have already experimented with conducting a dream interview by yourself or with a dream partner, you will have noticed that keeping in mind the core steps of the interview (eliciting a good description, recapitulating, bridging, and summarizing) is not as easy as it may at first seem. The questions on the cue card help a great deal in the actual practice of the interview, yet as you can imagine (if you've not already discovered it), dreamers' responses can be very surprising, and at times rather confusing and disorienting.

Then there is the problem of the especially loquacious, shy, or defensive dreamer whose responses don't appear to be very enlightening. Learning to cope successfully with these difficulties in interviewing other dreamers is the best possible training in learning to understand the dreams of one of the most challenging dreamers you will ever work with—yourself.

Following is a description of several basic strategies that you will frequently be able to use to facilitate your dream work. If you practice using these in conjunction with the cue-card questions, you will be able to take full advantage of the advanced strategies described in my book *Breakthrough Dreaming*.

STRATEGY NO. 1: AMPLIFYING THE FEELINGS

When the dreamer is not forthcoming about her feelings, opinions, or judgments in her descriptions of any dream element, you must get her to amplify what little she can express so that both of you can get a better picture of what is going on. Try to give the dreamer permission to exaggerate her feelings. Ask her to amplify them, to exaggerate them for just a moment. Tell her you could imagine having strong feelings about such a thing. Tactfully tease a dreamer you think would respond well to words such as "Come on now. I'll bet you have some feelings about that." If a dreamer seems on the verge of tears from thinking about a particular image or part of the dream but has no response to being asked what she is feeling, try asking something like "What is the saddest part of this scene [*or* image]?" or "If your tears had words, what would they say?"

STRATEGY NO. 2: GUESSING THE ABSURD, OR THE OPPOSITE

When a dreamer has trouble finding words to describe a dream image or action, it is sometimes helpful to make a guess that you are quite sure is wrong. By your suggesting an absurdly silly or clearly inappropriate descriptive word, the dreamer is almost always jarred and responds with a quick and very telling correction. This is an amusing and enjoyable strategy. For example, one of my clients just couldn't find much to say about turnips beyond describing them as a boring vegetable. I asked her if they were a favorite dessert among humans. She replied, "Good heavens, no! You only eat turnips if your mother forces them down your throat. They are disgustingly bland." The dream in which one of her prospective employers offered her turnips shed new light on certain turniplike aspects of this career opportunity that had been overshadowed by her desire to move up the career ladder even if the new position might not be as exciting as she would like.

STRATEGY NO. 3: "HOW IS IT DIFFERENT FROM . . . ?"

When a dreamer can describe a dream image—say, a gym he found himself in—only vaguely, ask him how the gym he dreamt of differs from the last one he belonged to or how it is different from others he knows of. Think about what category of things, people, feeling, or action the dream falls into, and ask how it is different from another thing, person, feeling, or action in that category. If the image is a cat, ask how cats are different from dogs. If the image is fencing, ask how that sport is different from soccer, horse racing, or football.

STRATEGY NO. 4: CORRALLING THE DREAMER

When your dreamer becomes loquacious or tangential in her descriptions, you can help her to refocus her energies, return to relevant material, and keep on the scent of the dream by saying something like "Let me bring you back to the dream." You may have to interrupt some dreamers with a line like this one or risk wasting much time and losing your way in the forest. When you interrupt the dreamer, it is often appropriate to reassure her that she has done nothing wrong, that her job is to say what comes to mind in response to your question and that it is your job to corral her when she seems to move too far from the dream. Freud and Jung wanted a full personal history (anamnesis) of the dreamer and a detailed description of the current life situation as background information for dream work. Freud then asked for copious free associations, and Jung for more focused associations. I agree with Boss that relevant history and current situational material will be offered by the dreamer, or can be selectively elicited as the dream poses its issues. The interviewer asks highly focused questions that in most cases bring out the necessary relevant information in the emotional and conceptual context of the dream. This can save time, and encourages the dreamer, rather than the interpreter, to point out relevant bridges or parallels between waking and dreaming realities.

It is true that in corralling the dreamer you risk cutting off a line of thought, feelings, or associations that could lead to relevant and useful material. But as a rule, even if you do make a mistake by corralling the dreamer too soon, you will get stuck at the bridge and realize you must return to get a fuller description of the image. A good interviewer is part bloodhound. With practice you will learn to follow the scent of the dream and not allow anything to get you off that track.

STRATEGY NO. 5: SHEEPDOGGING

A decade ago or so I demonstrated the Dream Interview Method in one of Arthur Hastings's classes at the Transpersonal Psychology Institute. Arthur, who is a very sensitive psychologist and a skilled student of dreams, later told me that I worked like a sheepdog. In the class, I was working with a particularly defensive woman and had to use all my wit. Arthur said something like "You work like a sheepdog. You gently get her to lay out a description, then try to get her to go over the bridge [or through the gate]. But if she looks like she is going to resist, you back off immediately and go at her from another image. You warm her up through her description, then try again to get her to the bridge. If that attempt fails, you go to another image, or back to a formerly explored one, each time backing off just before her defenses rally and she might bolt. After a while she has laid out so many suggestive descriptions that you've got her. She crosses the bridge because it seems the only thing to do." It wasn't until eight years after this discussion with Arthur that I first went to a county fair and saw sheepdog trials. Arthur was right. An interviewer needs to be insistent, focused on getting the dreamer to cross the associative bridge, but she must be agile, backing off quickly when resistance is high, and she must know how to use any number of strategies.

STRATEGY NO. 6: RESTATEMENT

Simply restating the dream action or the dreamer's description of a dream element can be a powerful strategy. Diana's response to my repeatedly saying "The caretaker gets interested" at the end of the interview on her dream about the exuberant, foolish woman precipitated a bridge between Ron and her fiancé, Jeff, that had badly needed confirmation. To work a restatement into an interview, you might say, "So then Z happened, right? Wait, let me write that down . . . Let me see if I've got that straight. It's interesting [odd, curious] that . . ." With your tone of voice you can use these lines to gently invite useful comment from the dreamer.

Six

COMMON DREAM THEMES

If dreams are so special, and if we really must learn to interpret them in light of the dreamer's particular associations and life circumstances, why do we have common dreams? The best answer I can give is that since dreams express our hopes, fears, conflicts, and efforts to solve problems, we, as humans, are bound to share common concerns. It makes sense to me that these concerns would now and again be represented by images that conjure up for most of humanity certain core emotional responses. Humans are prone to experiencing fear of being eaten, of falling and losing control, of being socially embarrassed, and so on.

If a human being was suffering from the common fear of being attacked, the chances are high that a dream of being chased would express that concern. Modern man might put some new twists on this dream, such as being chased by a car rather than a tiger, but the theme remains the same. However, there is usually much more useful information in these dreams than the basic theme. Many of your common dreams have their own personality—your personality. The fact that you dream a common dream on a particular night is the first clue to its special meaning for you. You almost always dream about issues that were of concern to you on the day preceding the dream. So you might dream of being smothered the same night you met a woman who was very attractive but deep down reminded you of your smothering mother.

Your common dreams and nightmares are generally customized, and include details and variations on the common themes that offer you a more specific look at what is going on in your heart. In interpreting these dreams, don't be satisfied with broad, general platitudes such as "You have dreams of falling because you fear loosing status in your life." Find out how the way you fell in your dream really felt and how that bridges or parallels some specific situation in your life. Maybe your falling dream was tinged with feelings of shame or loss of control. The dream events that led up to the moment of your fall will also offer you clues about the meaning of falling for you on this particular night in this particular dream.

Throw away the old-fashioned, superstitious dream dictionary you bought last year. Its rigid interpretations can never give you the answers you need. Here are some examples of common dream assistance, most of them taken from my book *In Your Dreams,* my answer to those one-interpretation-fits-all prescriptions.[1] You can look up your particular dream here, just as you would use a dictionary. But instead of pat responses you will find lots of ideas and the sorts of questions you can use to unlock your private, specific meaning.

What about the fact that most of our common dreams are also common to us—in other words, they tend to recur often or from time to time. In most cases, our common dreams represent a recurring theme or problem in our lives. Often this is a theme we share with many other people. By understanding our particular version of a common dream, we can resolve a recurring problem and at the same time appreciate that many of us at one time or another share similar difficulties in living.

Dream Themes: How to Interpret Any Theme in Your Dreams

Almost every dream you will ever dream will have a plot or theme to it, common or uncommon. Without understanding the theme, you will usually be at a loss to make sense out of the individual images—the people and things you dream up. This first section is dedicated to helping you figure out any theme you conjure up. The rest of the chapter will deal with the most common dream themes and their variations. You will see how different people who have worked with me have interpreted their versions of common dreams, and you will find a short list of questions that you can use and modify to interview yourself or another dreamer about the particular meaning of a common dream.

Try using the interview questions listed below to explore the meaning of any theme not listed in this book. They will help you follow the basic interview steps, which are:

1. Getting a good description

2. Restating that description

3. Bridging or connecting the image described to something in your life.

Remember, if you pretend that the interviewer comes from a different planet, you will find it much easier to give concise answers that get to the point about what you really feel and really think about the various images in your dream. This will work whether you give the role of interviewer to a partner or you play it yourself. These questions should provide you with the material to connect your dream experience to your waking experience, and thus interpret your dream according to your own meaning system—which, after all, is the one you went to sleep with before you created the dream. Good luck!

1. *Describe the main theme in your dream.*

2. *Exactly how did you feel in that situation?*

Are you being suffocated? Is someone chasing you? Have you lost your purse? Do you find yourself naked in public? Describe as fully as you can your specific feelings and attitudes. Just how did you feel as you stood there stark naked in the dream? Remember, I, your interviewer, come from another planet and don't know how a human like you would feel in such a situation. Can you find three adjectives to describe your experience?

3. *Is there any situation in your life in which you have the same feelings you just described?*

4. *What led up to your finding yourself in that situation?*

5. *Is there any way that in your life you are doing things analogous to the things that led to your dream predicament?*

6. *How so?*

7. *What parallels do you see between your dream theme and feelings, and your hopes, fears, habits, and concerns in your waking life?*

BEING CHASED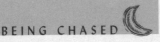

Variations

This is usually a frightening dream. We are chased by all manner of people, animals, and sometimes elements like storms, lightening, and thunder. Very often dreamers do not remember much detail, only that they were trying to escape from a mean beast or a huge bug, or a threatening man. The pursuer might carry a gun or a knife or simply exude a sense of ominous threat. Dreamers almost always awaken before they can find out what will happen. Some manage to outwit their pursuers before awakening. In some cases the dreamer is caught by the pursuer, and in some the dreamer decides to stop running, turns around, and asks his assailant, "What do you want, what are you doing in my dream?" at which point any number of surprises may occur.

Sample Dreams

"Thug Chases Me"

Joseph dreamt regularly of a thirty-year-old thug (about his own age) who was running after him, trying to get him. Sometimes he'd have a gun, sometimes a knife, sometimes just his bare hands. Joseph would awake full of anxiety, his heart beating fast. This is a very common version of a chase dream. When Joseph described the thug in his dream as a rough, uncouth, inconsiderate oaf who was very self-centered and unconcerned about the needs of others, he saw a parallel to himself—to the part of himself that had yet to be civilized and that drank too much, drove while drunk, and could be extremely hostile toward people who angered him. In the dream he felt threatened by this aspect of his personality, which was threatening his career and his relationship.

"Chased by Men with Knives"

Elena dreamt the following dream perhaps three times a year over the period of more than a decade:

> I was walking down a street in the city. It was night, and two young men brandishing knives were chasing after me. I woke up terrified.

This is a common dream in which women feel threatened by men carrying guns or knives. Very often the dreamer can't say much about the pursuers, only that they are threatening. It is not clear what they want to do to the dreamer, perhaps kill her, but certainly they have ill intent and the dreamer feels simply terrified. In this case Elena said that the feelings in the dream describe her feeling of vulnerability, in the urban environment she lives in as well as in the general sense that she feels threatened by a variety of situations in her life in which she feels unprotected and alone.

What Do You Say?

1. *Describe, being as specific as you can, just how you feel as you are being chased in the dream.*

2. *Can you say why this person is chasing you and what his or her intent is?*

3. *What is the person or thing that is chasing you like?*

4. *Does this person or thing, which you describe as* [restate the description], *remind you of anyone or anything in your life that you are running away from or that seems to be after you?*

5. *Do the feelings you experience in the dream remind you of any situation in your life?*

6. *What would be a better way than fleeing to deal with the conflict or the problem?*

Variations

Many common dreams come in both pleasant and unpleasant versions, but a dream of having your teeth fall out seems always to give the dreamer an awful feeling. The good news is that if you can figure out why you are having your particular version of this dream at this particular time in your life, you may be able to understand something important and resolve a conflict or two.

This is a very common dream; almost everyone has had it. Sometimes people dream that their teeth are crumbling into their hands, or worse yet that they can feel the teeth totally loose like stones inside their mouth. Some dreamers say that it is just at the point of smiling that their teeth spurt out of their mouth. Almost everyone feels either shocked or terribly embarrassed.

Sample Dreams
"Teeth Crumble"
Claudio dreamt:

> I was sitting with a group of friends when I suddenly felt all my teeth crumble in my mouth. I knew that as soon as I opened my mouth they would all fall out.

Claudio asked himself if his feelings of anxiety and imminent embarrassment that he felt in the dream reminded him of any recent life situation. Sure enough, the dream seemed to be exaggerating his new position as manager at his office and making him look at how he felt in it. He dreamt this dream the night after his first meeting as the new manager in his office. He interpreted the dream as pointing out to him that he was not as confident as he pretended to be—that in fact he was terribly worried that he had been prematurely promoted and was bound to say something so stupid that all would know he was too inexperienced for the post. The dream helped him recognize and work with his anxiety.

"Teeth in Hand"
Katherine dreamt:

> My teeth suddenly fell out into my hand. All of them!

When she asked herself exactly how she had felt in the dream and why this situation might lead to such feelings, Katherine got to the meaning of her dream. Katherine was in the process of getting a divorce after twenty years of marriage. The dream feelings of dread at having to be seen toothless and old vividly pictured her worst fears as she reentered the singles world. She knew that she had better come to terms with the realities of being fifty and single if she wanted to be able to date with any self-confidence—the quality that most attracts men.

What Do You Say?

Now it's your turn. Here are some dream-interviewer questions that will help you find out why you dreamt of your teeth falling out when you did.

1. *Why would a human like you (remember, I come from another planet) care if his or her teeth fell out? In other words, what's wrong with having your teeth fall out?*

2. *If you know, describe which teeth fell out and how it came to happen.*

3. *How do you feel in the dream about all this?*

4. *Do the feelings you have in your dream remind you of any feelings or of a recent situation in your life?*

5. *How so?*

Check to see if you have made a good match or bridge between your dream and your life feelings. If not, describe your dream feelings more fully until you see the parallels in your life.

BEING NAKED IN PUBLIC

Variations

We are sometimes totally naked, sometimes only partially undressed, but in all these dreams we feel embarrassed, ashamed, and, oddly, usually incapable of making an exit or finding some clothing. Another strange thing about these dreams is that usually the people who see us don't seem to care. They seem indifferent both to our nakedness and to our suffering. Sometimes we know the people who are looking at us; they might be friends or family members. This dream almost always seems to end badly in more or less frozen embarrassment, and we wake up feeling wretched. Only very rarely do dreamers tell of not being embarrassed and of actually finding an unexpected comfort in nakedness.

Sample Dreams
"Emilio in the Streets"
Emilio dreamt that he was standing in the middle of a busy street in Rome (his home) between four lanes of traffic when he suddenly realized he was naked from the waist down. He felt very embarrassed and didn't know what to do.

When I asked him how he felt being naked in the middle of a Roman street, he said, "Well, I was embarrassed." I asked, "Why were you embarrassed?" He responded, "Well, the cars go very fast, the drivers are very aggressive, and I felt very vulnerable." He was then able to bridge the dream feelings to those that he was having in his waking life in his new job, where he was surrounded by very aggressive people and needed to learn how to gird his loins for his professional battles.

"In the Green Bathtub"
Susanna dreamt that she was at a beautiful party at a posh ski resort in Switzerland. She was in a spectacular private home, and everyone was dancing and having a good time on the first floor. She decided to go upstairs and take a bath in her hostess's luxurious bathroom. The bathtub was emerald green, about ten feet by ten feet square and about four feet deep. She slipped into the tub as beautiful music was playing. She was happy to just relax and soak in the tub, but then she noticed that other people were walking by the bathroom and the door was wide open. At first she was embarrassed, thinking she should get out of the warm tub, close the door, and make sure no one could see her. But then she thought, "Ah, it's no big deal, I don't care if they see me. I am having such a wonderful time."

Susanna described her feelings in the dream and realized that they parallel perfectly her growing sense of confidence in her own sensuality and her ability to go after what she wants in life. She was surprised that in the dream she was able to stop worrying about being seen, which reminded her of her own determination to become more comfortable both in public and in private with her sensual, sexual side.

What Do You Say?

1. *Describe the setting in which you are naked.*

2. *How do you feel being naked in this setting? Remember, I come from another planet and have no idea how humans feel in such situations.*

3. *Is there any situation in your current life in which you feel as you do in the dream—for example, overexposed or vulnerable?*

4. *In the dream, does anyone else care that you are naked?*

5. *If no one else in the dream cares that you are so exposed, could it be that in your waking life you are overly concerned with being vulnerable or feeling emotionally exposed?*

BEING UNABLE TO RUN

Variations

Almost everyone in an audience will groan when I mention the dream of wanting to run but being unable to. Your legs feel like they are mud or water, and you just can't run! This dream is sometimes a variation on the being-chased dream, because very often people recognize they are unable to run as a response to the effort to flee from a pursuer. This dream is usually both frustrating and frightening.

Sample Dream
"Leaden Legs"
Patrick dreamt:

> I was playing softball with a community team and hit the ball into left field and went to run to first base, but my legs wouldn't go—they felt heavy and leaden—and I was unable to get to first base before I woke up.

In interviewing himself Patrick described his feeling of having hit the ball as one of satisfaction and achievement followed by a terrible feeling of not being able to move his legs because they felt so heavy. He felt he was working against tremendous forces in trying to move. He asked himself where he had similar feelings in waking life and realized that it was a recurring situation for him that, having achieved something in his life, he would often feel somewhat paralyzed to follow through. In his work he would win a contract and then have a difficult time motivating himself to do the follow-up. He had always thought this was just laziness, but the feelings in the dream had more to do with anxiety. Perhaps some of his paralysis after achievement came from a fear that the achievement was just a fluke and he wouldn't be able to live up to his promise.

What Do You Say?

1. *Why are you running in this dream?*

2. *If you are being chased, can you describe who or what is running after you?*

3. *Describe as specifically as you can, using three or four adjectives, how you felt at being unable to run in the dream.*

4. *Is there anything or anyone in your life that is like the pursuers in your dream?*

5. *Is there anywhere in your life where you feel just as you do in the dream* [for example, paralyzed, leaden, frozen]?

6. *If you find a parallel situation, can you imagine a way to mobilize yourself to take appropriate action, to liberate yourself from a fear or from someone else's control?*

MAKING LOVE TO AN UNEXPECTED PARTNER

Variations

Haven't you been surprised in more than one dream at finding yourself making love to the most unexpected people? These dreams can be nightmares or sweet romance depending of course on whom you are making love to and how you feel about that person. You might make love to your mother or your father, your sister or your brother; you might have sex with someone of the same sex if you are heterosexual or someone of a different sex even though you are homosexual or lesbian. You might find yourself in bed with someone you had a crush on in childhood, someone from second grade or high school or college. Very often people find themselves making love to an old boyfriend or girlfriend or a former husband or wife. This can be a rather shocking experience, or it can be a semisweet one of sadness and longing.

Helpful Hints

These dreams are easiest to work with if you first describe the personality of the dream lover as well as the quality of the dream encounter. See if there are any parallels in waking life. The dream lover could indeed represent a part of you, a part of your personality. In cases in which the dreamer is making love to an absolutely marvelous, wonderful person of the same or different sex, the dream lover could represent an idealized self-image of the dreamer. Or the lover could represent a situation in which the dreamer feels honored and flattered that such a lover would be interested in him or her. Such dreams come at a time when the dreamer is moving to a new level of self-confidence and competence either in relationships, in career, or in general self-image and self-esteem.

In cases where a heterosexual person dreams of being with someone of the same sex, the key to interpretation, as in the other dreams, is to describe the personality of the dream lover. The dreamer will usually find that this dream lover is a person whom the dreamer admires and would like to emulate, who often has achieved a bit more than the dreamer and is a bit more accomplished. The dream can suggest a desire to be accepted by, to be on the same level as, such a person. This could for example be true of a heterosexual man dreaming of having a homosexual encounter. Of course these dreams can also mean the obvious: that the dreamer really does have very strong heterosexual (if the dreamer is homosexual or lesbian) or homosexual or lesbian (if the dreamer is heterosexual) leanings. However, this is rare in my experience. By the way, lesbians and homosexuals who dream heterosexual dreams are usually just as uncomfortable as are heterosexuals who dream homosexual dreams. You will find many different types of sexual dreams discussed in my book *Sensual Dreams*.

Sample Dream
"In Bed with My Ex"
Larry was surprised to have had the following dream:

> There I was having sex with my ex-wife. I couldn't believe it. I woke up and said, "What am I doing here?"

When we asked Larry to describe his ex, he said she was an extremely controlling, critical, and talkative woman whom he had married when he was too young to know any better. We asked why he had married her. He admitted that it was because she was the sexiest, most desirable woman in his college class but that he had failed to notice some of her more enduring and obnoxious personality traits. In order to find out why Larry would have had this dream on the particular night he had, we asked him if there was anyone in his life now whom he would describe as originally attractive and highly desirable, but also critical, controlling, and talkative. Larry said that he was dating one of the prettiest women in the city and that two of his friends had commented that she was somewhat like his first wife.

It was very hard for Larry to consider that he might be in bed with the same woman again, only this time she had a different name and a different face.

Dreams of being in bed with former lovers usually do point out a pattern we are repeating as we pick different people in different bodies. There is a very strong tendency to pick similar personalities over and over again until we resolve the needs or conflicts that led us to get involved with that sort of person in the first place. If one asks the dreamer, "When was the very first time you were involved with a person who has the basic personality style of the lover in your dream?" the answer is often a shocked "Oh, my heavens, it was my mother" (or "my father," or "my older brother [*or* sister]"—some early person in the dreamer's life on whom the dreamer has imprinted and with whom the dreamer seems compelled to connect again and again).

LOSING YOUR PURSE OR WALLET

You may be anywhere at any time in your dreams and suddenly notice you've lost your purse, your wallet, or your briefcase. You might feel mildly concerned, but more likely you feel something close to panic and are unable to remember where your purse is or when or how you lost it.

Sample Dreams
"Lost Purse"
Marjorie dreamt:

> I was walking downtown, and I suddenly noticed that I had lost my purse. I don't know if it had been stolen by a pickpocket or if I had dropped it, but I realized I had no money left with me at all and I started looking everywhere. I realized that I would never find it.

In interviewing Marjorie, I said, "Now, pretend I come from another planet. Why would a human such as yourself care whether or not she loses a purse?" She said, "Oh my, if I lost my purse I would lose all of my identity papers, my credit cards, my money, I would have trouble getting anywhere, making phone calls, buying anything, or proving who I am." I asked her, "Is there anywhere in your life where you feel that you have trouble proving who you are, that you don't have any money, that you don't have any credit cards?" "Oh, yes!" she said. "I don't work any longer, my children are married, and they have children who are almost grown, and I don't think I count for much anymore. I don't know how to tell people I am an important person: I have thoughts, I have desires, I have plans. People treat me like an old person. Actually, I'm not really sure what my plans are, but I want to have plans. I want to be taken seriously, but I do feel old, and maybe I don't even take myself that seriously anymore."

In a somewhat unusual version of this dream Nicolas dreamt that he was walking in a particularly beautiful plaza in Rome when a very handsome young man rushed up to him, stole his wallet, and then disappeared. I asked Nicholas, "What are wallets, and why do you feel a need to carry them?" He said, "You carry a wallet to put the money you need for the present, your credit cards, and your identification papers in one place." When asked what the problem would be in losing your wallet, he said, "Well, I could replace everything in it, but it would be a lot of trouble. I'd have to go through a lot of bureaucratic red tape to get all my papers replaced. The cash money wouldn't be a problem and the credit cards wouldn't be a problem, but it would be a big bother."

I asked Nicholas if there was anything in his life that he felt would be a big bother to replace, that gave him a sense of power in the world, like a wallet—something that allowed him to identify himself. He answered, "It's funny, but . . . my

girlfriend, I think of my girlfriend. She is extremely beautiful, and everyone notices whenever I go to a party with her. I think it makes me look good. Actually, last night she was flirting with a handsome younger man, and I was afraid that he would steal her from me. It would be a bother to find someone else who is as pretty as she is, and as easy to get along with." It is interesting to note that Nicholas was not panicked in the dream; his focus was on what a bother it would be to replace the materials in his wallet. The cash outlays he had made for his girlfriend he felt were not that great, wouldn't be that big a loss.

What Do You Say?

Keep in mind that as in any common dream, although there may be common interpretations that are most often on the mark for most dreamers, you may have a very idiosyncratic twist to your common dream. The only way you will find out is to interview yourself. This will also help you find a more specific understanding of the general nature of your dream. Why not try asking yourself these interview questions?

1. *What is a purse [or wallet, or briefcase]? Pretend I come from another planet and have no idea what one is, why humans use them, or what they carry in them.*

2. *Why would a human such as yourself care if your purse was stolen [lost, etc.]?*

3. *How do you feel in the dream when your purse is lost or stolen?*

4. *Is there anywhere in your life where you feel the way you feel in the dream when you realize that your purse has been stolen?*

5. *How so? Be as specific as you can.*

6. *Having identified the relevant area of your life, is there anything you could do to change the situation?*

Almost every time I give a lecture or talk about dreams on radio or television, someone in the audience wants to tell me about a dream of entering a familiar or an unfamiliar house and discovering more or new rooms. The dreamer's face lights up, and even without knowing what the dream means specifically, he or she understands that something good is going on. The new rooms are often filled with sunlight and fresh air, and the dreamer is amazed to discover that all these extra rooms exist. Now and then the new rooms discovered are in need of repair, but the dreamer almost always feels hopeful and confident of being able to fix them up and make them look wonderful. Very often the dreamer is aware of having known the house well but never having realized that the house had all this room in it. These dreams usually carry feelings of happy surprise and optimism for the future.

Sample Dreams
"More Rooms"

> I am walking through a familiar house and discovering new rooms on the left, new rooms on the right. They are big, beautiful, and flooded with sunlight. I was so amazed; I had had no idea that these rooms had been here all the time. I was delighted to think I would have this much space and shocked that I hadn't realized this before.

Pasquale had this dream within the year that he had decided to retire from an extremely workaholic lifestyle. He had begun to suspect that there might be more to life than working and achievement. He was beginning to get interested in the arts, sports, and deeper relationships with women. He wanted to travel. He interpreted the house as a representation of himself and of large spaces within himself he had not previously enjoyed. All that remained now in the dream was for him to furnish the rooms, to live in these rooms, to use the space. The feeling was one of expansiveness and delight in discovering new space, new possibilities.

"Room with Potential"
Gia dreamt:

> I am walking through my house, and I discover a corridor that I had not realized existed. I went into the rooms off the corridor, and I was amazed to see very big

rooms. One in particular was a bedroom that was very big and had lots of potential, but it looked like it was in serious need of repair. Parts of the walls were peeling, windows had been broken, and it was pretty messy. But it wouldn't take too much work to make it a beautiful, lovely, romantic bedroom. I was very happy when I woke up.

Gia described the bedroom as a place that had been boarded up for a long time after having been terribly abused—just as she had been sexually abused as a child. The bedroom had to do with her own sexual self, one that she had boarded up for a long time and now in therapy was repairing. This room had great potential to be beautiful and romantic, and to provide her a space in life for her sexuality. She was happy to note that it had always existed, and now all she had to do was repair and refurbish it.

What Do You Say?

To find out what your dream of discovering new rooms in a house means, try asking yourself these questions:

1. *Describe the house in your dreams.*

2. *Does it remind you of any particular house in your life?*

3. *Describe the new room or rooms you discover.*

4. *Does this room have a particular purpose?*

5. *How do you feel about this room?*

6. *Are you discovering new parts of yourself or of your life that you would describe as* [restate the description]?

TAKING AN EXAMINATION

Variations

There you are, frantically looking for the right room, about to take an exam for which you are totally unprepared.[2] The test may be terribly important, such as the bar exam or the graduating exam from a school system, or it may be relatively unimportant, one course in a college curriculum. The test may take the form of a high school test, a doctoral exam, performing lines in a play, or singing an aria in an opera. The test may be reading at a bar mitzvah or confirmation ceremony. The exam may be illegible, or on the wrong topic. Perhaps you forgot to study all term. You stand onstage, everyone is waiting for you to sing, but you can't remember a single line. You wake up at that terribly anxious moment relieved it was only a dream.

Sometimes the dreamer who is struggling with an exam or a karate test realizes that he already passed this test, perhaps years ago. Why is he struggling through it again? An amusing variation is one in which the dreamer is about to take a test, realizes he hasn't studied and is unprepared, but decides to take the test anyway: since he couldn't do worse than getting an F, he might as well try it and see what he has absorbed. He does not wake up until he has found out that he got an A on the exam. You can imagine how this common dream with its many variations can have very many different meanings.

Helpful Hints

At the Dream Center we teach people to check to see if this dream comes the night before an actual test, and if so, we ask the dreamer, "Are you prepared or unprepared for the test?" You may be well prepared and simply overly anxious. Some dreamers are such perfectionists, so anxious about winning approval from the people around them, that no matter how well prepared they are for an actual test in life, they are unable to develop an appropriate level of confidence. This in itself is indicative of work to be done on self-esteem and perfectionism issues.

Next we would ask the dreamer to describe the circumstances of the examination and explore the possibility that the exam could act as a metaphor for tests in the dreamer's life or a sense of being tested or being examined. The specific details of the dream then can offer clues to a particular part of the dreamer's life, with indications of the dreamer's mode of coping. If the dreamer has this dream frequently, it is important to consider whether or not the dreamer is living a life with so many deadlines and so many demands that she realizes she is never fully prepared, never able to really keep up.

If the dreamer within the dream begins to protest the unfairness of the exam— that it is illegible, or on the wrong topic—the interviewer would ask for good descriptions of the test givers to see whom or what they represent in the dreamer's life. If the dreamer copes well, saying that he is unprepared and would like to take the exam later, or if the dreamer chooses to go ahead and take the exam anyway just to see what's possible, this could indicate that the dreamer is beginning to learn how to cope with either too busy or too demanding a lifestyle. Or perhaps he is learning to deal with his own needs to succeed or is beginning to take responsibility for his own procrastination or lack of preparation for life's challenges, be they specific tests or encounters with people in his career or private life.

Sample Dreams
"Crazy Exam"
Charlie dreamt:

> I am supposed to take a test in one of my courses in high school, but I can't find the room where the exam is supposed to be given. I look all over. I arrive about ten minutes late and pick up the exam, but it doesn't make any sense to me. Either the writing isn't clear or it's the wrong language, but I'm not going to be able to take the exam.

Charlie, a member of one of my dream study groups, told us, "The funny thing about this exam dream is that I'm sure I was prepared, but the school had put it in the wrong room. I don't think it was my fault, and furthermore, the exam wasn't legible. It wasn't at all what I had prepared for." When an interviewer asked Charlie, "Well then, whose fault was it that you were in such a predicament?" Charlie said, "It had to be the school's fault." He felt responsible in the dream, but in fact he was not, and he was being tested unfairly.

Asked where in his life he felt he was being tested unfairly, where obstacles were being put in his way, and where there was a bait-and-switch situation, he said, "My whole life I've felt like that. I could never please my father. He was always testing me, he was always testing me beyond my abilities as if he were playing games with me. In school I always tried to show him that I could do well, but even when I did he'd always have another test for me." The interviewer asked him, "Why do you think you had this dream recently? Is there anything going on in your life now that reminds you of these feelings and of these circumstances?" Charlie responded that his job felt like that. He trained for one activity, mastered it, and the next thing he knew he was transferred to a higher level but expected to perform well immediately. This dream helped Charlie see how he was continuing a lifestyle he had started as a child. As an adult he was not taking action to manage his life better. His unsatisfied need for approval was getting in his way.

"Forgotten Exam"

Alvin dreamt:

> I'm in a classroom and am about to take an exam on English poetry when I realize that I had forgotten to study over the weekend. In fact I had watched football all weekend, and I had forgotten all about the exam. I woke up with a start because I knew this was an important test. Without it I would not graduate from high school.

Alvin was asked to describe English poetry. He said, "My wife loves it a lot. It's beautiful and romantic, but I don't really know very much about it. It's all right, I guess." When asked to describe football, he said, "Oh, that's just fun. Guys really like that stuff a lot, and I really love the game." When his interviewer asked, "Are you feeling that you have to be tested on something that's romantic and that your wife really loves, but you've been spending your time watching football with the guys?" Alvin just laughed and said, "Well, that's pretty obvious, isn't it? My wife has actually put me on notice that if I don't become more attentive and romantic with her she is either going to take a lover or leave me."

How many versions of the "examination dream" have you dreamt? Do you remember ever having to run like mad to get to an exam you had forgotten you were to take and then being unable to find the right room? Or how about the dream of sitting in the examination room knowing that you are totally unprepared for the test? Have you spent the semester studying the wrong material, or just goofing off? Are you back in high school, college, or graduate school? And do you, like most people, wake up before you actually take the test?

The anxiety of these dreams is so unpleasant, and the theme seems so nonsensical, that many people cite such dreams as examples of the irrelevance of dreaming to our waking state. A number of adults have told me that such dreams can't possibly "mean" anything because they haven't had to take a school exam in years. But when asked if they feel they are about to face some current, adult-life "test" in their professional or personal life for which they feel unprepared, they can usually relate the dream's elements to a pressing concern in waking life.

Freud saw in such dreams a reflection of our childhood fears of punishment, fears that might have been reanimated by our having done something wrong or improperly a day or two before the dream. Only now, in the exam dream, the school authorities are in the superego role the parents used to fulfill. Freud also thought that since these dream exams seem to recall only the waking exams we actually passed in our youth, they offer the waking consolation that we need not worry because we have passed a similar exam before, and will do so again.

It was Alfred Adler who added to Freud's consolation theory the interpretation that the exam dream might mean "you are not prepared to face the problem before you." Adler insisted that one person's symbols must not be used to interpret those of another dreamer. And he believed that the mood of the dream and its coherence in terms of the whole of the dreamer's style of life are the best guidelines for interpretation.

Most of us could figure out these dreams on our own if we followed Adler's advice. If there are specific details noted in your exam dream—such as the day of the exam or the particular subject matter—these usually are metaphoric clues to the specific "exam" situation in your life. Often the type of exam and the feelings it evokes in the dream will point to an area in your personal, interpersonal, or professional life in which you are not doing well and into which you need to put more effort.

People who frequently have these dreams are often living lives overloaded with stress and near-impossible deadlines. In these cases, frequent exam dreams can be a signal that it is time to reconsider one's lifestyle. Sometimes people have these dreams before an actual exam in waking life. The dreamer can then heed the dream's anxious mood and prepare for the exam with new motivation. However, if the dream comes the night before the exam, it may have nothing to do with the dreamer's study habits but with his or her intense anxiety.

Examination dreams, like all common dreams, sometimes have very uncommon endings. One dreamer dreamt that she was about to take an exam for which she had hardly studied at all and which she was sure to fail. She thought about not even taking the test and accepting an F, since there was no hope of passing. Then an idea occurred to her: "Well, why not? What have I got to lose? I can't do worse than an F." She took the test, and to her profound amazement she passed, with an A! (It is interesting to note that this dreamer actually had a similar experience with a college history exam that she had considered skipping but then took and on which she received an A.)

This dreamer's exam dream occurred, as Freud noted they always do, just before a real-life "test" in the form of a presentation of her academic research to her colleagues. The dream, by reminding the dreamer of her "lucky" history test, did in fact reassure her and reduce her anxiety about her presentation. The dream also led her to take a closer look at her tendency to underestimate her competence in ways that threatened her confidence and her ability to achieve things of importance to her.

Lina, a counselor and a member of a small, long-term dream study group, surprised us with an exam dream in which she was observing and supporting a friend who was taking his oral exams for his license to be a marriage, family, and child counselor. She noted that the exam room was too dark, and that in this case the examiners were unprepared and disorganized! She had interrupted the proceedings and confronted the examiners about how badly the exam was being managed. The examiners told Lina that she didn't understand how much stress they had been under. Lina felt bad about this but decided she was still going to report them.

During the dream interview that followed, Lina recognized what the dream was about when she described the examiners as incompetent, guilt-evoking judges. Her parents were like those judges, and she was like the fellow she was supporting in wanting approval, especially in family matters. Lina herself had already passed the real-life exams for her counselor's license, but she hadn't passed the "test" of earning her parents' approval.

And, yes, Lina had decided to report her parents' mishandling of her childhood. She already had an appointment with a therapist to have at least one joint session with her mother and father so she could try to tell them how she felt. Working with this dream strengthened Lina's wavering resolve to do whatever was necessary to convince her parents to come to a therapy session at least once.

What Do You Say?

1. *Is there any actual exam or test you are about to take for which this dream could express anxiety?*

2. *Are you prepared or not for the actual exam, and is the dream a realistic concern or an exaggerated expression of your insecurity?*

3. *Describe the kind of test or challenge you are being confronted with in the dream as if you were describing it to someone from another planet.*

4. *What's wrong? Are you ill prepared? Is the test illegible?*

5. *Do you have any idea why you are unprepared?*

6. *Is there any situation in your life in which you feel like you are being tested in the way you are in the dream and for which you are unprepared for the same reasons you have just stated?*

7. *Taking the larger view on this dream, do you think you have an overly perfectionistic need based on insecurity to pass exams and in fact put yourself in too many testing situations? If so, is there anything you would like to do about that?*

8. *If you understand your dream to be reminding you of how you are in fact unprepared for a life challenge or an actual test, what might you do now or before your next test to be better prepared?*

PLEASANT FLYING DREAMS

Variations

Whenever I talk about dreams in a lecture or to a live audience on a television show, all I have to do is mention flying dreams and I hear a delighted *ah!* ripple through the audience. I see smiles on many faces, because flying dreams are among the most pleasant, delightful, and thrilling life experiences a human being can have. If you have had pleasant flying dreams, you know how wonderful it is to remember the delight, the thrill of soaring, the pleasure of flying effortlessly through the air, doing acrobatic stunts, flying high, flying low, seeing beautiful sights, and feeling unbelievably free.

If you haven't had a dream like this, just you wait, you are very likely to have one once you recall your dreams more fully. Some people fly at night. I have flown over San Francisco Bay, and out on the West Coast over the cliffs and the ocean with the stars and the moonlight. Other people fly in daytime, seeing bright sun and beautiful mountaintops. People fly to friends' houses and visit. Some people just float in their bedrooms and seem to be able to pass through walls and in and out of closed windows. Many people say that their earliest remembered flying dreams were pseudo–flying dreams in which they might be swimming or water-skiing and feel like flying, or snow skiing and say, "Ah! I think I'm flying." I had my earliest flying dreams of swimming and flying, but also of ice-skating. In the ice-skating dreams I would take off for a jump in the air and find that I could use gravity at my will. I had to learn how not to overjump out of the skating rink into the bleachers and how not to hit my head on the rafters above. It was quite a delightful challenge.

Many people have particular techniques for initiating flight in a dream. Again, early on in their dream-flying careers, dreamers usually expend a lot of effort to get airborne. People flap their arms really hard, as if they were wings. Some people use a bent right leg as a rudder; others take a one-two-three jump, à la Superman, to get into the air; and still others spin in order to take off, sort of like a helicopter. What is amusing to note is that, as time goes on, dreamers become aware that they really don't have to go through all this fuss to take flight, that just a slight movement of a finger will do it. And then later on dreamers say that actually all they need is the right attitude to get into the air. They have to know that they can fly and not worry about it, not doubt themselves; they just take off and everything works out fine.

Sample Dreams
"I Fly"
Marilyn regularly has this dream:

> I am flying above my colleagues and my friends, and I am the only one who can fly. They all marvel at my ability, and I am very proud of it.

When I interviewed Marilyn about this dream, I didn't suggest an interpretation by saying that she wanted to be a man, that she was proud of her sexual prowess, or that she wanted to be free or transcend. Instead I asked her, "How do you feel in the dream?" She responded that she felt very happy to be able to do this in front of her friends and show them that she had an ability no one else had. I asked her whether in her waking life there was any way in which she does the same thing. She said, "Actually, in my career, and maybe also with my social friends, I do show off and try to show myself as more spiritual than they are." As she spoke she realized that this may not be one of her more endearing qualities, that perhaps her need to be superior in the eyes of her friends was a compensation for feelings of inferiority, a compensation that could be rather distasteful to a number of friends and especially to her colleagues.

"Flying with Churchill"

Frank dreamt that he had a chance to fly in the company of Winston Churchill. He was very excited, and he was trying to show Winston how he was able to complete complicated acrobatic feats in the air. He was having lots of fun and enjoying showing his prowess to Winston. Now and then he worried that he might not be able to keep his altitude, but he knew that if he worried for an instant he would lose altitude. So he just kept his mind focused on the pleasure of showing off his skills.

Frank described Winston Churchill as a man who had the enormous courage to say what needed to be said, knew how to encourage vast numbers of people, and was a man whose ability to thrive under enormous pressure was legend. When I asked him to describe what his flying felt like, he said he was simply and enormously pleased that the time had come in his life when he could finally do this: "I'm at a level of achievement in my life where I feel really competent. I didn't feel obnoxious, I felt proud, and Winston was happy to see me, as if he were encouraging me to join the ranks of men who performed extraordinarily well." Frank didn't mention, nor would I insinuate, that this was a primarily sexual dream. It may have had little or nothing to do with sexuality; it certainly had a lot to do with Frank's growing sense of himself as a mature man of great achievement and skill.

What Do You Say?

1. *What is it like when you fly? Do you have any trouble getting or maintaining your altitude? Are there any other obstacles, concerns, or happenings in the dream?*

2. *How do you feel while flying in your dream?*

3. *Tell me more about these feelings.*

4. *What, if any, are the obstacles* [include attitudes, doubts, etc.] *to your flying or to your feeling great about flying in your dream?*

5. *Do the obstacles in your dream remind you of any obstacles in your waking life?*

6. *When was the last time you felt in waking life the way you do in the dream?*

7. *So, does your flying, which feels* [restate the description], *remind you of any situation in your life? Does it remind you of any feelings you wish you felt in your life?*

UNPLEASANT FLYING DREAMS

Variations

It's a shame, but anxiety, hostility, and insecurity can spoil even flying dreams. Instead of feeling delight in dream flight, some people dream of trying to fly and not being able to get off the ground. Or finally, after having made a lot of effort, flapping arms and struggling, they become airborne only to worry about losing altitude, or about bumping into things or getting tangled up in high-tension wires. Other people have trouble getting out of an enclosed space; they want to fly but can't get through the window or the ceiling, and feel stuck. Sometimes the dreamer is trying to fly, trying to take off, but is unable to because someone is holding on to his or her foot and won't let the person go! Such dreams can be filled with frustration and anxiety. Another common version of this dream is one in which the dreamer is running away from a pursuer, a bad guy of some sort or an animal, and in running, the dreamer is able to take off and start to fly. In this case, the flight is used as escape from fear and anxiety.

Helpful Hints

At our Dream Center we have found problems in flying dreams to have telling meanings. Men and women who fear losing altitude often are afraid of losing their sense of well-being, of losing their ability to feel free and to soar emotionally; some even fear losing their financial security. When people dream of flying in order to escape difficult situations, demons, or wild animals, it is often useful to ask the dreamer if that is his or her current way of coping with difficult situations. In other words, does the dreamer have a habit of trying to escape, trying to get above it all, rather than dealing effectively with the situation? When there are obstacles in the way of the flight or people who hold the dreamer down, the meaning of the dream is entirely dependent upon the dreamer's description of the obstacles or the people who are obstructing the flight.

Sample Dreams
"He Won't Let Me Fly"
Carol dreamt that she was in her backyard and trying to take off for flight but couldn't get any higher than about six feet. She kept flapping her wings, or her arms, until finally she looked down and saw that her husband was holding on to her ankle and wouldn't let her go. When I asked her to describe her husband and how he was acting in the dream, she said he was a loving man, but one who was extremely possessive and could not stand the idea of her starting a career. He had been resisting her idea of going to night school for that purpose. "I feel like he is holding me down, and I feel very frustrated in my waking life, just as I do in the dream."

"Bailing Out"
Hasse dreamt:

> I was flying in an airplane, and I thought the airplane was going to crash, so I pushed the eject button and I bailed out.

I interviewed Hasse, asking him how it felt knowing that the plane was likely to crash. He said it was very uncomfortable, that he didn't want to go down with the plane, so he bailed out. I asked if there was any current situation in his life that felt like he was on a flight that was going to crash, the plane was going down and he didn't want to go down with it, so he decided to bail out. He said, "Yes, I've decided to leave my alcoholic wife, and I am bailing out. I can't save this marriage, and I'm not going to go down with the plane. I really do have to leave, and it's very difficult, but the situation is dire."

What Do You Say?
See "Pleasant Flying Dreams" for the basic interview questions. Some additional questions for unpleasant flying dreams would be:

1. *Describe the person or obstacle that is inhibiting your flight.*

2. *Describe the feeling or insecurity that is inhibiting your flight.*

3. *Is there anything or anyone in your life that is like the thing in the dream that is causing you trouble?*

4. *Describe how you use flight in the dream [to escape, show off, etc.].*

5. *Does the way you use flight in your dream parallel ways you have of coping with pleasant or threatening situations in your waking life?*

People in Dreams: How to Interpret Any Person in Your Dreams

Since no book or even computer software could ever list the cast of thousands who have appeared in the course of your dream life, you will need a method for exploring the meaning of any dream person. The following dream-interview questions will help you or a dream partner discover the meaning behind the dramatis personae of your nights.

1. *Who is _____? Pretend I've never heard of him or her before.*

2. *What is _____ like in waking life? Describe _____ with three or four adjectives.*

3. *What is _____ like in your dream, and what is he or she up to?*

4. *So, _____ is [restate the description], right?*

5. *Does _____, whom you describe as* [restate the description], *remind you of anything or anyone in your life?*

6. *Does _____ remind you of any part of yourself? How so?*

Test the bridge by asking the dreamer (or yourself) to elaborate on how the dream image fits the waking one. See if this is a good metaphoric match. If not, get more description of the person to see if you can clarify the connection. You need to add to this list additional questions specific to your particular dream. Or you may not need to ask all these questions, since sometimes one or two questions will bring forth the meaning of the dream. Keep in mind that your imagined dream interviewer pretends to have come from another planet and knows nothing about the people, even the very famous people, in your dreams. This will encourage you to give concise, honest answers in describing what you do and do not like about the person and his or her behavior in your dream.

MOVIE AND TV STARS

Variations

Most people are usually thrilled to dream about movie and TV stars. Usually the dreamer feels flattered by attention from someone who is seen as glamorous and exciting, but not always. Sometimes they act out of character. Sometimes famous people appear in your dreams as the character they play on the screen, and sometimes they appear as the actor in his or her real and private life. There is no limit to the various roles these famous people can play, nor, really, to the various meanings they can carry for you. You might make love to your favorite movie star and feel greatly flattered, or you may be told that you are not welcome at a party given by your favorite screen actor. Then again, in a dream your favorite actors or characters may be in dire straits and in need of your help.

Sample Dreams
"Jerry Seinfeld and George"
Linda dreamt:

> I need to go to school and register for classes. I have a pressing urgency to get to school. I'm registering late as it is. I have a transportation problem and get the idea

that I will go to Jerry Seinfeld's apartment and then use George's car. George has a somewhat faded red Volkswagen. I do get to school on time.

Linda described Jerry Seinfeld as a funny, cynical, and disparaging man whose humor was always a put-down. She bridged that description as fitting none other than her husband. She described George as Seinfeld's sidekick, who was always around, also cynical, and not the main star. She bridged George to herself, saying, "My husband has the primary position in our business, and I feel like the sidekick and his assistant." Linda described George's faded red Volkswagen as a car with an engine in the back, no trunk, no room for storage or place to carry anything extra, whose red lifeblood was faded from being outside and not having its own garage. She said, "My body and my self are like George's car. My role in the company is not primary, and I feel that I really do need to start school and start a career of my own. I think that while I am attracted to Jerry Seinfeld, I really do not need to play George to him, I need to have my own career that is separate, where I feel that I am the primary mover rather than the assistant."

"Faye Dunaway"
Anna dreamt:

> I am trying to save a wonderful woman from being executed. She is like Faye Dunaway in *Don Juan de Marco* [a current movie]. I am pleading for her, but no one will listen or change his mind. They think she is different, strange, maybe bad, and therefore she must be killed. Suddenly someone says to me, "It's too late, she's already dead." I am so upset that I wake up crying.

Anna said that Faye Dunaway in her dream was the character she played in *Don Juan de Marco,* so I asked her, "What is Faye Dunaway like in your dream?" She described her as an older woman, romantic-feeling and beautiful. Anna really liked Faye Dunaway's role because it reminded her of how she wanted to feel, but not how she did feel, in her current marriage. When I asked her what was happening to Faye in the dream, she said, "She is going to be executed for no fault of her own. She is just being different, that's really all it is. They call her bad, but she isn't. She's a being of romance and beauty, and it's terrible that they are going to kill her."

Then she asked me, "Do you think the fact that in the dream she is already dead means it's too late for me? Is that part of myself dead, and will it never live again?" I reassured Anna that dreams often exaggerate to get their point across, then returned the question to her, saying, "Do you think the Faye Dunaway in you is dead?" She said, "Oh no, I still feel it, but I am afraid that if I act on it I will want to leave my husband, and I will be terribly criticized by his family and perhaps by everyone. I will also have a difficult time earning a living. And that's why I have been putting off my decision for so long. But this dream makes me think that I really must act, because I love, because I don't want to live the rest of my life without feeling what Faye Dunaway felt in the movie: romance, beauty, and happiness with a man she loved."

What Do You Say?

1. *Is the star in your dream acting as him- or herself offscreen, or is the star staying in the role as a character you are familiar with on-screen?*

2. *What is* [name the actor or screen character] *like in your dream?*

3. *How do you like this star? Why?*

4. *What is the star doing in your dream, and how do you feel about this?*

5. *Does this star, whom you describe as* [restate the description], *remind you of yourself, or of anyone else in your life?*

6. *How so?*

7. *If the star does not remind you of anyone in your life or of a part of you, and if the main feeling in the dream is that you are incredibly flattered to get the star's attention, have you been needing a boost to your self-esteem lately?*

MAFIOSI, NAZIS, FASCISTS, AND DICTATORS

Variations

Powerful men whose main interest is total control, who will do anything to get what they want, may appear in dreams in the form of Mafia men who kidnap the dreamer or who impersonate businessmen and friends. Some of us dream of Nazis who threaten execution if we don't do what they want, of Fascists who export Jews to the Nazis, or of dictators who are ruthless, threatening to kill our families. Sometimes non-Jewish dreamers will dream of being sent off to concentration camps or of trying to liberate Jews who are being murdered by the Nazis. I have even heard dreams of dictators trying to mend their ways, explaining to the dreamer that they had turned into such ruthless despots because of early childhood feelings of inferiority that they were now beginning to overcome.

Helpful Hints

At the Delaney & Flowers Dream Center, many of our dreamers have told us that Mafia men represent caricatures of people in their lives who will do anything to get their way. They will stop at nothing to get what they want. Nazis, fascists, and dictators fall into similar descriptive patterns, although Nazis are often described as the most repressive, controlling, hateful of people, who sometimes remind dreamers of their parents or of the dreamers' own rigid, repressive personality aspects. Dictators may represent a part of the dreamer's own personality that is very dictatorial and rigid, or the dreamer may use such images to represent parents, employers, or spouses.

Frequently the overcontrolling, rigid fascist or dictator is used as an image by women to represent their feelings of being controlled by a man or of being power-less in a relationship with a man.

Sample Dream
"The Mafia Is Going to Kill Me"
Mimi dreamt:

> Because of my attachment to a Mafia man, I am to be killed by his henchman. At one point I expect to be strafed by planes overhead, and I try to prepare myself for the inevitable. I awake in the middle of the night terrified.

Mimi had gone to sleep incubating a dream, asking herself if the man she loved was indeed a con man, as her friends all thought. In describing a Mafia man, Mimi said, "They are 100 percent self-centered, they think of themselves first no matter what they say to the contrary, and they have no scruples about taking advan-tage of other people, even to the point of killing them for personal gain." Since the dream opened with the declaration that her attachment to a Mafia man was the cause of her impending death, she added, "Well, the only man I'm attached to right now is Michael, and my friends all think he's a con man. They have lots of reasons to think that he is. I have lots of reasons to think that he loves me and he is just going through a difficult time in his life. But my friends may be right." She described a henchman as someone who does the dirty work for the Mafia, the power man. She thought that the henchman was the part of her boyfriend who was used to taking advantage of women, even if there was another part of him that was loving and kind. She thought that perhaps the henchman would win out, and she knew that she could be financially ruined by this man. The dream was a wake-up call.

Objects in Dreams: How to Interpret Any Object in Your Dreams

The following dream-interview questions should be very useful to you as you try to figure out the meaning of any object in your dream. If you dream of a blended object, one that seems to be both this and that, describe each object in turn, and then ask yourself how you would describe a motorbike that is both motorbike and wheelchair. Describe first one and then the other object, and then see what the blended object would be like.

As always, remember to keep in mind that the interviewer comes from another planet and wants a straight, simple answer that includes the facts as well as your feelings about the particular image.

1. *What is a _____? Pretend I come from Mars.*

2. *Why do humans have or use _____s, and how do they work?*

3. *How do you feel about _____s generally?*

4. *What is the _____ in your dream like?*

5. *How do you feel about the _____ in your dream?*

Variations

Car dreams are very common. Even though in the section on dream themes we have discussed general car dreams and dreams in which someone else is driving, we have yet to discuss the very memorable dreams of malfunctioning cars. Typically we are in cars that break down or have no brakes, or we can't figure out how to use the brakes. The car may belong to us or to someone in the family, very often a spouse, or a boyfriend. Sometimes we consult mechanics to help us repair the cars, mechanics who may or may not be very helpful, and sometimes we just try to fix the cars on our own with varying degrees of success.

Sample Dreams
"Let My Wife Fix the Car"
Vincent dreamt:

> I've gone on vacation with my wife. My wife's car is broken down. It's my job to get it fixed. This was the beginning of a long dream, but it certainly set the tone.

Asked what in his life was like the broken-down car, Vincent was quick to bridge to his marriage. He said that his marriage was certainly broken down and that he had taken the responsibility to fix it since she was not interested in helping. As you might imagine, the rest of the dream did not go very well for Vincent, who throughout the dream was being overly responsible and was not getting the support or assistance he would need to repair his wife's car (marriage). The dream highlighted his general tendency to take responsibility and his wife's general tendency to sit back and let him do all the work. In a later dream he took the car into a mechanic, who was a representation of the couples counselor they were seeing. Even with the mechanic's help Vincent was unable to repair his wife's car to its original state. It was time for Vincent to realize his limitations and the fact that his wife needed to get to work as well if she wanted to save the marriage.

"Personality Car"
Alissa dreamt a dream like many I have heard:

I dreamt I was driving a wonderful sports car. I was having so much fun, it was exhilarating, thrilling, and I felt strong and delirious to be alive. Then I realized the brakes didn't work, and I started trying to figure out how I would stop the car without crashing.

I asked Alissa to describe the car. She said it was a lovely, fun red car. I asked her what the personality of such a car was. She described it as racy, playful, and capable of high-performance achievements. I asked her if there was anything in her life that felt like this car, and she said, "Oh, yes. My new career. It's racy, high performance is very important, I'm really good at it, and it's very snazzy, like the car." I asked her if there was any way she had trouble putting the brakes on in her career. She replied that she did have trouble there. She was hoping it wouldn't cause her too much difficulty in the future, because right now she was so excited, traveling all over the world, doing things she never thought she would achieve. I asked her to pretend I came from another planet and tell me what was wrong with not having brakes in such a car. She answered that it would be a disaster, that one joy ride would be her last, that without good brakes such a car would be a death machine. Then she looked at me and said, "My husband has called my career a death machine. I'm going to have to figure out something. I don't want to give up my husband, I don't want to give up my life, and I don't want to give up my career." This was the first time Alissa had taken a serious look at the part of her career that threatened the rest of her life.

What Do You Say?

1. *Describe the car in your dream. What is the personality of such a car?*

2. *Describe what is malfunctioning in the car and why it is a problem. Pretend you are speaking to an interviewer who comes from another planet, and be very concrete and specific.*

3. *Whose car is in the dream?*

4. *Does your description of the car and its malfunctioning describe the person who owns the car, some part of yourself, or some situation such as your marriage or your career?*

5. *How important is this malfunctioning problem?*

6. *Does the malfunctioning in the car match any malfunctioning area of your life?*

7. *Is there anything you can do to repair or rectify the situation, and are you sure it is your responsibility to do so?*

DRUGS, CIGARETTES, AND ALCOHOL
Variations

We sooner or later dream about substances that we use inappropriately. Smokers dream of cigarettes, alcoholics of alcohol, drug users of drugs. People who live with those who abuse these substances also tend to dream about them. The dreams can show craving and portray near temptations. They can show the dreamer falling off the wagon, suddenly indulging in something she has given up. Or, in very lucky circumstances, the dream may motivate the dreamer to give up the habit once and for all, or at the very least may encourage the dreamer to start working on the possibility of giving the substance up or getting its use under control.

Very frequently the emotional color and the action of the dream describe in metaphoric terms the emotional habits that lead one to maintain a destructive habit. These dreams can also be warnings that the dreamer is getting involved again in circumstances or in relationships that could lead to falling off the wagon once again. Less frequently, people who do not have a particular problem with a substance will dream of it as a metaphor for unhealthy ways of relating to others or to themselves.

Sample Dream
"Smoking Some Grass"
Dottie dreamt:

> I was at a party, there were lots of fun people around, but all I could think of was going into a back room and smoking some grass. As I went to the back of the house, I was sorry that I would be missing the party.

I asked Dottie, "What is grass, and why do humans smoke it?" She said, "It's a fairly harmless substance that is overly regulated by the government. It helps you to relax and makes you feel content with the world." I asked her how she felt about going to the back room. She said she felt compelled to smoke, but she regretted it because "really, I would have had more fun being straight and staying at the party with my friends." I asked her if there was anything in her life that was like grass, that made her feel good, relaxed, but at the same time pulled her away from being with her friends in a partylike straight environment. She said her boyfriend was like that; she withdrew from a lot of her friends to be with her boyfriend, who indeed made her feel wonderful, who was sexy and very attentive to her. But she also thought she had given up a lot of her life to be with him, since he was not very gregarious. Then she looked surprised and said, "You know, I use him as a drug, as a security blanket to avoid challenging and threatening situations, because I feel so safe with him." Now, that's interesting!

What Do You Say?

1. *Describe the drug in your dream as if you were describing it to someone from another planet. Why do humans use it?*

2. *If you use it, why do you do so, and how does it make you feel?*

3. *Describe the dream context in which this drug appears.*

4. *Does something like this drug, or the drug itself, play a role in your life as it does in the dream?*

5. *How do you feel about the drug in your dream?*

6. *How do you feel about it when you are awake? If the drug seems more dangerous to you while dreaming than while awake, consider the possibility that you are at greater risk of damaging yourself or your life by using this drug than you may realize.*

7. *How do you feel when you awake from a dream in which you are using the drug? Do you awake relieved that it was only a dream and you aren't*

actually using it, or do you awaken disappointed that it wasn't the real thing and crave using it during the day?

CLOTHES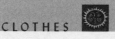

Variations

Have you ever dreamt of being in a different time and place where people were dressed in, say, Victorian clothes or Roman togas? Perhaps clothing has been an important image in your dreams in more specific ways. Have you ever forgotten your overcoat or had your jacket stolen? Perhaps you've dreamt of particularly interesting shoes, or of wearing shoes that were not yours or didn't fit. Many, many women have dreamt of wedding dresses and of veils. Some wedding clothes were forced on them by their mothers, others fit poorly, others fit like a dream. Have you dreamt of looking in the mirror and seeing yourself dressed in an unusual fashion? Perhaps you were wearing a beautiful red dress you would normally never have the courage to wear in waking life, or perhaps you were wearing your sister's clothing, which really didn't become you at all. Many of us have dreamt of being barefoot and of experiencing great inconvenience, discomfort, or anxiety as a result.

Sample Dreams
"If the Shoes Don't Fit"
Veronica had the following dream:

> I am getting dressed for my wedding. The problem is, the wedding dress doesn't look right, it doesn't fit me properly. My mother keeps coming up to me and giving me shoes, and I keep giving them back to her, saying, "Mother, they don't fit, they don't fit." Every pair of shoes she comes with is the wrong size.

When I asked Veronica what it was like to be in a wedding dress that didn't fit, she said, "Well, it wasn't bad, but it wasn't right, either. It just didn't feel comfortable. Some parts were too tight, some parts were too loose." I asked, "Is there anything in your life that doesn't fit like your wedding dress—too loose here, too tight there?" She said, "Sometimes I think my fiancé doesn't fit me quite right, but then nobody is perfect and nothing is totally easy, so I don't know if I should let that bother me." I asked her about the shoes that don't fit and about her mother's insistence that she try one pair after the other. She said that reminded her of her mother's encouragement to marry. Veronica felt a lot of pressure from her mother to get married, even if the fit wasn't right. She understood her dream: if the shoe fits, wear it; if it doesn't, don't.

"Barefoot in the Parade"
Kristin, in her late twenties, dreamt:

> I was taking a midday break from school, and I noticed a wonderful parade that was coming by. I wanted to go up and see the parade, but I noticed I was barefoot and enjoying the warm sun. That part was nice except that now without any shoes on I had to walk very slowly and very carefully to make sure I didn't hurt my feet on glass and other debris in the street. I had to get through the crowd to see the parade. I really wanted to see it, but I didn't think I'd get there in time because I had to take such care in walking.

I asked Kristin, "Why do humans go barefoot?" She said, "To enjoy the freedom and the wonderful feelings of sand." I asked, "How does it work to be barefoot in your dream?" She said it was a problem because it made her feet vulnerable to injury. When I asked what shoes were for, she said, "In this case shoes would be to protect my feet so I could walk wherever I wanted to. This parade was like the parade of life." I asked, "Is there any way that you're not able to join or take a look at the parade of life because your feet are unprotected and your feet are vulnerable to injury?" She said that yes, in fact this past year of her life she had been taking a break from regular work and schooling to explore her feelings. Her psychotherapy had been so intense that she felt extremely vulnerable. She told me, "I feel that I am much more focused on my feelings and am turned inward too far, although, like the warmth of the sun, I love to feel the freedom to experience my deeper emotions." Kristin said that the parade was a metaphor for the excitement of life. Her missing dream shoes were helping her reflect upon the level of extroversion that would allow her to move out into the parade of life.

What Do You Say?
1. Describe the _____ in your dream. First give a generic description. Why do humans wear _____s, and how do you like them?

2. *What is the _____ in your dream like?*

3. *Do you or would you wear a _____? Why or why not?*

4. *Let me recap this description. A _____ is* [restate the description], *and your opinion of it is* [restate the dreamer's opinion]. *Is there anything you would like to add or modify?*

5. *What is happening regarding the _____? Are you looking for it, wearing it, showing it off?*

6. *How do you feel in the dream regarding the _____? Are you proud or puzzled, or are you feeling ashamed or embarrassed by it or by its absence?*

7. *Is there anything in your life that is like a _____? Or is there anything that makes you feel like you are wearing* [or *have lost*, or *are not wearing*] *a _____?*

Settings in Dreams: How to Interpret Any Dream Setting

Here are the basic dream-interview questions you can ask yourself about any setting in your dreams in order to discover why you dreamt of being in Seattle or London, or in Aunt Sue's house. Your dream setting is never coincidental and can set the tone and indicate the part of your life under discussion in your dream. Remember that as you interview yourself or a friend, the dream interviewer pretends to come from another planet and has no idea what Seattle is like or who your Aunt Sue is. Instead, he or she asks you to give a precise description of the setting, one that will include how you feel about the setting, both in waking life and in the dream. Feel free to add to, modify, or skip questions when it seems appropriate. Just be sure to get a definitive description of the setting before you try to interpret its meaning.

1. *Describe the opening [or next] setting of the dream as if I come from another planet and need to know its nature and function.*

2. *What is this place like in your dream?*

3. *Is it different from such a place in waking life? How?*

4. *How does it feel to be in this setting?*

5. *So, this setting is [restate the description]. Right?*

6. *Does this setting, which you describe as [restate the description again], remind you of any situation or area in your waking life?*

7. *How so?*

YOUR PARENTS', GRANDMOTHER'S, AUNT'S HOME

Variations

You probably can remember many dreams in which you were at the home of someone you used to visit in your childhood. A grandmother, an aunt, an uncle, or maybe even your neighbor. Perhaps your parents' home. You may be a child again in the dream, but more likely you are your current age, following adventures that unfold on the porch, in the kitchen, upstairs in the bedroom, or anywhere in and around the house. The dreams can be pleasant or unpleasant, but usually they are simply curious dreams. You wonder why you were back there again.

Let's take a look and see what others have had to say about that.

Helpful Hints

When in a dream you are in the house of someone, it is useful to first get a good description of the person to whom the house belongs. For example, if you dream you are in Aunt Matilda's house, you would want to know who Aunt Matilda is and what she was like as well as in what period of your life you visited her home. Then you would want to have a good description of Aunt Matilda, to find out if the attitudes and ways of living pictured in Aunt Matilda's house are relevant in your life right now.

If you are dreaming of your childhood home, you would want to know during which years you lived in that house, because it's highly probable that the issues that the dream is dealing with had their origin in that particular period of your life. If going to visit your mother-in-law feels like going back to visit rigid, strict, unloving Aunt Matilda, you can imagine why you would dredge up the memory of Aunt Matilda in dreaming about your relationship with your in-laws. If on the other hand Aunt Matilda was a warm, loving person who understood you when no one else would, you may decide that she reminds you of your current husband. Or Aunt Matilda might remind you of how it feels to be with your best friend. As you can see, it all depends on how you answer your own questions.

Sample Dreams
"Grandmother's House"
Tanna dreamt:

> I was back at my grandmother's house as an adult, and I was wondering where I would sleep tonight. When I asked my grandmother, she told me I could sleep anywhere I wanted. I was shocked, because she was always so compulsive she would have every-thing planned down to the last detail. I rather liked her relaxed style. Then I woke up.

We asked Tanna to describe her grandmother, who had died fifteen years previously. Tanna said that her grandmother had been a very rigid woman—very loving, but a woman who tended to alienate the people close to her because she was so controlling: "Even when she tried to celebrate a happy holiday event, we would sort of dread going there because it was sort of like going to a happy police state, but a police state nevertheless." Asked if there was any part of her own per-sonality or anyone in her life who was like her grandmother, Tanna said, "Well, I guess you could say that I have become like that. I have four children, and I even dread my own Thanksgivings. I get them planned out in great detail, I make sure that everyone will have plenty to eat, the right place to sleep. But I think I'm too heavy-handed, like my grandmother." Asked how she felt in the dream, Tanna said that she was surprised at her grandmother's relaxed style. She told her dream-group members that perhaps it was time for her to relax and not worry that everything would fall apart if she failed to control every single moment of the day. She said her grandmother would have been fantastic if she just could have relaxed a little.

"Home Bombs"

David dreamt that he was back in his childhood home when he heard two bombs going off. He ran upstairs to find his wife, and then he heard a third bomb. He woke up with a start.

David said that the flavor of his childhood home, which he lived in until he was out of high school, was one of constant upheaval and anger. His parents had regular shouting matches. He said that the bombs in the dream reminded him a great deal of his parents' fights and of his waiting for the next bomb to drop and the next fight to start. In the dream, David was his own age, and he wanted to escape the house with his wife. Asked if there was anything going on in his current life that was like this situation, David said that he and his wife were having shouting matches just like his parents, and he thought the dream expressed his desire to "get us both the hell out of there." David was giving himself a strong dream message to do something about his relationship with his wife, in which he was repeating patterns from childhood, before it was too late.

What Do You Say?

1. *Describe the house in your dream. Describe the personality of the person whose house you are dreaming about. During what years of your life did you live in that household?*

2. *Try to remember what major issues were going on in your life during the time you lived in that house or the time you visited that house regularly. Is there anyone in your life or any part of yourself that is like the owner of your dream house?*

3. *Describe the action that occurs in the dream. Is there any situation in your current life that is like the action in the dream or that takes place when you act or feel like the owner of the house?*

4. *Is there any situation in your current life that is like the issues that were going on at the time you lived in or visited that house?*

5. *Describe the major people, actions, and feelings that arise during this dream, and ask yourself what current life situation could bring these memories back to life.*

6. *Does this dream help you to identify patterns of behavior learned in childhood that you are now repeating to your own benefit or detriment in your adult life?*

A PARTICULAR TOWN, STATE, OR COUNTRY

Variations

Isn't it wonderful how real and vivid dreams seem? Think how real it seems when you dream of being on a tropical island, in your hometown, or in Brazil. The dream paints the scene for you, with all the feeling of the familiarity or strangeness of the place that you choose to dream about on a particular night. You may see locals, or you may be a local yourself. You may be in this particular place with people from your hometown, or you may meet exotic strangers who themselves are traveling from place to place. In any case, the particular location you choose for your dream sets a tone and often identifies the area of your life that your dream is going to deal with.

Sample Dreams

Before you read about this dream, let me invite you to write down on a piece of paper a two- or three-line description of the state of New Hampshire. What kind of state is it, what kinds of people live there, how do you like it? Then take a look at Pia's dream to see how her description compares with yours.

"Far Away to New Hampshire"
Pia dreamt:

I am on a plane headed for New Hampshire—because, it turns out, that's where my boyfriend is from, and I'm going to meet his family and try to understand his lifestyle. That's all I remember of the dream.

When a dream-group member asked Pia to describe New Hampshire, she said, "It's the furthest part of the United States away from my home in San Francisco, the furthest part away geographically, morally, and spiritually; it's very far away. New Hampshire people are very straight, they're stuck, they are moralistic, and they tend to be older and of course very conservative. Independent, and I like that part, but all the rest would be very stifling to me." Asked if the attitude that

Pia associates with New Hampshire describes the origins of her boyfriend's family, she said she was afraid so. Pia felt that the dream was making her look at this highly improbable match. She said that if indeed her new boyfriend turns out to be as New Hampshire–esque as she was afraid he might be, even his good looks, good humor, and high intelligence would not be enough to overcome a mismatch on such a fundamental level.

"Sophisticated San Francisco"

Bernadette told her dream in one of our weekly study groups:

> I once dreamt of simply seeing the Golden Gate Bridge at different times of day, sunrise to sunset, saw the daylight changing, the fog coming in, the mist. The whole dream simply consisted of appreciating the beauty and the grace of the bridge and these constantly changing scenes and atmospheres. As I dreamt the dream I understood that the bridge symbolized something I shared with my new boyfriend. A sense of grace, elegance, and changing lights—for want of a better word. I woke up delighted by the dream.

In interviewing herself she asked, "What are the San Francisco bridge and bay like?" Her answer was "San Francisco is one of the most beautiful places on earth. It feels like home. I'm not in a foreign country. It feels like part of my homeland. The bridge that connects the San Francisco Peninsula with Marin County to the north connects the excitement of city life with suburban country life. The very special thing about it is that it never stays the same. The weather changes all the time, the light changes, the view of this area is so varied that it's forever fascinating—sometimes restful, sometimes exciting, but always beautiful. I realized that my description of the bridge as a connection between the excitement of city life and the beauty of country life really did articulate some of the special qualities I thought possible with my relationship with my new boyfriend.

"He has both the sophistication of the city and an appreciation of the country. His personality is mature enough to be varied and wise, yet exciting and young enough to be always interesting. I dreamt of the San Francisco and not other lovely bridges and bodies of water in the world, I think, to emphasize the fact that there was no lack of excitement with this man even though he lives near my hometown. The aesthetic pleasure in the dream is one I associate very strongly with San Francisco, and in fact describes very much my aesthetic connection with this man."

What Do You Say?
1. *Describe the place in your dreams as if you were describing it to a person from another planet who has never heard of it before. Use at least three adjectives.*

2. *Do you like or dislike this place? What kinds of people tend to live here? Give your impression, not just the facts.*

3. *How does it feel to be in this setting in the dream?*

4. *Is there any area of your life or any relationship in your life that feels like this setting?*

5. *How does this setting highlight certain aspects of your current life?*

Animals in Dreams: How to Interpret Any Animal in Your Dreams

No matter what animals you dream about, there are basic questions that will help you unlock the meaning you invest in that image. It's extremely helpful to consider what you imagine to be the personality of your dream animal—what its personality is like generally in waking life, and what its personality and traits seem to be in your dream. This will be determined by how the animal acts and by the general condition and look of the animal, as well as by your feelings toward it in the context of the dream.

The examples of specific animals that follow after this general entry will give you an idea of how to work with specific images. All you have to do is modify your questions to the specific kind of animal you dream about, no matter how unusual or bizarre.

Following are interview questions that will help you interpret any animal in your dreams. Remember to ask these questions as if you were someone from another planet and had no preconceptions about the image. Then when you answer the questions, remember that you are speaking to someone who comes from another planet and is unfamiliar with your particular web of associations and impressions. Just give as direct and as informative an answer as you can to the extraterrestrial, who really is interested only in knowing what you think about the images in your dream.

1. *What is this animal like? Pretend I've never seen one before.*

2. *How would you describe the personality of a _____?*

3. *What is a _____ doing in your dream?*

4. *So this animal is [restate the description], right?*

5. *Is there anyone in your life or anything or any part of yourself that is like a _____, which you describe as [restate the description again]?*

6. *How so?*

Test the bridge.

CATS

Variations

People dream of cats that are healthy, that are starved for attention or for food, cats that are mistreated, cats that are lost, cats that act in certain surprising ways. Dream cats have been known to wreak havoc in a bedroom, play hard to get, suffer and cry out, "Love me, love me," and of course bite and attack the dreamer. Sometimes the cats are orange, sometimes they look like a cat as well as another animal, sometimes they limp, and sometimes they gracefully leap over a fence. There seems to be no end to the various roles cats can play in dreams.

Sample Dreams
"Hissing Cat"

Kim dreamt that she walked into a big empty hall and out of a dark corner came a cat, hissing at her, hostile, trying to get her to leave. She thought that perhaps the cat had had a litter, but then that didn't seem to be the case. She wanted to be in this room when suddenly she realized that she was in the classic position of two cats in a barn. This cat was very jealous of her space and didn't want anybody else in her territory.

When I asked Kim to describe the personality of the cat, she said, "Well, I don't like cats. They're territorial, they're jealous, they're nasty, they scratch, they hiss, they're not warm and generous and open like dogs. I really don't like them." When I restated that description to her, she said, "You know, that description of a cat describes one of my friends. This friend has a very annoying habit of trying to claim as her territory almost any attractive man we meet when we go dancing together. She looks like a friend, she is a friend in certain ways, but whenever we're around men she becomes just like a hissing cat. There are plenty of men to go around. Just as in the dream there is plenty of room, but she won't let me into the space. She doesn't want me anywhere near, and I have this awful feeling . . . I've been humoring her, but I think I've really had enough. I have to talk to her about the fact that I'm not willing to play this game anymore."

"A Cat Moves In"

Tony dreamt that a very furry cat entered the house and planned on staying there. He woke up very distressed.

Tony described cats as selfish, demanding, very allergenic creatures. He hates cats and was more than a little upset to think of one moving in with him. When he heard the restatement of his description, he said, "Oh no, that sounds like my new girlfriend. I don't like to think that, because she is also very sexy. But she is selfish, she is demanding, and she is very controlling. I think I'd be as allergic to her as I am to cats. I wouldn't be able to breathe in the same space with her."

"Starving Kittens"

Jan dreamt that she walked out onto the porch of her house in the middle of winter to find several starving kittens in a box. They were hers, but she hadn't realized they

were there. They were hungry, neglected, and nearly freezing, and it made her so sad to see them in this condition that she wanted to cry.

Jan described kittens as defenseless, playful creatures that need to be well cared for. As she described them she cried, realizing that she felt very much like an abused and neglected little kitten. She had felt that way growing up. Even now as an adult she still felt that inside her were these kittens that needed to be nurtured and cared for. She had only now discovered the depth of the sadness she had carried with her from a very difficult childhood.

What Do You Say?

1. *Pretend I come from another galaxy. What are cats like?*

2. *Do you like cats? Why or why not?*

3. *What is the cat in your dream like? What is its personality?*

4. *Is there anyone in your life or any part of yourself that is like this cat, which you describe as [restate the description]?*

5. *What is the cat doing in your dream?*

6. *How does the cat's activity parallel the actions of the person in your life who is like the cat?*

SNAKES

Variations

Is there anyone who has never dreamt of snakes? Most often snakes in a dream frighten a person. A snake may threaten to poison you, to squeeze you to death; sometimes they actually do kill the dreamer in the dream. In other cases snakes are the objects of adoration and care. Some people who like snakes as pets will even dream about snakes as having particular personalities and moods, and will find them playing very specific roles within a dream. Some dream snakes are poisonous, while others are harmless. Some are hidden in the grass, and others are on display as in a zoo.

ALL ABOUT *Dreams*

Sample Dreams
"Snake Fangs"
Carla had the following dream:

I walked past a man who was carrying a serpent. It curled around me and attacked me. I could feel its fangs sinking deep into my leg. I was in more shock than pain. I looked at my leg to see the mark of where the bite had been. Was the snake poisonous? My leg was sore. When I came to, I was told that an acquaintance of mine had just suddenly died for no apparent reason. It made me realize how temporary our existence is. It can all vanish in a moment. My misadventure with a snake wasn't that final. I was alive, and I would be all right.

Carla described the snake as venomous; it had a good grip on her, it went deep into her. She saw it as evil and disabling. Carla asked herself, "When have I been attacked by something that's venomous and could sink its fangs into me and also had a good grip on me?" She responded, "I most closely bridge this type of experience to the mean and malicious attacks from my boyfriend, Clement. I was surprised when a similar incident happened over the weekend, after the dream, with my sister, in which I felt my character had been attacked. I realized that both my sister and Clement attack because they feel defensive. I have tried to learn not to take this too personally, but the dream seemed to be letting me know that these kinds of encounters are more toxic than I realized. It seems I should stay clear of snake territory."

"Eek! A Snake"
Beth dreamt:

I screamed as I opened a small box containing some of my jewelry and some of my pens and pencils, because I found a live snake in the box. It was small, thin; it was probably harmless. I asked who put it in there, and a very pretty, young, sexy acquaintance of mine said she did, and said that she kept larger snakes among her own things. I wanted her to get rid of them all.

Beth described the snake in her dream as frightening, squirmy; she didn't like it, she didn't know what it would do next. Although she was afraid of it, she also realized in the dream that it was harmless. She described her young acquaintance as

sexy, appealing, and a little mysterious, a person who was not at all afraid of snakes. Beth laughed and said that this dream must be about sex: "I grew up in a time when sex was not a topic anyone ever talked about, and I feel uncomfortable dealing with sexuality. I wish it would just go away." The acquaintance in the dream offered her a chance to consider another way of relating to sexuality that might be more fulfilling. Beth also thought that the harmless nature of the snake in her dream referred to her husband, who, though sexual, was indeed not going to hurt her.

"Jowly Snake"

Cici dreamt that she was riding in a train and at an intersection saw a snake. The snake was huge, and had a big head with a fat and jowly neck. It was green and ugly. But she was glad to note that it was far enough away not to pose any threat to her as she passed by in the train.

After recapping her description of the big, fat, jowly snake, Cici bridged easily to her former direct boss at work. She was a dangerous, envious, jowly creature who had made Cici's work life difficult. Now, however, Cici had repositioned herself both administratively and geographically such that her return to work after a break no longer troubled her. The serpent would no longer threaten her.

What Do You Say?

1. *What are snakes like? Pretend I've just come from another galaxy and have never seen one before.*

2. *What is the specific snake in your dream like?*

3. *How would you describe the personality of the snake in your dream?*

4. *What is the snake doing in your dream?*

5. *So, this snake is* [restate the description], *right?*

6. *Is there anyone in your life or anything or any part of yourself that is like this snake, which you describe as* [restate the description again]?

7. *How so?*

   Test the bridge.

Many common dreams take the form of nightmares.[3] They are frightening, and most of us would just as soon forget them. But your nightmares could be the most important dreams you will ever have. If you can learn how to recognize their meanings, they can save you years of suffering and frustration.

A gentleman in his forties had had a recurring nightmare, a version of the common "the corpse who is not quite dead yet" variety of dream. In the dream, which occurred twice a month for twenty-two years, he was at a wake. When he looked at the corpse, he was horrified to see that it was moving its fingers. Then the dead man would slowly sit up in the coffin and stare at the dreamer, who would try to hide from the not-so-dead man's gaze. But wherever he would hide—behind plants, behind other people—the corpse, the dreamer knew, could always see him. He would never find a safe hiding place.

For over two decades the dreamer had awakened in terror from this frequent nightmare, which would suggest that the conflict represented by the dream had existed in the dreamer's life in one form or another for at least that long. When I asked him if he knew of a problem that had haunted him for many years, he said he was not aware of any. I asked him to describe what major things had happened in his life during the year the nightmares began, but nothing came to his mind. He described in detail the feelings he had in the dream of wanting to hide.

When I asked him if he had made a major decision that year, one that might have resulted in his trying to kill off some aspect of himself, he interrupted energetically. That year he had made a fateful career choice. Instead of becoming a musician, as he had hoped to do, he accepted his father's counsel and became an engineer. From that day on he had played no more music and in fact rarely attended concerts! Greatly relieved to have understood his nightmare, our dreamer resolved to let the musician in him live just a bit by taking time to enjoy great music, even if he could not now become a great performer.

Very often nightmares are triggered by our efforts to deny a part of ourselves, our needs, and our experience. If you dream of being chased by strange men, ask yourself, "What am I running from?" If you dream of being imprisoned, ask yourself, "How am I allowing myself to be contained, locked up?" If you dream of being mauled by a wild beast, ask yourself, "Deep inside, do I feel I am being devoured?"

Nightmares are like flashing red lights signaling trouble and conflict that have reached the point of becoming a significant problem. Recurring nightmares are symptoms of a problem that the dreamer has been unable to resolve and that is crying out for attention. The fact that you are having frequent nightmares, especially recurring ones, is a very good reason to seek professional help with your dreams. Frequent nightmares could be indications of extreme conflict and stress in your life. Or as Ernest Hartman, in his wonderful book, *The Nightmare*, points out, "a lifetime of frequent nightmares could reflect a highly sensitive, vulnerable, creative, thin-boundary nature, which might benefit from psychotherapeutic coaching in coping with the slings and arrows of daily life."

Some analysts believe that a nightmare is a failed dream in that it does not produce some resolution to the frightening situation; the problem-solving function of dreaming seems to be absent. Others would point out that the dreamer's defenses were inadequate to protect against the painful experience. In the case of a posttraumatic recurring nightmare, I would agree. War veterans who suffer agonizing replays of battle scenes are struggling with an inability to adapt to or integrate their painful experience. Most nightmares, however, contain several symbolic clues to the dreamer's problems. The recalled nightmare can be the dreamer's first conscious hint of trouble, as in the case of the engineer who had no idea how much he had restricted his experience of life by hiding from his corpse.

Nightmares often reflect extraordinarily accurate, perceptive, and emotionally vibrant appraisals of an important conflict. They can point the way toward resolution of the problem long before the dreamer could have figured it out for himself in the waking state. I would suggest that nightmares can be very successful dreams indeed, and that they are vital warning signals one would be unwise to ignore.

In my private practice, I have worked with many lay and professional dream workers who are embarrassed to admit that they "still" have nightmares. There seems to be a popular belief that nightmares are for the unenlightened and immature. Not at all! Even the most integrated, successful of my clients have dramatic nightmares from time to time. They attend to these signals and act on them before minor problems turn into major ones. Raymond Greenberg, a Boston psychiatrist, pointed out to me that sometimes nightmares have such relieving or happy endings that the problem the dream depicts is obscured. It is important to remember that realizing the happy ending in your waking life usually depends upon your insight into the dream conflict.

STOPPING NIGHTMARES

People often ask, "How can I get rid of my nightmares?" Repressing or aborting a nightmare by awakening or by forcing a happy ending onto it is to reject the offer of insight the experience offers. It is true that by becoming aware, within the dream, that we are having a nightmare, we can change the course of the dream. If we use this awareness or lucidity to paste on a Pollyanna ending, it is easy to lose the motivation to hear the message of the dream. If, instead, we use lucidity to stay in the frightening dream and explore its fearsome characters and events, we can enhance our chances of recalling the dream's details and gain useful insights from the clues they offer us. As you will see in chapter 7, repetitive nightmares that result from post-traumatic stress are another matter. In that chapter you will find dream control methods that have proven very effective in reducing nightmare intensity and frequency.

Seven

DIRECTING YOUR DREAMS

By learning how to direct your dreams, you will be able to use them to solve specific practical and emotional problems. You will find new ways to explore and play with your dreaming state of mind. And you will be equipped to reduce the frequency of your nightmares and the conflicts that give rise to them. The first time you succeed in directing a dream, you will feel a rush of delight and achievement. No doubt you'll tell all your friends about it. But most of all you will feel a new sense of partnership with your dreams. And the fact that your dreams are on your side, ready to help you out when you request assistance, will give you an enhanced sense of your power to thrive in your life. Before giving you simple instructions for incubating your own dreams, I shall present a few examples to inspire you.

Some Really Impressive Examples of Dream Incubation

In 1846, Elias Howe patented the lockstitch sewing machine, which he invented with the help of a dream. All of Howe's earlier models had failed because he had placed the eye of the needle in the middle of the shank. One night, he dreamt that

he was captured by a tribe of savages who took him a prisoner before their king.

"Elias Howe," roared the monarch, "I command you on pain of death to finish this machine at once."

Cold sweat poured down his brow, his hands shook with fear, his knees quaked. Try as he would, the inventor could not get the missing figure in the problem over which he had worked so long. All this was so real to him that he cried aloud. In the vision he saw himself surrounded by . . . painted warriors, who formed a hollow square about him and led him to the place of execution. Suddenly he noticed that near the heads of the spears which his guards carried, there were eye-shaped holes! He had solved the secret! What he needed was a needle with an eye near the point! He awoke from his dream, sprang out of bed, and at once made a whittled model of the eye-pointed needle.[1]

The creator of the periodic table, Dmitry Mendeleyev, told a close friend who was a geologist that in a dream he saw the periodic tables with which he had been struggling. In the dream, "all the elements are placed as they should be. I woke up and immediately wrote it all down on a piece of paper. Eventually there was only one place which needed to be corrected."[2]

Hermann von Helmholtz (1821–1894) was a famous physicist, physiologist, and philosopher who was to have an important influence on Freud via one of his principal proponents, the physiologist Ernst Brücke, who was one of Freud's teachers. Helmholtz taught that all knowledge is founded in experience that is hereditarily transmitted or acquired, and that purely chemico-physical laws governed neurophysiology and thus psychology.[3] W. B. Cannon reports that this empiricist, who among numerous other contributions invented the ophthalmoscope and formulated the law of conservation of energy, ". . . when near the end of his life, told of the way in which the most important of his ideas had occurred to him. After investigating a problem 'in all directions,' he testified, 'happy ideas come unexpectedly without effort like an inspiration. So far as I am concerned, they have never come to me when my mind was fatigued or when I was at my working table.' Rest was necessary for the appearance of the original ideas and they occurred as a rule in the morning after a night's sleep."[4]

Cannon, himself a famous physiologist, wrote that one of his inventions and some of his best ideas came to him when he would awaken in the middle of the night. For example, his formulation of the body's "fight or flight" mechanism came to him while he lay awake in the dark.[5] Cannon regularly asked his dreams to help him solve scientific problems and even to prepare lectures.

> As a matter of routine I have long trusted unconscious processes to serve me—for example, when I have had to prepare a public address. I would gather points for the address and write them down in a rough outline. Within the next few nights, I would have sudden spells of awakening, with an onrush of illustrative instances, pertinent phrases, and fresh ideas related to those already listed. Paper and pencil at hand permitted the capture of these fleeting thoughts before they faded into oblivion. The process has been so common and so reliable for me that I have supposed that it was at the service of everyone. But evidence indicates that it is not.[6]

Murder writer Sue Grafton *(B Is for Burglar, C Is for Corpse)* regularly incubates dreams for her alphabet novels as well as for her TV screenplays.

> I reach a point in many of my books, when I'm very heavily engaged in the process of writing, where I have a problem that I can't solve. And as I go to sleep I will give myself the suggestion that a solution will come. Whether this is from a dream state I'm not certain. I know that I will waken and the solution will be there. I attribute it to right brain activity. I don't know the relationship between right brain and dreams but I know when the analytical self, the left brain, finally releases its grip on us and gets out of the way, the creative side of us, which often surfaces in sleep, comes to the fore and in its own playful and whimsical manner will solve many creative problems.[7]

Novelist Stephen King knows how to incubate dreams, and for his long book *It*, he dreamed up the ending he had been unable to come up with while awake. He said of the welcome dream, "I really think what happened with this dream was that I went to sleep and the subconscious went right on working and finally sent up this dream the way that you would send somebody an interoffice message in a pneumatic tube."[8]

My colleague, Loma Flowers, M.D., has used dream incubation with considerable success in helping patients in her psychiatric practice to understand and cope with the psychological factors in various illnesses including headaches, high blood pressure, and allergies. She described one dramatic example that occurred in her capacity as a consulting psychiatrist. The patient had undergone abdominal surgery for cancer. The patient, who had initially done well after surgery, had been vomiting for two weeks when Dr. Flowers was called in to determine whether or not the vomiting might be psychologically triggered. If the patient continued to vomit, it would be necessary to operate again to see what had gone wrong.

In the second session, Dr. Flowers worked on a spontaneous dream about the patient's work problems. The dream work helped the patient feel more in control regarding her job situation. The next day her vomiting had somewhat decreased but was still present. Because of her long experience with the effectiveness of this dream-interpretation method, Dr. Flowers hypothesized a second, hidden issue contributing to the vomiting. She went over the personal history with the patient one more time, seeking evidence for this hypothesis. It became apparent that the patient needed to face some unresolved grieving she had failed to do for a son. The grief had apparently been stirred up by the emotional trauma of her own illness and hospitalization.

Dr. Flowers instructed her on how to incubate a dream to help work through the grief. That night, the patient dreamt that she was playing the card game old maid with her son as the small child he had been many years ago. He was cheating in the amusing way he had always cheated at the game. And he was laughing with exuberant mischief as he had always done in that situation. This dream and the strong feelings in it allowed the mother to get in touch with the good times of the relationship, long eclipsed by the subsequent tragedy. Only when one can reexperience the good feelings for the lost loved one is it possible to truly grieve and let go. The mother's dream helped her to reconnect with good, warm, loving, laughing feelings and thereby allowed her to proceed with the arrested grief work. The next day she was up and eating. The vomiting was over.[9]

Sleep on It, Incubate a Dream

Have you ever gone to sleep with a problem on your mind and awakened with the solution in mind the next morning? If so, you've already incubated a dream! More properly speaking, you have incubated a problem, but we say *dream* because humans have been using that term since the times of ancient Greece. You can quite easily learn to incubate a dream on a topic that is important to you. If you try to incubate a dream tonight, you will probably wake up tomorrow morning with a long or short dream or no dream at all—with just the solution in mind.

This is what happened to a woman we'll call Kathryn, whom I met at a cocktail party one night. Kathryn had been part of a conversation about dreams and heard me mention how easy it is to incubate a dream. The next morning she called me to say thank you. She had gone home the night before determined to try to incubate a dream to solve a pressing problem. It seems that a year earlier her family had bought a German shepherd puppy that had now grown too big and too boisterous for her family and her house. All attempts to find another home for enormous George had failed, and the only choice remaining was to take him to the pound. This alternative pained everyone concerned and led the parents to feel ashamed for not having foreseen the problem.

Following my cocktail-party instructions for dream incubation, Katherine wrote out her question and went to sleep repeating it to herself: "Is there any alternative to the pound?" She awoke in the morning with no dream recall, but with the winning idea. She went to the newspaper lost-and-found section and found a family that had lost a year-old German shepherd. She called and said that although she had not found their dog, she had another adorable one looking for a happy home. The other family was overjoyed, and Enormous George had been saved from the pound.

I created my method of incubation in 1971 while a senior at Princeton. I first incubated dreams in the form of prayers to God asking why I was so very faint at the idea of marriage. At the time I had a wonderful boyfriend, psychologist Henry Reed (who would later design his own ritualistic form of incubation), and even though I was young I realized that my panic at the mere thought of marriage was clearly neurotic. My dreams responded immediately. Unfortunately, my Jungian analyst was terrible with dreams, and it would be several months before I figured them out for myself.

I realized that the world needed a simple, do-it-yourself, nonreligious method of interpretation that anyone could use comfortably. My phrase-focusing technique worked like a charm for my fellow students and me. And it's so simple! In a pilot study I conducted for a master's thesis on incubation in 1973–1974, students were able to dream on the topic of their choice eight out of ten times.[10] Robert Davé at Michigan State University conducted a study of the effects of hypnotically induced dreams on creative problem solving. He worked with twenty-four subjects. One group of eight was given hypnotic suggestions to dream a solution to an academic, vocational, avocational, or personal problem that stymied them at the time of the experiment. Another group of eight received rational cognitive treatment that consisted of very rational discussions on the subject's problem. The third group of eight subjects constituted the control group and was told that before employing any methods to enhance creativity, each of them would have an hour-long personality interview that would be analyzed before the enhancement procedures were begun.

Six of the eight in the hypnotic-dream group were successful in breaking through their impasses; in the rational-cognitive group, one of the eight; and in the control group, none of the eight. After the first week, four from the control group were assigned to a hypnotic-dream group and four to the rational-cognitive group. None of the latter four was successful in solving the targeted problem, but three of the four who entered a hypnotic-dream group were! Of nine of the successful subjects in a dream group, six attributed resolutions directly to one or more of their hypnotically induced dreams. Two said that their resolutions were due to their hypnotically induced dreams in conjunction with subsequent nocturnal dreams, and one credited her success to having visualized the elements constituting her problem.[11]

In England, Morton Schatzman invited people via a newspaper announcement to try to solve a brainteaser by incubating dreams on them. Although he has no way of knowing how many people tried the experiment and did not write him, he did receive many strikingly impressive solutions embedded in incubated dreams.[12] I hope he will soon find funding to do more detailed studies on this promising subject.

Dr. Robert Hoffmann, formerly of the University of Ottawa and now at the University of Texas at Dallas, and Dr. Kathy Belicki of the University of Ottawa have conducted dream-incubation experiments that show the process to work. Unfortunately, owing to lack of time, money, or, in the case of Dr. Hoffmann, access to certain files, they have yet to write up and publish their results.

Dr. Diedre Barrett at Harvard Medical School has conducted a pioneering study on incubation. Twenty-six college students were asked to incubate dreams on a problem of personal relevance as a homework assignment in a class on dreams. They used a method of incubation described by sleep researcher William Dement and presented in his classic book, *Some Must Watch While Some Must Sleep*. Using this method, students are instructed to work on solving their problem for exactly fifteen minutes before sleep and in the morning to write down on a questionnaire any dream recalled from the night. If the problem remains unsolved, the students are to work on the problem for another fifteen minutes.[13]

In Dr. Barrett's study, which I hope will be the first of many by this imaginative researcher on this topic, "approximately half the subjects recalled a dream which they felt was related to the problem."[14] Seventy percent of these students thought their dream contained a solution to the problem. Given my twenty-seven years' experience with incubation, both in my private practice and with Loma Flowers at our Dream Center, I would suggest that two modifications to this type of experiment would yield significantly better results.

First, I would have the subjects write out a brief discussion about the problem without making any effort to solve it. Second, I would have them write out a clear one-line question or request before sleep (see below). These two steps are, in my experience, of great value. Then, of course, we have the problem that some answers come embedded in metaphoric dreams that the dreamers and/or experimenters are often not able to interpret. If each subject could be given a standardized dream interview, I am quite sure that many more clear solutions would be uncovered. In fact, to make such studies easier and less expensive, I have been working on a computerized version of the dream interview that is extraordinarily adaptable to such a format. This would allow researchers access to relevant associative material as well as to coherent, well-founded interpretive efforts made by the dreamers themselves. But until more funding is made available to researchers, dream studies will remain few and modest in scope.

In the meantime, it may encourage you to know that in my experience most people who incubate a question they are emotionally eager and ready to learn more about can succeed on their first try. Follow these steps, and perhaps by tomorrow morning you will have incubated your first dream.

How to Incubate a Dream

Step 1: Choose the right night.

First, choose a night when you are not overly tired. In order to work with your dream self rather than against it, it is imperative that you be free of intoxicants like alcohol and drugs. Valium and most sleeping pills cloud the mind. Many users who take an active interest in their dream life find that they no longer need them. If you are currently taking these drugs, remember that it is dangerous to go off them abruptly. Since an interest in dreaming sometimes cures or alleviates insomnia, it is useful to consult your doctor for the best schedule for tapering off. If your doctor has prescribed more than one or two weeks' worth of sleeping pills, you might do well to get another doctor's opinion, since such long-term use of hypnotics is detrimental to your sleep.

Be sure you will be able to spend five to twenty uninterrupted minutes working with your dream journal just before sleeping. You will need at least ten minutes the following morning to record your incubated dream, unless you awake and record it in the middle of the night, so be sure to leave time for this.

Step 2: Day notes.

Before going to sleep, record your day notes. Write three or four lines about what you did and felt during the day. What were the emotional highlights of your day? Getting the thoughts and feelings of the day down on paper will clear your mind, relax you, and help you recall your dreams much better.

Step 3: Incubation discussion.

In this step, called the *incubation discussion,* you use your conscious mind (and heart) to take a close look at the various aspects of your situation. Direct your attention to these. Ask yourself if you are really ready to examine the problem, called the *incubation issue,* and if you are ready to do something about it. Discuss the matter thoroughly with yourself, writing down as much of the discussion as possible. You might consider such questions as the following:

What do you see as the *causes* of the problem?

What are the alternative solutions you now recognize, and why won't one of them do?

How are you feeling as you write this?

What "secondary gains" or benefits might you be receiving from perpetuating this conflict?

Does living with the problem feel safer than resolving it?

What would you have to give up (e.g., sympathy, martyrdom) if the problem were resolved?

How would things be different if the problem were resolved?

You may not be asking about a problem but rather seeking information or insight related to various life interests. In this case, ask yourself why you want or need the information and what you plan to do with it when you receive it.

Go as far as you can with the incubation issue while you are awake. Churn up your feelings. Get the thoughts out of your mind and onto the paper.

It can be very tempting to skip this step entirely. And in fact many people can omit it and still successfully incubate a great dream. However, this has proven to be one of the most important steps in the process for beginners. The more completely you use your conscious mind to grapple with the issue and actually write out the discussion, the better you will be at asking a question that goes right to the heart of the matter. And the more positive you can be of getting an answer to your question in the morning. Sometimes a brief discussion will suffice. Later, as you become familiar with the process, the written form of the incubation discussion can frequently be partly or entirely eliminated. More difficult and confusing issues, however, will require a written discussion. Remember, if you want to ensure that dream incubation will work for you on your first try, your incubation discussion will be a crucial factor in your success. Place the letters *ID* in the margin of your journal at the beginning of your incubation discussion for later reference.

Step 4: Incubation phrase.

On the next line in your journal, write down a one-line question or request that expresses your deepest and clearest desire to understand the dynamics of your predicament. This will be your *incubation phrase*. Make it simple. You may want to play around with several phrases until you find the one that feels best. Your incubation phrase might be "Help me understand why I am afraid of heights and what I can do about it," or "What are the dynamics of our relationship: what's *really* going on between *X* and me?" If you were hoping to discover new ideas for a project, you would clearly state your request, asking, for example, "Please give me an idea for my next painting." Whatever your question or request, find a phrase that expresses it as briefly and as clearly as possible. The more specific your incubation phrase, the more specific will be the resulting dream. Write your incubation phrase in bold letters and place a big star ✶ in the margin to the left of it. Be sure to write out this phrase on paper before sleep. Omitting this step leads to many problems such as "Now, what did I finally decide to incubate?"; "I forgot how I phrased the question!"; or "I couldn't decide which thing to incubate."

Step 5: Repeat your incubation phrase over and over to yourself as you fall asleep.

Now you are ready to place your journal beside your bed, turn off the lamp, and close your eyes. Having done this, focus all your attention on your incubation phrase. Imagine that you are about to begin production of a dream scene that will answer your question. You direct the camera to zero in on a close-up of your main point of interest, your incubation phrase. You take control of the camera, your consciousness. It focuses exclusively upon the phrase again and again. As you fall asleep, forget about the written ruminations of your incubation discussion. Concentrate on your question. If distracting thoughts occur, such as, "Will this work?" or "Tomorrow I must remember to . . . ," let them go. Keep bringing your focus back to the incubation phrase, which is the distillation of your query. Let all your feelings focus on this phrase. Keep it in your mind up to the very last second before you fall asleep. If you do this, sleep assured that you will most likely dream about your problem the first time you try. This is the most important part of the incubation procedure, so be sure your camera is focused well.

Step 6: Sleep!

This step is the easiest. Just sleep. In ways we do not understand, a portion of our consciousness that usually appears *un*conscious from the point of view of the waking self will make contact with sources of experience and wisdom most often available only in the sleeping state. As we quiet the daytime barrage of sense perceptions and fall asleep, we tune in to a subtler level of experience.

In our sleep states, we apparently have access to the great storehouse of all our personal history (deeds, attitudes, memories, impressions) as well as to information concerning our probable future. As many psychologists, psychiatrists, and countless students of dreaming have found, our inner self sees our life and problems more clearly, more objectively, and from a far broader perspective than we usually do while awake.

On rare occasions, you may even become aware enough or conscious enough to witness your dream producer at work. You can become aware of a part of yourself that's busily choosing just the right cast of characters and associations from your personal memories in an effort to translate your experience with the non-three-dimensionally oriented parts of your inner self into terms that will make sense to your conscious mind. This encounter with your inner self apparently takes place in highly symbolic form. The dream-maker self has the task of breaking down these powerful symbols into more specific guises that we can relate to our daily experience. The dreams we remember may be no more than the tail end of the sleep process.

Your incubated dreams will usually come the same night you ask for them. The dreams may redefine your problem, translating it from the way you consciously see it into the way your inner self sees it. The discrepancy can be very enlightening. The dreams may present alternatives to your dilemma that you've not considered. They might introduce you to whole new areas of psychological awareness and understanding. Finally, some incubated dreams will seem to have a resolving, soothing, healing effect in themselves. The very experience of a dream may change your mind or feeling in a way that resolves your conflict. Trust your dream producer to do the job well. This creative part of you is aware of your incubation concerns and quite capable of responding to these with skillfully crafted dreams.

Step 7: Record.

Record in detail all your dream memories *as soon as you awake with them*, whether it is in the middle of the night or in the morning. Make no judgments at this point regarding the relevance to your incubation question of the dreams or pieces of dreams you recall. Include any feelings, thoughts, songs, or fantasies that come to mind. *Try to reexperience the dream.*[15]

Step 8: Interview yourself about your dream.

Use the guidelines in chapter 4 and conduct a good dream interview. Don't try to force your dream to answer your question. Since your dream could possibly be about another topic, explore your dream with an open mind. It would be a shame to miss the point of a dream that was important enough to override your incubation request. When you figure out what your dream is about, only then ask yourself if it sheds light on your incubation phrase. Remember that dreams don't tell you what to do. Your dreams are your own mind working. Let your dreams give you insight—that is, let them open your eyes. Armed with new insight that makes sense to your waking mind, you will be better equipped to make more-enlightened decisions with your conscious, waking mind.

THE SHORT VERSION OF HOW TO INCUBATE A DREAM

1. Write out your question before you go to sleep.

2. Repeat it over and over to yourself as you fall asleep.

THE VERY SHORT VERSION

1. Repeat your question to yourself as you fall asleep.

As people get better at focusing their attention on a topic and as they gain confidence that the process works for them, they can streamline the process to just a moment's attention before sleep. Some can even order up the incubation by having suggested it to themselves during the day! But if you want to maximize your chances of success, put pen to paper and follow each step of the process.

SAMPLE INCUBATION

Most people start incubating dreams because they want insight about a difficult relationship. Fortunately, dreams are almost always quick to respond to such requests.

Les had been hoping to salvage a relationship with Betty for over a year. Betty had told Les it was over, although she periodically gave him hope that he still had a chance with her. Even though she had another boyfriend, Les could not let go. He told Betty to take her time, that he would be patient while she worked things out in her heart. Les's self-study, which included working with his dreams, had already pointed to the role of unloved but ever faithful suitor that he had played more than once in his life. One night he incubated a dream by asking, "What should I do regarding Betty?" He dreamt:

Muhammad Ali is standing at a curb next to a limousine. He is waiting for Ella to come out of the front door of the house behind him. The people in the house like Ali a lot. He stands there, waiting patiently. A pure, God-like voice comes from behind me. It is filled with great wisdom, strength, and certainty. The voice says, "Everyone knows that Ella will not come out the door. But Ali waits. She is no longer there, but the great warrior waits. Ella is dead!"

Everyone knows, but the champ waits. He stands strong, but Ella is dead. Boom! This is crushing, humiliating, and humbling. Ali has lost this bout. Alas, even the great warrior Ali, who has fought and won so many bouts, has to concede that Ella is dead. He had to accept it.

Les did not at first understand the dream, but he suspected that he was not going to like its message. Our interview proceeded as follows:

GAYLE: Who is Muhammad Ali? And what is he like?

LES: He is the greatest fighter who ever lived. He had the strength to say what he believed, and was a super boxer. Ali lost three championships, and I've had and lost three important relationships in my life. And I'm a fighter, and willing to say what I believe. And like Ali, I can't believe that Betty will not come back to me.

G: What is Ella like?

L: She's a woman I used to know in Oklahoma. Now she's a writer in her seventies in Arizona. She is a kind, thoughtful woman who likes me.

G: Does this kind, thoughtful woman who likes you remind you of anyone?

L: Sure, Betty was like that when we were going together. I guess I've got to accept it, don't I? The part of Betty that was good to me is dead. She's never coming back.

Les was sad after this dream interview, but he understood that the first thing he had to do was to accept that no matter how loving and strong he was, Betty would not return to him. A few weeks later, Les dreamt that he saw Betty again and discovered that she was only twenty-two years old instead of her actual age of thirty-eight. This dream helped Les see that Betty, whom he tended to idealize, was really quite immature for her age. Not only did these dreams help Les let go of his addiction to Betty, they helped free him to look for more satisfying romantic choices. Les was getting tired of his Muhammad Ali hero role, loving where there was no hope. Sometimes a sad dream can be remarkably liberating.[16]

Here is another incubated dream that caught the dreamer's attention. Lila was like a co-alcoholic (a codependent) in the ways she enabled and reinforced her boyfriend's temper tantrums. When he was angry, she would try everything to mollify him, even when that meant giving in and apologizing for a fight he had initiated. She had long ago lost interest in sex with her boyfriend, and had often thought of leaving him, but couldn't bring herself to because he was generally very kind and gentle and only rarely flared up. She had ignored many dreams of being threatened by unpredictable snakes, and by aggressive, vicious animals. But this dream was the one she could not ignore. It came the morning after she had incubated a dream by asking, "Why don't I have any sexual interest in my boyfriend?"

As if watching a nature-show documentary, I hear the deep voice of a narrator who says, "Some people try to save, to cure their rabid dogs. But this is an organic brain syndrome." Then I see illustrations of skulls of dead rabid dogs. The brains had been eaten away by the disease.

The narrator continued: "But, in fact, the only thing to be done is to hold their heads, comfort them, then put them out of their misery and remove the threat they pose to society."

Then I see body parts of humans who had been attacked by rabid dogs. Arms and legs bitten, shredded. Very horrible. I understand that "rabid" here refers to a temper disorder—anger and rage—NOT to a rabies poison that is transmitted by saliva. The lesson of the scene is that one mustn't take half measures. This disorder is too dangerous, and there is no cure.

Lila was crying when she awoke. As she worked with the dream she began to see that her boyfriend's difficulty in handling his anger, his "temper disorder," was indeed more severe and more threatening to her than she had previously admitted to herself. If things were really this bad, no wonder she didn't want to have sex with him. For years Lila had clung fast to the role of placater of the irritable beast, and she had taken some pride in her skill at improving his moods and averting explosions. To an unhealthy extent, her life had centered on the care and management of her boyfriend, and she had lost sight of her own needs. She took the first steps toward taking definitive action to protect herself by learning to communicate to her boyfriend that she would no longer tolerate his temper tantrums. This was not easy for her, because she was good at soothing bad tempers, not at asserting herself in the face of them.[17]

I am always happy to hear from readers who incubate their dreams. If you would like to share your experiences with me, write to me at the Delaney & Flowers Dream Center (the address is given in the appendix) or visit my Web site, *www.gdelaney.com*. You will find more on incubation in my book dedicated to the topic, *Living Your Dreams.*

Lucid Dreaming

When you realize that you are dreaming *while you are dreaming,* you are having a lucid dream. This can be a wonderful, colorful, liberating experience. Remembering a lucid dream may also make it easier for you to figure out what your dream is trying to tell you, and its intensity may have a significant impact on you. If you don't remember ever having had a lucid dream, you can probably teach yourself to have them. Achieving and maintaining lucidity is much more difficult than incubating a dream, but it is a learnable skill. Lucid dreaming occurs spontaneously in about 1 to 3 percent of university students,[18] and we don't know yet if it is more common among older people. However, if we were to study large numbers of people who record their dreams daily for years, we would probably find a much higher percentage.

Professors Sheila Purcell, Alan Moffitt, and Robert Hoffmann are among the most sensible and interesting researchers in the field of dreaming. In one of their experiments at the University of Ottawa Sleep Lab, they found that those of their subjects (let's call them the sleepers) who had the highest rates of recall during the experiment were the ones who achieved lucidity in their dreams.[19] They describe lucid dreaming as being part of a continuum of self-reflectiveness in the dream state. Instead of seeing lucid dreaming as something very different from normal dreaming, they consider it as a form of normal dreaming—one that is characterized by a greater ability on the part of the dreamer to reflect on the dream situation and to reflect on herself and her role in the dream while she dreams. If you look at the dreams and nightmares you remember, you will probably be able to identify dreams in which within the dream itself you recalled having had a similar dream before, noticed odd "only in your dreams" characters and events, managed to end or alter the dream, or simply asked yourself what you might do in such a dream situation.

In some dreams you probably have noticed that you can to some extent control your dream. You might decide to end an unpleasant dream and wake up. You might choose to turn an uncomfortable dream into another, more pleasant one by deciding to dream about your favorite vacation spot and movie star. Some people use their lucidity to explore how their consciousness works and even try to meditate while asleep. As you dream lucidly, you notice things almost as you would if you were conscious and awake. This lucidity is usually fleeting and may come and go over the course of a dream. When you move into dream control, you take a more active part and change the course of events to a greater or lesser degree. You may be able to change an entire ending, or just one image or action before the dream takes off on its own again.

Many writers suggest that anytime you have a bad dream, you should try to become lucid and then change the dream into a happy one. With very few exceptions (see below), I strongly disagree with this Pollyanna approach to lucid dream control. Usually when you have a bad dream, it is because there is something bad going on inside you and in your life. Most of the time, our bad dreams offer us the best, most direct, and most accurate information about feelings, attitudes, and situations that are getting us into trouble. While awake, we often close our eyes to these things, and our dreams are like a smoke alarm—one that we should not disable. Take as a simple example the nightmare of a smoker who dreams of being diagnosed with inoperable lung cancer. This kind of dream can and has scared people enough to give up smoking cold turkey. If this dreamer had changed the offending plot into a day at the beach, would he have awakened frightened enough to quit? I doubt it. The same holds true for more complex bad dreams that point out to you emotionally self-destructive behaviors, attitudes, and relationships. If you have these dreams, and if you are not clinically depressed or the victim of trauma suffering from posttraumatic stress, which can put you and your dream process into a rut, then for heaven's sake be thankful for these dreams. Taking the time to understand them could save your life, or greatly increase your happiness.

Having said that, I would encourage you to try to become conscious in your dreams. Paying attention to your dreams, recalling and recording them, suggesting to yourself that you will note unusual events and things in your dream and realize that you are dreaming, will help you have more lucid dreams or at least show you that you are already having them. One of the most creative researchers in lucid dreaming is Dr. Jayne Gackenbach, coauthor of *Control Your Dreams*.[20] Dr. Gackenbach describes several methods of inducing lucid dreams in chapter 2 of this book.

MILD

MILD, a mnemonic technique for the voluntary induction of lucid dreams, was developed by Stephen LaBerge. The basic steps are as follows:

1. Tell yourself to awaken early in the morning.

2. If and when you do, recall and run through in your mind any dream you remember.

3. Get out of bed and do something for fifteen minutes that demands your full waking attention, such as reading a book or making a "to do" list.

4. Return to bed and say to yourself as you fall asleep, "The next time I'm dreaming, I want to remember that I'm dreaming."

5. While doing this, visualize your body lying in bed asleep, and at the same time see yourself in the dream that you just rehearsed, recognizing that it is a dream.

Though some people report that this method has helped them recall more lucid dreams, especially at first, numerous students at the Dream Center and those in my private practice have been disappointed with their results. I wonder if the fifteen minutes of waking activity might distract the dreamer too much. Perhaps reading about lucid dreaming during that period would yield better results. Another method that may be more effective according to Dr. Gackenbach was developed by Paul Tholey, a German clinician who has used the same method for over thirty years. Whereas LaBerge, an extraordinarily inventive physiological researcher, has little to no training or experience with psychotherapy, Tholey has worked with patients in clinical settings in the context of psychotherapy. This usually gives one a much better feel for a subject's feelings, and for the meaning and interpretation of dream experiences in the context of the dreamer's life. Here is Tholey's method as summarized by Gackenbach:

THOLEY'S METHOD

1. Ask yourself, "Am I dreaming or not?" at least five to ten times a day.

2. At the same time, try to imagine intensely that you are in a dream, that everything you perceive, including your own body, is merely a dream.

3. While asking yourself, "Am I dreaming or not?" you should concentrate not only on contemporary occurrences, but also on events that have already taken place. Do you notice something unusual, or suffer from lapses of memory?

4. As a rule you should ask yourself the critical question in all situations characteristic for dreams—that is, whenever something surprising or improbable occurs, or whenever you experience powerful emotions.

5. If you have a reoccurring dream event or subject—frequent feelings of fear, for instance, or appearances of a dog—you should ask yourself the question whenever in your waking life you find yourself in a threatening situation or see a dog.

6. If you often have dream experiences that never or very rarely occur in a waking state, such as floating in air or flying, then you should, while awake, try to imagine that you are having such an experience, telling yourself all the while that you are dreaming.

7. If you have difficulty recalling your nonlucid dreams, you should employ methods to improve your memory of them. In most cases, though, practice in obtaining the critical-reflective frame of mind will improve your dream recall.

8. Before drifting off to sleep, don't try to will lucidity by force of thought; simply tell yourself you are going to be aware or conscious in your dream. This method is especially effective when you have just awakened in the early morning and feel as though you are falling back asleep.

9. Resolve to carry out a particular action while dreaming. Any simple action is sufficient.

To facilitate steps 8 and 9, Tholey suggests ways of retaining waking consciousness while falling off to sleep by focusing on the so-called hypnogogic imagery of early sleep. These include the following:

* The image technique. Concentrate only on visual images while falling asleep.

* The body technique. Concentrate entirely on your body while falling asleep. Notice your breathing, the way your leg muscles relax, the heaviness of your arms.

* The image-body technique. Concentrate on both imagery and your body.

* The ego-point technique. Imagine that you are only a "point" from which you perceive and think in the dream world.

* The image-ego-point technique. In addition to the ego point, also concentrate upon imagery.

Although Tholey's method is more comprehensive than LaBerge's MILD, it is also complicated and time-consuming. It may, however, be far more effective. Two French scientists who worked with Tholey's technique found that even those participants who dropped out of their study often obtained good results.[21]

HYPNOTIC INDUCTION

A third method employs a formal hypnotic induction. Actually, most forms of lucid-dream induction, of dream incubation, and dream control use forms of self-suggestion. If one thinks of hypnosis as a process of suggestion by oneself or another with or without accompanying rituals, then most of us make use of it all the time. A psychologist at the University of Virginia, Joseph Dane, was able to induce lucid dreams in each woman in his study on the night she spent in the sleep lab. After having hypnotized her, he told each woman, "Tonight, you're going to turn off the automatic pilot in your dreams and fly with awareness. Tonight as you dream, you will somehow manage to recognize that you are dreaming while you're dreaming. Something will happen in your dreams to trigger your awareness, and you will remember that you are dreaming."[22]

Some of my clients have had success with this method, which is very pleasant and brief. Some have recorded the induction with their own, their beloved's, a friend's, or my voice and played the recording beside the bed before sleep. Some use a formal hypnotic induction or a simple relaxation exercise in the first part of the recording.

In her wonderful book, Dr. Gackenbach recounts the dream of Fariba Bogzarin, a friend and artist who is very active in inspiring and organizing the Association for the Study of Dreams's theatrical and artistic shows.

> Artist Bogzarin suspects that at least in some of her lucid dreams it is the absence of strict boundaries that allows unexpected creativity to fill her works. "While awake," she explains, "I feel in some sense limited by my body's boundaries, but while lucid and creating, the separateness no longer exists."

> She illustrates her point in the following dream:

> "I am in a studio making a sculpture. There are about seven different life-size sculptures that are not yet finished. The sculpture that I am making is a life-size Greek-motif male sculpture. As I am working on his hand, I say to myself, "How did I get to make this sculpture? I am not a sculptor." As soon as I say that, I become lucid. A rush of excitement rises up my spine. While I am holding on to the sculpture, it starts to move in my hand. The upper part of the sculpture, which I had sculpted, starts a graceful move and I start moving with it, dancing a harmonious dance. Then I woke up. I wrote in my journal that I felt one with my creation. It was both an external and an internal oneness."[23]

Lucid dreaming has its magical, inspirational, and practical sides. Many of my clients learn to ask themselves while dreaming, "What does this dream mean?" Oprah Winfrey told me while we were doing one of her many shows on dreaming that ever since reading *Living Your Dreams* she can interpret her dreams while she's dreaming them. Others have told me that while dreaming they ask themselves dream-interview questions or hear my voice asking them the questions that unlock the metaphor of the dream. Here is an example from Gackenbach's book of a man who used his lucidity to solve a technical problem.

> Electronics maintenance technician and exhibit designer Bob Rosengren of Seattle, Washington, had the following lucid dream when he was having problems with the electronic design for a museum exhibit.

"I was working on a very tight timeline before the exhibit opened last December 26, and ran into a problem with a circuit design. I could not solve it, and time was running out. About a week before opening day, I had a lucid dream in which I was in my small town, in a waterfront restaurant with my dream associates. I told them my predicament, as they saw I was upset. They told me to just 'slow things down,' and made some references to certain things not being ready at the same time other things were. None of that made much sense to me, but the words kept popping up in my head that morning at work. On a hunch, I decided to search through the data books on a couple of the integrated circuits I was working on, and suddenly realized that in my design I had neglected to allow for a twenty-two-nanosecond 'setup time.' After including a small delay, my circuit design worked perfectly."[24]

Sheila Purcell, Alan Moffitt, and Robert Hoffmann have found that subjects who learned to have lucid dreams in one of their studies "experienced less confusion about a waking issue after waking from a dream about it."[25] These lucid dreamers also reported that after writing out their dreams, they had greater understanding about their waking issues. Their lucid dreams clearly had positive effects on their self-understanding and motivation.

Although you can live a fine life without ever having or recalling a lucid dream, such dreams are fun to experiment with, and can be very useful in learning more about your dreams and your life issues. Some of my students and clients have suffered from an exaggerated sense of the importance of lucid dreaming. Some have tried several methods and many gimmicks without success and have concluded that they were less spiritual or less skilled than other dreamers. I have probably worked with more dreamers than anyone on the planet, since I do only this, and I can say with no reservation that lucid dreaming does not equal spiritual or psychological superiority. I have worked with the dreams and the lives of gurus and others who have regular lucid dreams, and some of them have little psychological maturity, love, or generosity in their hearts. Others are indeed beautifully evolved people. Some people who focus great efforts on having as many lucid dreams as possible do so because they have an unhealthy need to control all their experiences and have little knowledge about who they really are. They avoid serious exploration of their inner feelings either through dream work or psychotherapy. I reassure my lucidity seekers that their spontaneous dreams are rich beyond imagination and that learning to understand their normal dreams will tell them what they need to know. If they then have lucid dreams in addition, great. But they shouldn't miss seeing Paris by deciding instead to take an arduous trip up Mount Everest.

Nightmare Control

Rosalind Cartwright, an ingenious and thorough dream researcher at the Rush-Presbyterian Hospital Sleep Laboratory in Chicago, has found a way to employ dream control to help people who have suffered traumas like rape, war, and divorce. Her research has important implications for depressed patients as well. In *Crisis Dreaming,* a book she cowrote, she describes her form of dream therapy, which she calls RISC. It has been especially helpful to people she studied who were suffering from a recent divorce.[26] Here is her description of the method.

> The premise of dream therapy is straightforward: If bad dream scripts make you awaken discouraged and downhearted, rewriting the scripts to improve the endings should lead to better moods.
>
> Dream therapy has just four steps that you can learn on your own:
>
> * Recognize when you are having a bad dream, the kind that leaves you feeling helpless, guilty or upset the next morning. You need to become aware while you are dreaming that the dream is not going well.
>
> * Identify what it is about the dream that makes you feel badly. Locate the dimensions within your dreams that portray you in a negative light, as, for example, weak rather than strong, inept rather than capable, or out-of-control rather than in control.
>
> * Stop any bad dream. You do not have to let it continue. You are in charge. Most people are surprised to find that telling themselves to recognize when a bad dream is in progress often is all it takes to empower them to stop such dreams when they occur.

* Change negative dream dimensions into their opposite, positive sides. At first, you may need to wake up and devise a new conclusion before returning to sleep. With practice, you will be able to instruct yourself to change the action while remaining asleep. . . .

The RISC treatment, like other techniques of psychotherapy, works both by what it does and how it does it. In most psychotherapy treatments, therapist and patient focus on changing waking attitudes and behavior. The therapist helps the patient generate the "right stuff" to talk about and work on. In the RISC program, we also seek to change waking attitudes and behavior, but we do it by spotlighting the negative aspects of the underlying identity displayed in each patient's dreams. I met with my patients for hour-long sessions at weekly intervals, usually for eight weeks or longer.[27]

Cartwright notes that it is important that the dreamer choose the better ending:

The way they define "better" sometimes proves surprising. One meek young man often had a nightmare in which a bus ran him down. When he changed this dream, he gave himself a machine gun so that he could attack the bus and shoot its driver. He felt much better afterward and never had the dream again. Why not? In his dream, he could retaliate aggressively against the bullies who had picked on him when he was a youngster and destroy them. His dream success rebuilt some pride he sorely needed. . . .

Altering the outcome of a dream is a tall order, but our studies show it's an achievable goal. There's an active give-and-take between the conscious and the sleeping mind. Even if you don't change a particular dream while asleep, your waking exploration of the depressive elements of your dreams, and your awareness of what you can and should change, may have a payoff. People who do their homework, who devise several possible solutions to familiar dream dilemmas, report that they often manage to incorporate some of these new waking attitudes into their dreams.

Such success reverberates with waking life. Becoming more active in dreams helps people to become more positive about the future. A successful night of dreaming produces immediate benefits for mood in the morning. Stopping a bad dream and changing it lifts the spirits. People gain a sense of empowerment from knowing they are not at the mercy of their bad dreams. Then, as they begin to change the image of a rejected, helpless self to one that is more in control, waking behavior begins to improve. They start to try out the new roles, the underdeveloped better aspects of themselves, that they first practice in dreams.[28]

THE RISC METHOD OF DREAM CONTROL

Here are the steps Cartwright has developed to teach dream control aimed at feeling a person whose dreaming process had got into a rut. One reason many people get into these ruts is that they don't have an effective method of interpreting their nightmares. Pay special attention to your nightmares, and interview yourself carefully about them. Get the help of a dream partner or good dream analyst if necessary. If, after you have tried to understand your dream and to take meaningful action on it with or without the assistance of a good dream analyst or therapist, you find that your nightmares are stuck, not progressing, repeating the same dreadful endings, try following these suggestions. They come from an experienced, very sensitive and effective research psychologist.

* With your dream diary and your day journal in hand, start by reviewing the dreams that trouble you the most and try to figure out why. As you learn to identify your negative self-talk, you will become more proficient at doing so.

* Look at the message each dream displays and focus on its dimensions. Each dimension will have numerous images that illustrate its opposite pole. Initially you may see more negative dimensions in your dreams, but as you explore in your waking life the positive side of the dimensions you habitually use, you will program yourself to incorporate more self-confident images into your dreams at night.

* When you locate a problem dream, imagine different endings. You're the scriptwriter. How else could the dream have turned out? Consider several endings. Which do you prefer?

* Think of times when you've been in a similar situation that turned out well. If you can't find many positive images in your memory bank to draw on, you will need to create new images for yourself. If you're stuck in the past, for example, mentally rewrite your dream scenarios so you are an adult, not a

helpless child. If you find yourself a victim in your dreams, practice standing up for yourself in fantasy, where you can do it safely. Ponder the new possibilities at bedtime.

* Tell yourself, "Next time I dream, I want to recognize that I'm dreaming." Even more importantly, tell yourself, "Next time I have a bad dream, I want to recognize it, stop it, and change it." You always can stop a dream just by opening your eyes.

Here is an example of the RISC method in action.

Judith was a single woman in her forties who had lost her job as a traveling sales representative when her company made sweeping recessionary cutbacks. After searching unsuccessfully for months for a new job, mainly by responding to newspaper ads and sending out dozens of resumes, she was feeling depressed about the lack of opportunities and was running out of money. The longer Judith was out of work, the more she began to feel that something must be terribly wrong with her, that she was unemployable. She felt disgraced, and she was embarrassed to see her former workplace friends; she stopped calling them, and they stopped calling her.

Judith frequently dreamed that her car had broken down and that she was in a remote spot, far from help. She would awaken feeling beaten down before her day even started. After learning the RISC method, she reported this dream:

"My car was stalled at a ferry debarkation point. It was rapidly getting dark. The car was completely dead and I was standing at a distance from it, full of despair, looking at the rough waves and menacing skies, desperately wanting to go home, needing my car to do so, feeling utterly powerless and deflated.

"I woke up feeling a sense of emptiness and failure, let down, very disappointed in myself," she said. "I was thinking, 'Here comes another bad day.' But then I thought about the dimensions I kept repeating in my broken-down car dreams: dead versus alive, helplessness versus taking charge, stuck versus moving forward. I kept thinking, 'What can I do to help myself?'

"The next thing I knew," she reported, "I was back in the same dream:

"It was the next morning. My car now was in a garage. A mechanic approached me and said, 'Take your car. It's fixed and we threw in a full tank of gas, free.' This meant to me that the garage service was apologetic about having taken a full overnight to fix my car. I needed my car badly; it was my vehicle to getting on with my life. I was surprised and grateful."

This dream is a good example of the benefits of dream therapy. It showed Judith's gratitude for the "overnight help" she received. In the dream she turned night into day and her broken-down car into a functional one. Her dream dimensions came up on their positive side. She also saw that she didn't need to struggle entirely on her own. She recognized it was no disgrace to ask others for help, especially when they, like the man in her dream, had knowledge she lacked.

After this dream, Judith realized it was necessary to swallow her pride. Although she cherished her independence and didn't want to be in anyone's debt, she took out her address book and contacted her former co-workers and clients. She returned to a businesswomen's lunch group she always had enjoyed and told everyone she could buttonhole that she was looking for work. Within two weeks a job offer came from what Judith thought was a surprising source: one of her former clients had long thought she was one of the better sales representatives calling on him and now wanted her to represent his company.

In one of Judith's most recent dreams, she was driving across a big bridge. In another, she was traveling down a busy highway, keeping up with traffic and enjoying the trip. She now has new images of strength to store in her memory bank. The more such images you can create for yourself, the more likely you will be to draw on them, and the more likely it is that the dream process will function well on its own when you next find yourself in a situation in which the same emotional buttons get pushed.[29]

THE KRAKOW AND NEIDHARDT METHOD OF NIGHTMARE CONTROL

Drs. Barry Krakow and Joseph Neidhardt have developed a method similar to Dr. Cartwright's RISC dream therapy, one that is also based on cognitive (thinking) and behavioral (specific actions or behaviors) principles. They developed this method to help relieve sufferers of frequent nightmares from the dread of unhappy nights. I first heard about their method a few years ago when a Los Angeles–based TV producer called asking me to use it with a dreamer on her show. I was asked to work with the dreamer on the air and about two months later to come back to the show and meet with her again to see if her nightmares had become less frequent. I called Barry Krakow, received the simple instructions in his method, and went down to L.A.

The dreamer who volunteered for the experiment had been the victim of a carjacking. The thug had held a gun to her head, terrifying her. Somehow she managed to run away and was not wounded physically, but she had recurring nightmares about the event that were making her miserable. Before we went on air the first time, she told me she had taken some self-defense classes in order to regain her courage to walk the streets. But to my shock, I learned that the fellow who was teaching the course had taught her to look defiantly into the eyes of the men she passed on the sidewalk! Since I had always understood that this behavior is often interpreted as a challenge on the streets, I asked her how things were going for her on the streets of L.A. She responded that she felt better, but that oddly enough she had men saying hostile or challenging things to her, which had never been the case before. I told her that I thought her self-defense trainer must have been trained on another planet and that assertive eye contact on the streets could get her into trouble. Then we went on the air, she told us her dream, and I suggested she try the following steps of this method of dream control.

Imagery of pleasant scenes.

This step teaches imagery rehearsal. You can practice imagery of pleasant scenes at any time regardless of what's happening with your nightmares. Some people find it relaxing, especially if you do it for ten or twenty minutes. Others describe imagery as useful in such activities as problem-solving, golf or treating insomnia. . . .

Recording.

Recording helps in two ways. For some, it eliminates bad dreams. For others, it provides a clear picture to use in step three when you create a new dream. You may record a nightmare at any time after you've had it. The sooner you record it, the more details you will remember.

Changing/Imaging the new dream.

Change the nightmare in any way you wish, then image only the new dream. You can do this at any time. If you are awakened in the night, you will already have a clear picture of the bad dream. You can immediately decide how to change it. Then write down your new dream and image it. This is an ideal time to practice for three reasons.

First, many people complain of insomnia following a bad dream. If so, use this time to your advantage by changing the nightmare, then imaging the new dream. This produces confidence because it provides an immediate plan of action for dealing with bad dreams that awaken you.

Second, some people discover that imaging the new dream promotes relaxation that will help you return to sleep.

Third, many nightmare sufferers report the upsetting experience of returning to sleep after a bad dream only to find themselves right back in the same nightmare. We know several individuals who have prevented this "instant nightmare replay" by using imagery of the new dream before returning to sleep.

If it proves more convenient, you can change and image the new dream the next morning. This is an ideal time, too. You can also practice later in the day. Remember, though, the longer you wait to work on the dream after you've experienced the nightmare, the more likely your busy daytime schedule will interfere with your sessions.[30]

At our next meeting a month or so later, on the same television show, we discovered that our dreamer's nightmares were significantly less frequent, and that she had been able to change the ending while dreaming one or two times. She was very happy and, I think, much better off putting her assertiveness into her dreams than on the streets. She told me that she had much more peaceful walks now that she was no longer giving strangers that "I'll fight you if I have to" look.

* * *

This brings us to an interesting question. In the two methods of dream control described above, what role does assertiveness training play? Could rehearsing the new ending in the waking state bring about a small change of attitude away from victimhood toward competence, effectiveness, and mastery? Would the dream then reflect that change, and act as a reinforcer of the assertiveness training? If so, these procedures would work best for people who need confidence building and a greater sense of power in their lives. They do not, on their own, help a dreamer understand the causes and dynamics of the problem the nightmare expresses. In these cases, as both researchers recognize, some form of therapy or dream interpretation is called for to help the dreamer work through the underlying causes and habits of mind that give rise to the nightmares. Dream control for nightmares makes the most sense when the dreaming process is caught in a rut, and I think it is best employed only after the dreamer has understood the nightmares. In those cases in which the nightmares just keep on coming in spite of effective interpretation, dream control can bring great relief. But if it is used instead before the dreamer has had a chance to gain an understanding of the issues explored in the dream, a precious opportunity for growth will be lost.

Eight

WHAT'S NEW IN DREAMS AND PROBLEM SOLVING?

ost people have no idea how influential dreams have been and continue to be in the development of culture. Religions have been born and molded via the dreams of prophets and writers. Muhammad said he received the first part of the Koran in a dream; Judaism and Christianity taught that God warns and informs man through dreams. The arts, the sciences, and technology have been hugely influenced by people who had the wit to record and make good use of their dreaming minds. Although many uninformed people are skeptical and unaware of the problem-solving functions of dreaming, the historical and modern evidence is impressive. It is usually sufficient to ask someone who sneers at the thought of employing dreams to solve the practical issues of life, "Have you never gone to sleep with a problem on your mind and awakened with the solution in mind?" It is a rare person over thirty who can answer no.

I would agree that the vast majority of our dreams are about our personal emotional lives and focus on our relationships at home and at work. As Freud said, it's all about love and work. Within these all-important arenas, our dreams regularly help us to assess problems, understand their causes and development, point out their possible consequences, and sometimes offer solutions. I think the frequency of the problem-solving function of dreaming is most evident to clinicians and dream analysts like myself who actually do interpretive work with dreamers and can observe the progress of their lives as they make use of the natural problem-solving function of dreaming.

Since most of us never learn to understand and use our dreams as children, we grow up with the idea that dreams are nonsense. Their images seem bizarre and disconnected. Many of us feel uncomfortable even considering the possibility that those dreams that are so confusing, and often frightening or embarrassing, have anything at all to do with *our* minds. We usually fail to see the rich metaphoric links between our dreams and our current life challenges, and let our dreams fade into the thin morning air. We have seen in our work at the Delaney & Flowers Dream Center, as have almost all the clinicians I know, that most dreams don't make sense, and that rarely do they reveal specific solutions until their metaphors have been fleshed out through associations and descriptions.

When we can look at the dreamer's metaphorical descriptions and bridges, the problem-solving nature of most dreams becomes clear. Usually people dream about their feelings about themselves, their work, and their relationships. Apparently more rare are the dreams that help us solve concrete problems. Yet I wonder whether, if more people were taught to incubate and remember their dreams, and if they were encouraged to use their dreams for concrete problem solving, this would still be the case.

Almost every one of the thousands of clients I have seen in my office for over twenty-five years has had at least one story to tell about having solved a work-related problem. I lecture on dreaming all over the United States and Europe, participate on television and radio shows all over the world, and everywhere I go, people tell me stories of how they have used or learned to use their dreams to solve practical, concrete problems. These problems include ones in math, physics, engineering, creative writing, speech giving, architectural design, construction, software design, computer troubleshooting, contract writing, organizational design, business management, sports, child management, and so on and so on. My books on dream incubation and interpretation are used in business schools and management-training programs around the world because learning to solve problems with the use of dreams is easy and very practical.

It is not necessary to incubate dreams in order to benefit from their natural tendency to help you solve problems. Many spontaneous dreams have presented their dreamers with prize-winning results in many fields.

Dr. V. S. Rotenberg, at the Abarbanel Mental Health Center in Bat Yami, Israel, has conducted fascinating research into the problem-solving functions of REM sleep. REM sleep, or rapid eye movement sleep, consists of the major dreaming periods of our nightly sleep. They usually occur every ninety minutes and last from five to thirty to forty minutes, each episode becoming longer over the course of the night. Rotenberg notes research that has shown that REM sleep increases in people who are doing well in a course of intensive language learning, and that people who are prevented from getting their full REM sleep are less able to solve creative problems.[1] Rotenberg's research shows that dreaming functions at least in part to help us search for solutions to problems and to facilitate learning and consolidation of that learning. It also has positive effects on our physical and emotional health by jump-starting our active search for solutions when we fall into a state of renunciation of our search. The physiological effects of the state of renunciation include a marked reduction in our resistance to disease and stress. The practical ramifications of such a state are, of course, a diminished capacity to solve all manner of problems.[2]

Dream Problem Solving and Creativity in the Business World

Since the 1979 publication of my first book, *Living Your Dreams,* I have received fascinating letters and telephone calls from people in business who have used the Dream Interview Method and my method of dream incubation to resolve problems and generate new ideas at work. A few management-training programs and business schools around the world have begun to explore the potential of enhancing creative problem solving through dream work. They have also used dream workshops to facilitate trust and communication among various work and management groups.

At Stanford University's Graduate School of Business, Professor Michael Ray and Michelle Myers, authors of *Creativity in Business,* introduce students to the use of incubation by distributing a one-page instruction sheet I created for their class. Once, after the students had been instructed to try to incubate a dream on a business-related topic, I came to the class to lead the discussion. About 80 percent of the class members who had tried to have a dream on their chosen topic felt they had been successful.

I asked for a volunteer to tell his dream without disclosing to any of us his incubation question. Little did I know that the volunteer was not really a student but James Schrager, a professor and the chief financial officer of a trading firm in San Francisco, who was there to show how silly it was to use dreams in business. His dream was of a visit to a beloved uncle who, it seemed in the dream, had sold out to the desire for financial success and had given up his creative work. As the dreamer responded to my interview questions he described his sadness at the fact that such a creative man had given up so much for money and worldly success. In a flash the dreamer said that the dream was a shockingly meaningful response to his request, although it came from an unexpected angle.

James's incubation question asked for a new idea to further an invention he had worked on for some time, but had abandoned several years earlier. He excitedly understood his dream to be a metaphor or parable about his own life, about how he himself (like the uncle in the dream) had abandoned his inventive pursuits to become famous and successful in corporate America. "He was my favorite uncle," James said. "But he sold out. It showed what's keeping me from getting into the state of mind to create." He announced with conviction that his dream was not completing his invention, but that it was, more importantly, making him see why he was no longer inventive in a way that had so thrilled him. After confessing his original purpose, the professor became a client and learned to use his dreams to his great benefit. He credits his dreams with, among other things, the creation of a method for taking companies public in Japan, and a corresponding new business. His invention, covered in a story he wrote for the *Wall Street Journal*, gave its creator a new sense of inventive potency.[3]

In 1985, at the second meeting of the Association for the Study of Dreams, I met Dr. Francis Menezes, director of the Tata Management Centre in Pune, India. In the years following, he has used dream work as one of his favorite training tools. At a large Indian chemical corporation he used dream-interview and dream-incubation techniques as well as experiential dream-group practices to identify major problems facing fifty-two scientists at its research-and-development center. Dreams were used as a diagnostic tool to discover why these highly trained professionals were not contributing much to their fields. Their dreams quickly revealed feelings of powerlessness, frustration, anger, and anxiety. These feelings related to a lack of trust within the scientific community itself, a lack of motivators for creative work, and a lack of freedom to make decisions. The data collected from these groups were used to restructure the organization. The center went on to target a dozen mission-oriented projects to which the scientists could direct their energies, adding dream work to their discovery tools.

In her new book, *Daring to Dream*,[4] Anjali Hazarika, a colleague of Frances Menezes in India, has described her pioneering work with the National Petroleum Management Programme. This government-owned oil-industry organization consists of thirteen state oil companies engaged in the exploration, production, refining, and marketing of oil and natural gas. In an effort to help these companies, which constitute a major segment of India's economy, to become globally competitive in a new era of deregulation and reform, a variety of new strategies are being explored. Dr. Hazarika includes dream study in her work with executives, management, and engineers.

In 1995–1996, Dr. Hazarika conducted management and dream workshops with thirty-five senior managers of cross-functional departments in Engineers India, Ltd., southern Asia's leading design-engineering and consultancy company. These managers, who learned to recall, discuss, interview, and incubate dreams, worked on creative problem solving in their company and industry. At the end of the workshop, 84 percent said that they would continue working with dreams. Fifty-five percent felt that it is possible to enhance creativity through dream work, and 72 percent stated that the workshop has definite application as a new method for management development.[5]

Using my phrase-focusing method of incubation, Dr. Hazarika has helped managers and scientists target and understand unproductive management styles and generate new ideas for management and market positioning. She uses a combination of group dream discussion to increase openness, and incubation and dream-interview methods to empower the participants to tap their own wells of dream ideas and insights. It is interesting that she is able to demonstrate the practical side of dreaming quickly enough to intrigue her clients in a few days' time.

Though it might be argued that India's philosophical and religious traditions would lead Indian businesspeople to be more reflective and less prejudiced against exploring their dreams, we are making inroads into the American business psyche. It is surprising to many that business schools call on me to give workshops in problem solving in dreams.

My colleagues Kent Smith and Ilona Marshal and I once conducted a three-week course in dream work for a graduate business school with eight campuses. At the home campus we worked for about four hours once a week with the president and six managers. Before our first session, the members of the group were instructed to read my book on dream incubation, *Living Your Dreams,* and to incubate a dream about a work issue. Each person had a private dream session followed by a group meeting. To the surprise of some of the members, each person was successful at incubating a dream.

One of the managers with whom I met confused me. After I had interviewed him about two dreams, it seemed that the dreams dealt with two distinct issues. One had to do with problems in his management group and was very helpful, and the other brought him to a decision to leave his present job! Since I generally ask dreamers not to tell me what question they incubated before sleep until we interpret the dream, I remarked that his dreams responded to two incubation questions, not one. The manager laughed and said, "I cheated. I asked two questions on the same night. I really wanted feedback on the possibility of quitting this job!"

In my work with the president, I was struck by his openness in a field that was so new to him. In response to an incubation asking about the problems in his management group, he dreamt that he was being forced over to the right on the freeway. As he exited, he saw a number of pedestrians crossing at the light on the off-ramp. He knew he couldn't stop the car and awoke with a start, thinking that he would surely kill them.

With the help of a series of interview questions the president interpreted his dream this way:

I am being forced to be more conservative in the way I run this graduate school by various economic and political forces. I really am afraid that some of the pedestrians, the people who work under me and who are used to a more liberal environment, will be hit—fired, or made very unhappy. What the dream shows me is that I am out of control and need to put on the brakes to protect them.

When I asked our dreamer to describe his recent management style, he used two words: "blunt ax." When we all met in a group, the president was surprised to see that his managers immediately recognized the meaning of his dream and identified with the victim-pedestrians. Before the president had shared his dream, everyone else in the group had been very guarded in their discussion. After his frank discussion of his concerns, and his admission of having been out of control, everyone else relaxed and told their dreams. Everyone, that is, but the man who was planning to leave the school.

Besides management problems, mechanical problems can threaten a business's viability. One of my clients owns a company that troubleshoots for big computer installations. This client had known how to use his dreams to review his unsolved problems for years when we met. But he had no idea that dream incubation was easily taught to others. He sent me a few of his key employees, who then taught everyone else in the company how to put their dreams to work at work.

A couple of years ago I was taping a television show about dream solutions in Los Angeles. One of the guests, Floyd Ragsdale, was an employee of Dupont in Virginia. He had been in charge of work related to a huge machine that broke down and was costing the company hundreds of thousands of dollars a day. No one could locate the problem. Then one night Mr. Ragsdale went to sleep asking himself, "What is the problem?" He awoke thinking of springs and coils. He thought that his incubation effort had failed, but he drew out his dream images anyway. He took the simple drawings to work. Then it came to him: one of the tubes in the machinery must have collapsed, and could be repaired by lining the tube with a Slinky-like coil! His solution worked, and his coworkers took a little more interest in their dreams. Mr. Ragsdale, the "dreamer," was given a handsome reward for his practical assistance.

And who says that engineers aren't creative? I know of many engineers whose nighttime creativity has solved many different types of problems. Norman Laurie, senior vice president of engineering at EMC Corporation, knows firsthand how dreams can boost creativity at work. He and the staff at EMC (a Massachusetts firm that designs and manufactures computer-enhancement devices) had been working on ways to remedy the fact that 50 percent of the company's projects were running behind schedule. This is a particularly troublesome problem in an industry where the rate of change is so fast that delayed projects can quickly become obsolete and unmarketable. One night Laurie dreamt up the following solution: an incentive plan that, at the beginning of each project, set the royalty figure, the date the project should be ready to market, and another date six to twelve months later on which the scientist-researchers would stop receiving their royalties. Furthermore, these royalty payments would be raised (or lowered) by 5 to 8 percent for each week the project was early (or late). The sooner the project was finished, the longer the workers would collect royalties and the higher these royalties would be.

Inc. Magazine reported that the results of this plan are such that now only 10 percent of EMC's projects are late, and 20 percent are completed ahead of schedule. Bonus payments to employees have been as high as fifteen thousand dollars.[6]

Even though deep down everyone is curious about the meaning of at least some dreams, many people are highly skeptical that dreams mean anything at all, much less that they are often pictures of our sleeping minds at work solving problems. One of my life goals is to introduce as broad a spectrum of people as possible to the riches of our dreaming mind. So sometimes I have to overcome a daunting disrespect for dreaming and a prejudicial ignorance regarding its applications. For example, the vice president of an advertising firm that had considered inviting me to give a lecture on the business applications of dreams was highly skeptical about paying anyone for such a lecture. But out of respect for those of his colleagues who wanted to invite me, he agreed to test the possibility of incubation for himself. He incubated a dream on how he might speed up the billing and collection process for the company's accounts. Upon awakening the next morning he forgot his dream. But he had the idea he wanted clearly in mind. He directed the branch offices to send out the invoices the same day the orders were placed, thus shortening by eight to ten days the procedure that had always been handled by the central office. He also called me to say I was hired.

Actually, my life has been touched in many ways by the dreams I have incubated, starting in 1970. In fact, my first book was sold to an editor at Harper & Row in 1978 thanks to an editor willing to experiment, Bill Anderson. His son had been undecided as to which high school to attend. Father preferred school A, and son was undecided between schools A and B. One evening Bill told his son he was reading a manuscript on dream incubation and that maybe he would like to try it. The son not only was open to such a suggestion, but recalled a dream the next morning that made it clear to him that he would be happier at school A. Bill was delighted and convinced. He bought and published *Living Your Dreams*.

Many of my client's business-related dreams deal with fleeting but important issues—issues such as reorganizing office procedures and programs, rewriting difficult contracts, preparing for and surviving ambushes at important meetings, and taking a clearer, more accurate look at associates' strengths and weaknesses. Then there are the dreams that help people see others more clearly in order to make better hiring and firing decisions and better assignments. Dreams also offer to help all of us to recognize and assess the impact that our work life has on our personal life and vice versa. The workaholic who dreams of being in bed with his boss is likely not having a great romantic life at home. Dreams can open our eyes before it is too late—if we give them half a chance, that is.

Dream-Generated Inventions and Designs

I have had a number of clients who as architects have used their dreams to design and redesign projects when changes needed to be made. Probably the first account of a building being designed in a dream dates back to 2100 B.C.E. The Sumerian governor of Lagash in Mesopotamia left us clay cylinders describing in cuneiform (one of the world's earliest writing systems) a dream in which he was instructed to build a temple to the goddess of one of his cities. Governor Gudea tells us that his dream also contained instructions on the special materials to be used for the temple. My clients don't report dreams of instruction; rather, they see good designs and come up with ideas to solve impasses. Sometimes, amateurs dream of their dream houses and give their vision to an architect to work out in wood and stone and glass. If you have ever seen photographs of the baron and baroness of Portanova's home, Arabesque, in Acapulco, you will surely agree that such collaboration can lead to fantastically beautiful results.

The now-famous examples of Elias Howe's sewing machine, Otto Loewi's Nobel Prize–winning design for the experiment that proved the chemical basis for the transmission of nervous impulses, Mendeleyev's dream of the periodic table, and D. B. Parkinson's dream of what became the M–9 gun director in World War II have been well documented.[7]

In the sciences, sleep and dreams were credited with contributing to the work of men who were often reticent to reveal their dream sources until later in life. The most famous example is that of August Kekulé, who discovered in "half-sleeps" both the process of the formation of carbon chains and the cyclic structure of the benzene ring, thus launching the science of organic chemistry. In 1890, Kekulé addressed his fellow chemists, who had gathered to honor him at a "Benzolfest," with these words: "Perhaps it will interest you if I let you know, through highly indiscreet disclosures from my inner life, how I arrived at some of my ideas." After describing how his ideas came to him while in half-sleeps on a bus once, and before his fireplace a second time, Kekulé closed by saying, "Let us learn to dream, gentlemen, and perhaps we will then find the truth . . . but let us also beware of publishing our dreams before they have been examined by the waking mind."[8]

Apparently the amazing case of the Hindu mathematician Srinivasa Ramanujan, who died in 1920, is well documented. In an article in *Scientific American,* James Newman describes the story of the poor uncouth Indian boy who became "quite the most extraordinary mathematician of our time." A mathematician's mathematician, though his name is not familiar outside the field, he left a memorable mark on mathematical thought. His greatest contributions were in the number system, "one of the richest, most elusive, and most difficult branches" of mathematics. Newman writes:

> Numbers, as it will appear, were his friends; in the simplest array of digits he detected wonderful properties and relationships which escaped the notice of even the most gifted mathematicians. . . .

> Ramanujan used to say that the goddess of Namakkal inspired him with the formulae in dreams. It is a remarkable fact that, on rising from bed, he would frequently note down results and verify them, though he was not always able to supply rigorous proof. This pattern repeated itself throughout his lifetime.[9]

Although I have found no reliable evidence whatsoever that Einstein really used his dreams in his work as is sometimes claimed, I know a number of mathematicians and physicists in the United States, Italy, and France who have worked out a variety of complex problems in their sleep.

For example, Elmer M. Tory, a professor of mathematics and computer science at Mount Allison University in New Brunswick, Canada, wrote me of a breakthrough he had while on sabbatical at Harvard in 1978–1979. At the end of the year, Tory turned his attention to a problem in Gaussian fields for a project his colleague D. K. Pickard had been working on.

> This was a problem with which I had no previous experience. I played with the problem for about two weeks and gained a little insight. Then I awoke one morning at

2:00 A.M. with the solution clearly in mind. I arose, wrote furiously for two hours and returned to bed. I then spent about a week filling in the gaps. Even then, I realized that there remained leaps of intuition, which needed to be filled in. . . .

As the author of almost fifty papers, I have to say that this was not my most important result. However, in none of my other work did the entire solution emerge completely, but rather in successive revelations, each getting closer to final understanding. This case was unusual because the final result was a quantum leap from my previous understanding. All the elements of the complete solution were revealed and my mind leapt intuitively from one result to another. (Formal justification was supplied later.) . . . I am amazed at the extent to which the solution went beyond my previous knowledge. Perhaps because it was so sudden and complete, it was my most exhilarating discovery.[10]

To give me a flavor of his exhilaration, Tory enclosed a letter to his colleague announcing his discovery that began with these words:

Cease your whoring after false gods! I enclose the definitive solution of the problem. It is not yet the definitive version of the definitive solution, but the definitive solution nonetheless. . . . In any case, I will send this now, so you can savour its beauty. In all modesty, I have to admit that it is brilliant, absolutely brilliant! FAAANNtastic!

Dr. Tory had placed a warning on the letter: "Don dark glasses before opening. Extreme brilliance may be harmful to your sight!"

Who says math isn't fun? I just wish we could convince our schools to teach children how to make use of their dreams so they too could feel some of the excitement and assistance of dream discoveries.

Unfortunately, I am not able to understand either the problems or the solutions sent to me by these happy mathematicians and physicists, and could never hope to tell you about them in an interesting way. Engineers, too, often regale me with stories of how they have gone to bed puzzled by a problem and awakened in the morning with a solution. Having written the first modern book on the subject of dream incubation, I have received letters from many in the sciences telling me of their experiences. For this I am very glad, but I wish their explanations could be simpler!

Philosophers, who like the rest of us spend their days trying to figure out what life means, continue their mental labors into the night. The father of our modern theory of knowledge, philosopher René Descartes, had three dreams in 1619 upon which he based his work in methodology, algebra, physics, and metaphysics.[11] In his *Meditations on the First Philosophy*, Descartes wrote: "I am now awake, and perceive something real; but because my perception is not sufficiently clear, I will of express purpose go to sleep that my dreams may represent to me the object of my perception with more truth and clearness."

Gottfried Wilhelm Leibniz (1646–1716) was an influential philosopher and writer on logic, mathematics, science, history, law, linguistics, and theology. In discussing the nature of the spirit he wrote: "For not to mention the wonders of dreams in which we invent, without effort but also without will, things which we should have to think a long time to discover when awake, our soul is architectonic also in its voluntary actions and in discovering the sciences according to which God has regulated things (by weight, measure, number, etc.)."[12]

Immanuel Kant (1724–1804) wrote, in *Dreams of a Spirit Seer,* that "ideas in sleep may be clearer and broader than even the clearest in the waking state." And Schopenhauer wrote, in his *Cogiata,* of a dream he had in 1830 that he interpreted as telling him he would die within the year. This dream motivated him to leave Berlin at the outbreak of cholera in 1831. Upon arriving in Frankfurt am Main he saw an apparition of his deceased father telling him that he would outlive his mother.[13]

Voltaire reports that he once dreamed a superior revision of an entire canto of his *Henriade* and commented: "I said while dreaming things I might well have said while awake. Therefore I had reflective thoughts in spite of my not having had the slightest conscious part in it. I had neither will nor freedom, and yet I combined ideas with wisdom and even with some genius."[14]

Nietzsche, too, appreciated the creative, problem-solving, and self-revelatory nature of dreaming. He delighted in and felt changed by his dreams of flying, and wrote: "How could a human being who had had such dream experiences and dream habits fail to find that the word 'happiness' had a different color and definition in his waking life, too? How could he fail to desire happiness differently? 'Rising' as described by poets must seem to him, compared with this 'flying,' too earthbound, muscle-bound, forced, too 'grave.'"[15]

Bertrand Russell, the philosopher, Nobel Prize winner, writer, mathematician, and historian, had a dream at the age of sixteen that dissuaded him from committing suicide. He described how he learned that when he was struggling with a difficult problem or concept in math or politics or philosophy, he would devour as much information on the matter as possible during the day. He would then go to sleep in the expectation that in the morning he would awake with a workable solution. He found that solution not every time, but often enough to practice his form of incubation regularly. Although he was skeptical of psychoanalytical interpretations, Russell appreciated dreams for their beauty and emotional impact.[16] In a letter dictated in 1929 he told of a dream that had filled him with more beauty than he had ever known before or after. It made a deep impression on him.

I dreamt that my bedroom was transformed into a vast cavern on a vast precipitous hillside. In the middle of the cavern I lay sleeping on my bed, while all round, tier above tier, innumerable hermits likewise slept. The next room was transformed into a similar cavern on the same hillside, connecting with mine, filled also with hermits but not asleep. They were hostile to us & might come to destroy us in our sleep. But I in my sleep spoke to my hermits in their sleep, & said: "Brother hermits, I speak to you in the language of slumber, & the language which only sleepers can utter & only sleepers can hear or understand. In the land of sleep there are rich visions, gorgeous music, beauties for sense & thought such as dare not exist under the harsh light of the cruel sun. Do not awaken from your sleep, do not resist the other hermits by their own means, for though you win you will become as they, lost to beauty, lost to the delicate vision, lost to all that ruthless fact destroys in the waking world. Sleep therefore; by my slumber language I can instill into you what is better than success & war & harsh struggle, & the worthless grating goods which wakers value. And by our magic, as one by one the other hermits fall asleep, we shall instill into them the bright vision, we shall teach them to love this world of gentle loveliness more than the world of death & rivalry & effort. And gradually from us will radiate to all the world a new beauty, a new fulfillment. Men's dreams will lead them through the livelong day along grassy lawns by sparkling brooks & through the dream night to the majesty of the stars, made gentle & warm & lovely by the rustling twigs through which they shine; to edifices of emblazoned glory, inaccessible mountain tops whose whiteness makes the blue of the sky more visible; & the mysterious sea, majestic in storm & gentle as a playful child in the sparkling calm.

In these visions mankind shall forget their strife, happiness shall come to all, pain shall fade out of the cruel world, & mankind shall come to know the beauty which it is their mission to behold.[17]

Dream Creations of Writers

From the early 1800s on, we find a growing number of artists who record dreams that have inspired their work and solved pivotal problems. We may have the greatest number of recorded examples of problem solving in dreams from our writers, since, after all, they as a group are sensitive to and like to write of their internal experience. Samuel Taylor Coleridge, in 1800, may have been the first to write of the unconscious, which he described as "something not known as existing in oneself,"[18] and he coined the words *psychosomatic* and *psychoanalytical*.[19] Coleridge also wrote an account of how a dream influenced the writing of his poem *Kubla Khan*.[20] Charles Dickens, who experimented with healing a friend through hypnotism, was interested in altered states of awareness and wrote *A Christmas Carol* as a revealing, stylized dream that transformed the personality of its dreamer.[21] Nineteenth-century Russian poets and novelists such as Pushkin, Gogol, Dostoyevsky, and Tolstoy used dreams in their writing with psychological insight of unusual sophistication.[22] The English artist and poet William Blake credited the discovery of his method of illuminated engraving to a dream. Blake also claimed to receive instruction in painting in his dreams and drew a portrait of his dream instructor.[23]

In my book *Living Your Dreams*, I have described how playwrights such as August Strindberg, Ingmar Bergman, Claude Lelouche, and Robert Altman, and writers such as Robert Louis Stevenson, William Styron, and D. H. Lawrence, used their dreams in their work.

Naomi Epel has recently written a wonderful book, *Writers Dreaming*, which describes the way in which many contemporary writers have been influenced by their dreams.[24] Isabelle Allende told Epel that she had been unable to find the right tone for the ending of her book *House of the Spirits*. She had written the last fifteen pages more than ten times when one night she awoke with a dream. In it, she was telling the story of her book to her grandfather, who was lying on his bed. When she awakened, she realized that the tone of the whole book was that of a conversation between herself and her grandfather. This gave Allende the exact tone she wanted. "So," she told Epel, "the epilogue has the tone of a person sitting beside her grandfather, who is dead, sitting by his bed, telling the story very simply. The dream gave me that."[25]

Horror writer Clive Barker recounts how he often uses dreams as the starting place for a story and that his story "The Age of Desire" and his book *Weaveworld* are examples of that process. Barker adds, "You don't even have to turn dreams into art. . . . Bringing it [a dream] kicking and squealing into the light and seeing the value of metaphor in your life, talking about the value of metaphor, that's what's important."[26]

Stephen King, the best-selling novelist, also uses his dreams and nightmares as seed ideas for settings and stories. King used a spooky house from a childhood nightmare in his novel *Salem's Lot*. He even tells of a nightmare in which a hideous mad woman jumps out of a door wielding a scalpel to get him if he doesn't finish the work he is doing![27] When King came to a lecture I gave in Maine, he enthusiastically told of his delight in flying dreams. He wanted us to know that not all his dreams are unpleasant, and that his flying dreams exhilarate him.

Bharati Mukerjee, winner of the 1988 National Book Critics Circle Award for *The Middleman and Other Stories,* says that endings for her stories and for her novel *Jasmine* have come to her in her dreams. She wrote in Epel's book that she had "come to trust very much the unconscious within the creative process and the efficacy, the value of dreams. Art really is quite often anticipated by or resolved by dreams. My husband, Clark Blaise [a writer at the University of Iowa], is a wonderful writer and trusts them even more than [I]. He actually sees the characters in very thick and solid ways."[28]

The children's poet Jack Prelutsky has received poems and frequent inspiration in dreams. Of the period in which he wrote *The Headless Horseman Rides Tonight* and *Nightmares: Poems to Trouble Your Sleep,* he said, "I wrote all the poems in [these two books] between about midnight and six in the morning. I would wake up in a cold sweat and I'd be dreaming about a witch or a werewolf, or a goblin or something like that. It was a particularly unpleasant time."[29] Prelutsky has dreamt whole poems, and fun ones as well. He says, "My biggest suggestion to writers is: keep a notebook . . . and a pencil by the bed. I mean I wake up almost every night and write something down. Sometimes you dream that you've found a cure for cancer or something and you think it's brilliant and, of course, . . . it's . . . garbage. . . . But about a third of the time there's a very good idea there."[30]

The prolific North Carolina novelist Reynolds Price, author of *A Long and Happy Life*, *The Use of Fire*, and *Blue Calhoun*, made these fascinating remarks:

> Sometimes, when I'm working intensely on a book, especially if I'm working on a particular character that I'm fascinated by, I'll find myself dreaming dreams which seem to me to be very appropriate to that kind of person. These dreams seem to be more appropriate to the character I'm writing about than to me. I really feel as though, not only am I creating that person's life in the daytime while I'm writing the book but I almost seem to be dreaming that character's dreams. I have literally transcribed some of those dreams and attributed them to the character.[31]

Price used such dreams in his novels *Love and Work* and *The Surface of the Earth*. He added, "I felt these dreams were some kind of deep unconscious response to my work on the book itself and therefore were appropriate to the characters."[32]

Price has also written directly from dreams, and has frequently gone to sleep not knowing where to go next with a piece of writing, only to find the answer right in his mind upon awakening the next morning.

There are many more examples of writers whose dreams have influenced all of us through their dreams, from Milton to Blake to Richard Bach, who wrote the second half of *Jonathan Livingston Seagull* in a dream eight years after having put the first part away on a shelf! The Swedish playwright August Strindberg said, "I believe in dreams, for my brain works sharpest when I am asleep."

Painters, Sculptors, and Moviemakers

The Swiss artist Paul Klee underlined that it was "the right of the painter to excite the imagination and to consider dreams, as well as still life, as material for their art."[33] Painters such as Jasper Johns and Salvador Dali, and many of my artist-clients including Tana Sommer, not to mention entirely untutored amateurs like myself, have seen paintings in our dreams that we then took great pleasure in making. Jasper Johns's dream-generated series on the American flag won him both acclaim and huge sums of money, while struggling artists' paintings have yet to become famous. Nevertheless, all of us, from recognized artists to rising ones to those of us who will forever remain painting primitives, are delighted by our dream inspirations.

My friend Rick Moss sent me notice of an art show in Santa Fe, New Mexico, that was to be held in April 1997. Called "Ladies of the Night: Dreamworks of Contemporary Women Artists," the exhibition included the paintings, sculpture, and mixed-media works of thirty-five artists at the Guadalupe Fine Art Gallery. Every year at the annual meeting of the Association for the Study of Dreams, we hold a showing of dream-related art from contemporary artists around the world. My guess is that most artists at one time or another have used their dreams but that in most cases we never hear their stories.

The flamboyant late-Renaissance writer, jeweler, and sculptor Benvenuto Cellini was dissuaded from killing himself by a dream. He had been in a wretched, filthy, dark prison cell in Rome, starving, losing his teeth and his health. The night after a failed suicide attempt, he dreamt of an angelic youth who rebuked him, saying, "Knowest thou who lent thee that body, which thou wouldst have spoiled before its time? . . . Commit thyself unto His guidance, and lose not hope in His great goodness!"[34] For the rest of his stay in prison, Cellini's attitude changed from that of tortured victim to that of accepting disciple. He wrote of being visited "with the gladdest and most pleasant dreams that could possibly be imagined." After his release, he went on to sculpt some of Italy's most beautiful works.

A good number of the movies we see, movies that reflect and shape our popular culture, are also dream inspired. Movies have been made from dream-inspired books such as *Dr. Jekyll and Mr. Hyde*, *Frankenstein*, and *Sophie's Choice,* and a few film directors have told us how their dreams have inspired or influenced their movies. Federico Fellini, Luis Buñuel, Claude Lelouche, Robert Altman, and Ingmar Bergman are but a few examples. In fact, Claude Lelouche is quoted as saying, "People don't realize that dreams are the most determinant elements in our lives. I dream a film before I make it." Bergman, when asked if he records his dreams, said, "Yes, now and again, when they may come in handy. Sometimes while I'm dreaming I think: 'I'll remember this, I'll make a film of it'—it's a sort of occupational disease."[35]

Good morning my dearest! Imagine what I dreamt during the night: I had used my abortive symphony in a piano concerto and was playing it. From the first movement and Scherzo, plus a Finale, frightfully difficult and grand. I was completely enraptured. I have also dreamt much about you and beautiful things.[36]

So wrote the twenty-one-year-old Johannes Brahms in 1885 to Clara Schumann about the inspiration that eventually developed into his spectacular First Piano Concerto.

Many of our classical composers have used musical scores and conceptions heard and experienced first in their dreams. Beethoven, Rossini, Robert Schumann, Mozart, Camille Saint-Saëns, Stravinsky, and Richard Wagner are just seven from our Western tradition. In fact, of *Tristan and Isolde* Wagner wrote to a friend, "I dreamed all this. Never could my poor head have invented such a thing purposely." And it was in a dream that Wagner solved the awful problem he was having with the opening of his Ring Cycle:

Trying to sleep on a hard bed, I sank into rushing water the sound of which formed itself into musical sound—the chord of E Flat major whence developed melodic passages of increasing motion. I awoke in terror recognizing that the orchestral prelude to *Das Rheingold,* which must have been long latent within me had at last been revealed to me.[37]

Mel Graves, the former director of the Redwood Empire Jazz Festival and a composer for avant-garde ensembles such as the Kronos Quartet, said of his piece *Soundtotem II,* "Much of the melodic material was directed by meditations and dreams on the subject."[38] *Soundtotem II* is part of a series on the totem art and legends of the Northwest Coast American Indians.

The classical contemporary composer Ellen Zwilich, who won the Pulitzer Prize in 1983, says the music runs through her unconscious all night. Once Zwilich was asked if she would compose a piece for someone's first concert. She said she was too busy. "But we kept talking for a while, and during the conversation I started to hear music. The trio was already beginning to take shape in my head. So I said I'd think it over, and I did, throughout the rest of the day and, I guess, through the

night as well. In any event, I woke up the next morning, and the whole opening section was waiting to be written down."[39] I once heard Peter Nero, conductor, composer, and pianist, say that his passion for writing computer programs is greatly aided by his dreams. Whenever he comes upon a problem he can't solve, he puts himself to sleep and almost always awakes with the solution to his problem.

Much of our popular music also flourished first in dreams. Steve Allen uses his dreams regularly in his multifaceted and abundant work in comedy, writing, performing, and composing. His most successful song, "This Could Be the Start of Something Big," was only the first song he remembers having heard first in a dream. Paul Frances Webster, who wrote unforgettable love songs for the movies, never went to sleep without a pen and paper by his bed. He would go to bed expecting solutions to problems in rhyming and metric schemes for his songs and regularly awoke with solutions. His credits include "Love Is a Many Splendored Thing," "The Shadow of Your Smile," "Secret Love," the love theme from *Dr. Zhivago*, "The Twelfth of Never," "April Love," and "Black Coffee." I learned all this from his son, Guy Webster, a photographer. Guy and I spent a day together around San Francisco and on Allan Watts's houseboat in Sausalito as he took my picture for a magazine. Guy also told me that he uses dreams for ideas for album covers for artists such as the Rolling Stones and Peter, Paul, and Mary.

Health: The Dreaming Body

The use of dreams in the diagnosis and treatment of physical illness has a long and checkered history. Many aboriginal peoples—the ancient Babylonians, Hebrews, Greeks, and Romans—believed that in dreams we could diagnose and sometimes be cured of illnesses. In his book *On Dreams,* Hippocrates (460–377 B.C.E.), the father of Western medicine, wrote, "The mind and body are interdependent parts of the human totality and . . . a physician gains a much improved chance of healing the mind/body organism if the aid of both parts is enlisted."[40] Apparently, Hippocrates was interested only in the medical value of dreams as a potent diagnostic tool in ascertaining the state of his patients' health. Hippocrates, along with Aristotle and the second-century Greek physician Galen, felt that dreams could give early warnings of illness and thus make diagnosis and treatment easier.

ALL ABOUT *Dreams*

Recently medical schools have been teaching the "Bio-Psycho-Social Model," which holds that all illness should be considered as a function of biological, psychological, and social influences. Perhaps we can learn how to discard the superstitions of the past and those of present-day, medically uninformed believers, and still remember that our emotions and our bodies are connected. Medical journals are beginning to publish articles with titles like "The Use of Dreams in the Initial Interview—A Guide for the Primary Physician," and more and more serious journals dealing with the psychosomatic side of medicine are being published. So we may soon be learning more about how dreams sometimes reflect a person's state of health.

Already there are fascinating reports from a few pioneers. At our open annual meetings of the Association for the Study of Dreams, creative, serious, well-qualified researchers have presented fascinating findings. For example, cardiologist Robert Smith, of the Department of Medicine at Michigan State University, has done research showing that the pumping efficiency (ejection fraction) of the heart has a direct correlation to certain dream images. And he suggests that some dreams may have specific biological meaning and can give warning of impending illness.[41]

Cancer surgeon Bernard Siegel, who is on the clinical faculty at the Yale School of Medicine and is the author of *Man, Medicine, and Miracles?* has also addressed the Association for the Study of Dreams with his experiences of his patients' dreams. Here are three dreams that made Dr. Siegel take notice.

Dream # 1:

Patient with breast cancer reported dream in which her head was shaved and the word *cancer* written on it. She awakened with the knowledge that she had brain metastases. No physical signs or symptoms were evident until three weeks had passed and diagnosis was confirmed.

Dream # 2:

Patient had dream in which a shellfish opens and a worm presents itself. An old woman points and says, "That's what's wrong with you." The patient, a nurse, sick with an undiagnosed illness, wakened with the knowledge that hepatitis was her diagnosis—confirmed by physician later.

Dream # 3 [Dr. Siegel's personal dream]:

> "At the time, I had symptoms possibly due to cancer. A group was present in the dream. Others had cancer but I was pointed out as not having it. I awoke with the knowledge that I did not have cancer. This was verified by later tests."[42]

Dr. Robert Royston, a psychoanalyst at Ticehurst House Hospital in East Sussex, England, has decided to investigate how widespread the experience is of people dreaming of an illness before its obvious appearance. He has asked readers of the *Sunday Telegraph* newspaper to send in their dreams, which, at least in hindsight, seemed to have predicted an illness.[43] But let me add that if you are currently concerned about a possible illness, you should consult a qualified physician near you. I think it is important to keep in mind that many of our dreams that carry plots of our having a particular illness such as cancer or AIDS are not literal. My clients sometimes use such illnesses metaphorically to represent a destructive relationship or self-destructive attitudes and behaviors. Nevertheless, cases such as those reported by credible people should inspire us to do further research, don't you think?

Dreams and Addictions

Loma K. Flowers, M.D., associate clinical professor of psychiatry, and Joan E. Zweben, Ph.D., clinical professor of psychiatry, both at the University of California at San Francisco, have conducted fascinating research on the use of dream therapy in assisting people in recovering from addiction.[44] They describe how they used the dream-interview method with people in psychotherapy, and in dream workshops and in addiction-recovery groups. Flowers and Zweben found that dreams in which the dreamer uses his addictive substance at first "seem to provide an indication of the psychological work necessary for recovery, then a warning sign of the intent or the urge to use again."[45] In later stages of recovery, they note, using the substance in a dream is often a metaphor for other, current issues such as repressed feelings or overspending. I have also observed this, and would add that in later recovery, "using" dreams can symbolize destructive behaviors and attitudes of all sorts as well as destructive relationships.

Flowers and Zweben state that "using" dreams, which are often very frightful, can be transformed through the dream interview from nightmares to be suffered into useful resources in the recovery process. They suggest that dream interviews of "using" dreams can be used in various treatment settings as a useful contribution in both relapse prevention and clinical management (therapeutic work). "In addition, with the increased potential for discontinuity in care within the managed care health systems, an ability to pick up the thread of treatment quickly and accurately midstream becomes more and more imperative for therapists and primary physicians alike. Moreover, the fact that pairs of clients can become proficient in dream interviewing without a therapist allows them to monitor their needs in recovery, and so correctly inform a new therapist or seek appropriate support in a timely fashion."[46]

Wouldn't it be wonderful if we could dream our way to losing weight and eating healthfully? Many people have asked me if this is possible. I can only say that I've never seen any obvious successes. Some habits seem more intractable than others. Although many of my clients have dreamt dreams of chastisement or encouragement to lose weight or to eat more wisely, dreams seem to leave the really hard work up to the dreamer. It may be easier to stick to a diet program once your dreams or your therapist helps you understand some of the emotional motives for your overeating, but the actual behavior changes remain huge mountains to scale.

The prognosis is less discouraging, however, when it comes to quitting smoking. Several of my clients over the years have incubated dreams or a series of dreams that have helped them quit smoking tobacco and marijuana. Some quit the very next day, some took a couple of weeks. Others never even got ready to ask their dreams for help and never quit. Bill Dement, one of the world's pioneers in sleep and dream research at Stanford University, tells how one of his dreams ended his enslavement to cigarettes. He dreamt:

I had inoperable cancer of the lung. . . . [I saw the] ominous shadow in my chest x-ray. . . . The entire lung was infiltrated. . . . [In a] subsequent physical examination . . . a colleague detected widespread metastases . . . [in the lymph nodes]. Finally, I experienced the incredible anguish of knowing my life would soon end, and that I would never see my children grow up, and that none of this would have happened if I had quit cigarettes when I first learned of their carcinogenic potential. I will never forget the surprise, joy, and exquisite relief of waking up.[47]

He gave up his habit after the dream in 1970, and is a smoke-free, vibrant, extremely productive man today whose work has improved many people's sleep and saved the lives of many who learned that inadequate sleep is the cause of countless accidents.

The novelist Robert Stone, acclaimed as the heir to Herman Melville and Joseph Conrad, tells of a recurring "using" dream that seems to have helped him stay smoke free for a decade. "I think everybody who's quit smoking dreams about it. The one I used to get all the time was: I find myself smoking which horrifies me because I've wasted all that time and suffering quitting and I'm smoking again. Then I get some screwy explanation like, It's the second Thursday of the month. You always get to smoke on the second Thursday of the month! I wake up with great relief to find out that I'm not really smoking again."[48]

I have also had a number of students who gave up dependence on coffee and too much sugar by using their dreams. Personally, when I dream of not having or of not being offered enough chocolate, it's a nightmare. Which just goes to show that in dreams, as in life, one woman's medicine is another's poison (cruel deprivation)!

Nine

Solo Dream Study

Most of the time, we all do solo work on our own dreams even if we also have a dream partner or are in a dream group. Since we dream every night, it would be a shame not to be able to figure out our dreams on our own, and it's not always possible to connect with other dreamers. If you plan to work privately on your dreams, I would suggest the following program of study:

1. Contract with yourself that you will study your dreams for at least six months, preferably one year.

   The first six months are the most difficult. A contract should help you to stick with it long enough to notice that you have learned quite a bit about interviewing and about yourself. Promise yourself that you will keep a dream journal and interview yourself on one dream a week, and that you will read at least one book on dreams each month. Attend lectures, and take as many classes in dream work as you can. If there are no dream classes available near you, see if your local community college or a local psychotherapist offers one. Even if the lectures or classes are of low quality or about theories and methods you do not agree with, they can help you to clarify your thinking about why you prefer other methods. And you may be pleasantly surprised to find that you can learn important things in surprising places. The better acquainted you are with a variety of theories and approaches, the better able you will be to take advantage of good ideas that you can incorporate into your own dream-work style.

2. Write out an entire self-interview at least once every month.

This takes time and discipline, but the rewards are great. When you write out an interview, you will be less likely to take shortcuts, which usually lead to confusion and frustration rather than to learning. A written interview should include a diagram as well as an outline, so that you will be less likely to miss important aspects of your dream. If you have my *Dream Kit* book, spread out in front of you the cue cards describing the interview steps and the dream-element question cards. Carefully follow each step of the interview, and remember to try to create for yourself an atmosphere of nonjudgmental curiosity, humility, courage, and humor.

3. Conduct careful dream reviews on a regular schedule of once every two to four months.

Every one of my clients and students has thoroughly enjoyed the review process. Once you begin rereading your dream journal, which includes day notes, interviews, and commentary, you will find it a fascinating and rewarding activity. When you complete a review, write at least a one- or two-page summary of the issues your dreams have been dealing with in this period and of the progress you have made in better understanding and resolving the problems related to those issues. Then note which areas of dream interviewing have become easier for you and which remain the most difficult. If you have my *Dream Kit* book, fill out the weekly, monthly, and quarterly review sheets as often as you can. Before you close your journal, ask yourself if you would like to work on your dreams with a dream specialist or a dream partner, or in a dream study group.

How to Choose a Good Dream Analyst

Working individually with a skillful dream analyst can be one of the fastest and most rewarding ways to learn to use the dream-interview method. You can arrange to work on an individual, hourly basis, or you can study with a dream specialist in pair, group, and class settings. Some dream study groups hire an analyst to get them started and to return every month or twice a year to speed their learning and enliven the group. I have often returned to coach ongoing groups around the country via speaker telephone! A word of warning: there are a number of dream teachers who have little experience or skill. There are also those who would be so authoritarian that you might feel worked over after a session. Here are some suggestions for finding a dream analyst who would work well with you.

1. Read two or three books on dreaming, and choose an approach that makes sense to you. Contact the authors you like, and ask for referrals to people in your area who teach dream skills.

2. Ask what education and training in dream work the analyst has had.

3. Ask her to describe her approach to dream interpretation.

4. Ask for three of her favorite books on dreaming, and take a look at them.

5. Ask how long she has been working with dreamers and in which contexts. Some analysts have had little or no experience working with actual, real-life dreamers, and their approach may have more to do with theory and less to do with the issues of real life.

6. Ask over what length of time she usually works with a client. It's helpful to have an analyst who sees the fruits of her work over time. This increases your chances of finding someone who gets results. Some analysts work only during weekend workshops, and they can never really know if they are doing a good job.

7. Ask if you can tape-record your sessions. I have found that my clients, professional and amateur alike, who do so learn much more quickly. While you are being interviewed by an analyst or dream partner, you are absorbed in searching out your feelings and making connections. When you then listen to the tape, you can focus on the process and note what your analyst said, when and how she said it, what she might have said, and how you responded. This will also reinforce insight you gained during the interview. It is very easy to forget new insights and slip back into our old ruts.

Remember that you are the client who hires a specialist to teach you how to do this for yourself. Don't get mesmerized and stuck with someone who plays the holier-than-thou guru or the wiser-than-thou therapist. Dreams offer you direct access to your own powers of insight. Don't hand them over to anyone.

Finding a Dream Partner

Whether you work with a dream analyst or not, finding a dream partner will be one of the most effective actions you can take to gain expertise in dream work. By playing the role of the interviewer for another person, you will learn how to ask the right questions at the right time much more quickly than you can by working alone. It's a riveting experience to work with someone's dreams, and it teaches you skills you will use on yourself, your toughest client! When you've found a partner, consider planning to work for at least one hour a week together. You can meet in person or over the telephone. Really, the phone is a great medium for dream work. I have clients who live all over the country and the world with whom I have regular phone sessions. It works very well. Even nearby clients, if their schedule is tight, sometimes meet with me by phone and avoid the commute. When you work with a dream partner, the phone may be more convenient, even if you are neighbors; you can have your sessions while you are tucked in bed!

Remember that working with dreams will bring out very personal material, so be sure you choose a partner you trust and respect. Keep strict confidentiality, and try to be reliable in keeping your appointments with each other. This will keep you both motivated. The most precious benefit you will gain from working with a partner is a kind of friendship that will knock your socks off. Your relationship will become more open, courageous, supportive, instructive, challenging, and, in time, incredibly sweet and strong.

If you don't have a potential dream partner among your friends, meet other dreamers at dream lectures, courses, workshops, and dream study groups. Check out the dream-related Web sites, and join the Association for the Study of Dreams. (See the "Resources" section.) Come to the association's conferences and meet hundreds of dreamers from all over the United States and the world. Presentations range from experiential workshops to lectures by therapists, researchers, authors, artists, and others from the most diverse of fields who have a keen interest in dreaming.

POINTERS FOR FORMING DREAM PARTNERSHIPS

1. Choose a compatible dream partner.

Obviously, a partner should be someone you can trust to keep all your work confidential and who will not be judgmental, but accepting and supportive. Ideally, your partner should be courageous when it comes to self-exploration, not too defensive, and patient. A dash of good humor would also be beneficial. Choosing a member of your family as a regular partner is problematic. Parents and children make better occasional dream partners, because weekly sessions would impinge on each partner's privacy, and the intimate nature of dream work is not usually appropriate for a parent to share with a child.

Working with a spouse can be wonderful—or it can be awful. The issues covered in some dreams may be too hot for a couple to work on together, in which case a less-involved friend would make a more impartial interviewer. For couples dream work to succeed, the pair must have an extraordinary degree of trust, acceptance, and confidence in themselves and each other, as well as patience. If either one makes the mistake of using material discussed during an interview as a weapon in a fight, their ability to work together will be greatly diminished because the dreamer's confidentiality and trust will have been violated.

Dream partners who are siblings sometimes do well together, if they are not too competitive with each other. Adults can sometimes work with their parents, but get into difficulty if the younger partner is dreaming about difficult parental relationships. As you can see, dream work with family members can be tricky. If, however, you manage to avoid the many pitfalls, you will find that you and your partner will establish a wonderful, trusting intimacy with each other. Remember that whenever you work with a family member you must be extra careful not to try to interpret his or her dream. Keep in mind that the temptation may be overwhelming to guide your partner to see the truth that you think you already know about him or her. Try to phrase your questions with special care in order not to "lead the witness" and cause your dreamer to feel pushed in a particular direction.

You may think that you don't have any friends who are interested in their dreams. If you simply let your friends know that you are reading a book on the subject, you may find that many are eager to talk with you about their dreams. Just under the surface, most people are very curious about dreaming. As you discuss the topic with friends, you will probably find one or two with whom you would like to form a partnership. If not, go to lectures and classes on dreams, and strike up conversations with as many people as you can. You may find a sympathetic soul among the attendees. Perseverance usually will help you to find a partner within a few months.

In the meantime, practice with anyone who seems amenable, even if it is only for one time. Be careful, however, to be sure you are in a private environment. Since people's dreams often expose more than the novice dream teller would ever expect, your dreamer may suddenly feel embarrassed and even tricked. Learn how to retreat before the dreamer reveals more than he or she might really want to reveal. In order to do this, you might have to say something like "The next question I would ask at this point may lead us into very personal material. Perhaps I could tell you my question, and you could ask it of yourself, then continue the interview on your own." In this way you will forewarn the dreamer, who can then decide whether or not to continue the interview.

I dare not leave this section without reminding you one more time that as a dream interviewer, you must not tell your partner what his or her dream means. Your job is to ask questions and help the *dreamer* discover the meaning. Only as a last resort, after you have completed all the steps of the interview, might you sometimes ask the dreamer if he or she would be interested in hearing your hypotheses about what the dream might mean. Your hypotheses are then to be based on all the information from the interview, and are to be offered as an aid in the dreamer's own exploration, which is momentarily blocked. Do not push your ideas if the dreamer rejects them. As Montague Ullman says, the dreamer always has final authority over his or her own dream, and an interviewer must always respect that authority.[1]

2. Contract with your partner that you will practice weekly for at least one month, and after that, six months or a year, if you both agree.

If you can schedule your practice sessions for the same time every week, you will find that you are most likely to remain faithful to your contract. Together you may want to schedule monthly sessions with a dream specialist, who can observe your interview techniques and coach you. Or you could each go to a specialist on your own, and compare tape recordings of your sessions for new ideas. Seeing a specialist is not necessary but will help you to improve your skills and keep your enthusiasm up, especially in the sometimes awkward early phases of your study.

3. Tape-record and periodically transcribe your interviews, then listen to them for a review of the dream and for a critique of the interviewer's technique.

In your first sessions, you and your partner may want to use cue cards (described in chapter 5 and in the *Dream Kit* book), which list the basic interview questions. This will help you get started with a manageable number of questions. If you transcribe the recorded session, you will get even more out of it, both in the understanding of the dream and in the development of your interview technique. I personally learn most about a dream of one of my dreamers and about my technique if I review a transcript of the interview. It is fascinating to go over every word we both said. Sometimes I find important points I overlooked in the session, such as statements from the dreamer that I should have followed up on, or times when my questions were much more leading than I had realized. Or I notice times when I came up with fabulous questions, and times when I was barking up the wrong tree and did not pick up on the dreamer's signals that could have let me know it sooner. Reviewing and critiquing transcripts of our work as dreamer or as interviewer is an important part of our training program for advanced and diploma students at our Dream Center. It is a powerful and extremely satisfying method of improving your dream skills.

4. Schedule monthly and biannual reviews of your dream journals, and compare notes.

Conducting your reviews at the same time will give you motivation and encouragement. It will also inform both the dreamer and the interviewer about important patterns in the dreams, and about images and issues that are consistently difficult to understand. If you have *The Dream Kit,* use the periodic review question sheets in the workbook.

5. Ask your partner if there is anything she would like you to change about the way you work with her dreams.

You could do this at each of your first sessions, and then, once you know each other and the method better, you could do this at each review.

6. Consider having more than one dream partner.

Since different dreamers have different strengths and weaknesses in technique as well as various defensive maneuvers that you will probably use yourself at various times, the more dreamers you work with, the more likely you are to become aware of a broad spectrum of dreamer and interviewer styles. We encourage all the advanced students at our Dream Center to practice with as great a variety of dreamers as possible. The students immediately appreciate how this sharpens their skills, as well as their awareness of their own behaviors as dreamers when they are interviewed.

How to Join or Organize a Dream Group

If you are fortunate enough to work in a good dream group for six months to a few years, you will learn much about dreams, about how to listen and how to relate without intrusion and control, and about human nature. Hearing people's dreams over time shows you their real insides. By watching other people interview dreamers, you will quickly learn what tone of voice, which questions, and which strategies work best in different situations. If your group is led by an experienced professional who acts as a coach, you will benefit not only from your own interviews, but also from observing how the coach corrects and encourages other interviewers. You will see how various dreamers deny and evade certain issues and how they struggle to get beyond their impasses, and you will be heartened to see how various members of the group make important strides in their lives as they review and practice the insights gained from their dreams. By working in a group, you will come to know your fellow dreamers in a rather intimate, quite trusting way that is very special and highly valued by group members I have known. Although joining a group led by a professional dream interviewer is the most efficient way to get started, it is not necessary to employ the services of a professional, and you may prefer to start your own group.

Recruiting motivated dreamers who can all meet at the same time once a week is not easy. But if you spread the word among your friends and among classmates at lectures and in classes on dreaming, you may be able to find four to seven people who would make up a good group. In choosing group members, consider the same things you would in choosing a dream partner, and make explicit the vital need for complete confidentiality within the group. I would discourage you from including members who are depressed or for some other reason need psychotherapy. These groups are instructional, not therapeutic, and unless you are a therapist, you will do much better working with people who do not suffer from psychological disorders.

Check with your favorite authors to see if they offer groups or know of some near you. Through the Delaney & Flowers Dream Center, Loma Flowers and I lead weekly and monthly groups in and around San Francisco. We also offer brief intensive study programs for groups of dreamers who come to work with us for a few days to several months at a time. My esteemed and beloved colleague Erik Craig leads groups in Santa Fe, Detroit, and Boston through the Santa Fe Center for the Study of Dreams; phone numbers and addresses are listed in the "Resources" section.

If you can't find a group near you, why not start one yourself? You do not need to be an expert. As a rank beginner you can render a great service to others looking for a group by providing a forum for all of you to learn together. The leader needs only organize the four to seven people, provide a meeting spot, and suggest good reading. I wrote my book *Breakthrough Dreaming* as a manual for people who want to learn well how to use the Dream Interview Method. Groups read one chapter every week and discuss the material at each meeting. The book includes a chapter on conducting group sessions.[2]

HOW TO ORGANIZE YOUR OWN GROUP

Having led dream study groups for twenty-four years, I have developed a format that seems to work well and that may give you a model to use and modify to meet your needs. Here are the main steps we follow:

1. Make a verbal contract with four to seven people regarding the nature and the minimum duration of the group.

I have found that a group will not survive if the dreamers do not commit at the time of joining the group to attend regularly for at least eight weeks. Most members stay in our groups for one or two years, and new members are admitted when a place becomes vacant. Each group should decide in advance if it wants to make any rules regarding attendance. The trick is to leave members free enough to miss group when they have a good reason, and to have an attendance that is regular enough to maintain the continuity and cohesiveness of the group. Our groups allow unlimited absences for vacations and for work-related functions and travel. We also accept two "frivolous" or emergency absences a year. You may be comfortable with a different arrangement, and experimentation will guide you in determining your group's structure.

If you are not a professional, you may not want to charge a fee for your services, since you may be acting more as a host than as a teacher. However, I have received letters from people all around the country who have said that charging a nominal fee of five dollars a session has worked wonders in providing structure and motivation for members to attend regularly. This money can be used for refreshments, to buy books, or to hire a lecturer or coach for one or more sessions. Some groups have used the money to join the Association for the Study of Dreams, which publishes a newsletter and journal and has wonderful annual conferences for amateurs and professionals.

2. Outline the group procedures at the first session.

Our groups usually meet weekly for one and a half to two hours. At the beginning of each session, we designate the person who will present a dream, as well as a backup dreamer, who will be prepared if the scheduled dreamer is unable to attend. These two dreamers bring photocopies of one or two dreams for each member. The dreams can be copied right from a scribbled journal, or they can be typed. If the dreamer can do so, she leaves huge margins on all sides of the typed or written page so the interviewers can jot down her descriptions and bridges during the interview. This allows the interviewers to be more careful and accurate in their recapitulations and summaries.

Dreamers are invited to record the sessions in which they work on their dreams. In some cases the group also invites the other members to tape the sessions so they can review their interview technique. We encourage group members to practice with each other or with another dream partner during the week over the telephone.

Beginning and ending the sessions on time is usually appreciated by the majority of the group. Members who are habitually late are usually encouraged to plan to arrive fifteen minutes early. One late dreamer can hold up the whole group even if it starts without her. The late member inevitably has difficulty following the proceedings and must ask to be caught up on the interview before she can become an active interviewer herself.

It is helpful for dreamers to have read *Living Your Dreams* and *Breakthrough Dreaming* by the time they enter the group. This provides each member with a basic introduction to our approach and avoids the need to give introductory lectures to new members who enter an ongoing group. The group may then decide to reread certain chapters from either book each week and to spend five or ten minutes in the group discussing the material. In our monthly workshops, which last two and a half hours, we focus on a particular element (settings, people, objects, etc.) or a particular strategy (corralling, schmoozing, etc.) in our discussions and interviews. If you prefer to have longer meetings like this on a monthly basis, you might want to decide on relevant reading in advance.

3. Decide on your group's format.

    Here is the format I use in my practice.

A. We open the session with a brief summary from the previous week's dreamer of her reflections on her dream. She tells us not only what she did with the dream, but what she avoided doing and how she felt about it. She also tells us whether she has any pointers for us regarding questions we did or did not ask, or regarding styles she especially liked or with which she felt uncomfortable while she was in the group or listening to a recording of the session.

B. We then ask if anyone else has a comment on the previous week's session or on a dream he has worked on with the group in the past.

C. Next, the dreamer passes out copies of her dream and is invited by one of the members to tell the dream with feeling. The group may or may not diagram and outline the dream.

D. Each member takes a turn at interviewing the dreamer for a section of the dream, while I coach the interviewer, suggesting strategies and questions when needed. (We shall discuss the role of the group leader below.) As the members of the group gain experience and become accustomed to each other's styles, one interviewer may share a turn with another, and two or more interviewers may work in tandem with the dreamer. This dual interviewing can confuse both the dreamer and the original interviewer, and should be practiced with care.

E.   In the last five or ten minutes of the session, the dreamer or an interviewer summarizes the interview and the group elicits the dreamer's reaction to the summary. When working with novice dreamers and/or novice interviewers and/or long dreams, we may not get to the end of the dream. The dreamer and the group then need to decide whether to omit the summary. Is the dreamer understanding the dream as she proceeds through the interview, and will she be able to conduct her own summary, or will she leave the session frustrated and confused if she does not summarize the work she has done so far? This can be a difficult thing to determine, and the only comfort I can offer you is that in time you will all be able to work through dreams more quickly as you refine your skills.

F.   At the end of the meeting, the interviewers offer their notes to the dreamer, who can use them in her review. Jane Cunningham, a therapist and a member of one of our groups, suggested this idea, and it has been a big hit. While dreamers are working on their own dreams, they are too concrete in their thinking and too busy to take notes. In fact, note taking can be very disruptive to the interview process for the dreamer, who must be free to follow new thoughts and feelings as they pop up. Reviewing other members' notes is especially helpful if the dreamer has not tape-recorded the interview.

THE ROLE OF A GROUP LEADER OR COACH

For dreamers who have attained advanced skills in interviewing, the role of group leader rather than host may offer the other members of the group the most assistance. We train leaders to act as coaches, people who know the rules of the game and have enough experience to be able to make helpful suggestions. Coaches (as well as intermediate interviewers) can reassure novices that we all flounder and flail about when we first start interviewing, but that in time good questions come to mind without much effort. If a new interviewer suffers from performance anxiety, the leader might ask, "Is there anything I can do to help you feel more comfortable? Would you like me to suggest the first two questions?" The coach can model different aspects of interviewing, including patience, humility, and the readiness to admit errors and confusion.

The leader helps the group to follow the dream step-by-step and scene-by-scene while commenting, when necessary, on the dramatic structure of the plot. By reminding the group not to lose touch with the basic thrust of the dream story, the leader helps the group not to get lost in the details and to keep in mind the dramatic context of each image. The leader is also in a better position than are the active interviewers to comment on the timing of the invitations to bridge and on the quality of the bridges made by the dreamer. The leader may be able to suggest that a given bridge may be worth exploring for a more general or a more specific significance to the dreamer. The role of the leader is to comment on and demonstrate the interview process, not to give pronouncements on the meaning of a dream.

GROUP STRATEGIES

Below are a few strategies we have used in groups. They can be initiated by a leader or by any of the members.

1. Signing

In order to avoid unnecessary distraction, the leader or an observing interviewer can use a simple sign language to coach the active interviewer. To suggest that the interviewer follow up on a description by asking for a fuller one, use your hand as you do to motion someone or a pet to "come here." To suggest a bridge, make an arch with your forefinger. To suggest corralling the dreamer, point to the text of the dream or to your palm. To suggest that the interviewer encourage more unpacking of a bridge, pretend you are opening a rotary combination lock with one hand. To suggest ending the interview, make a circular "wind it up" motion with your forefinger.

2. Humming

At various points in an interview, group members may want to put their heads together and discuss their ideas and difficulties, and devise strategies. There may also be times when the coach would like to suggest specific questions and strategies, or to help an interviewer formulate less intrusive questions that aim at proving or disproving her hypothesis. What the group needs at times like these is a time-out. Asking the dreamer to leave the room would be inconvenient and disruptive, so we ask the dreamer if she would be willing to close her eyes, hold her ears, and hum a tune while we discuss how the interview is going. By having the dreamer hum during this period, our conceptual discussions do not distract the dreamer from her more concrete focus on the dream experience. The dreamer is not burdened by hearing the hypotheses of the interviewers, and the dreamer has a moment to rest and reflect. In fact, when we tap the dreamer to bring her back into the group, we make it a practice to ask the dreamer if she has had any ideas or associations while humming. Not infrequently, the dreamer has benefited by the repose and come up with helpful connections. Now and then, the tune the dreamer hummed has a title or lyrics that make trenchant comment on the dream.

Obviously, the dreamer should hum only if she is comfortable doing so. We tell her that we need this time-out only to discuss strategy without distracting her, not to keep secrets from her. We will tell her everything we have said if she finds she is uncomfortable—as soon as she decides to stop humming, or at the end of the interview. If the dreamer is taping the session, we point out that she will hear it all on the tape. Because new dreamers take their turn sharing their dreams only after having heard the dream of each member of the group, by the time a new dreamer is asked to hum she usually agrees. This is because she has seen how well the process works and has sufficient confidence that we will not be talking behind her back.

3. Discussion Observed by the Dreamer

When all of the group members are new and might hesitate to hum, or when the material to be discussed would not be too distracting, strategy discussions among the interviewers while the dreamer listens in can be surprisingly fruitful. For example, as the dreamer listens to his interviewers ask each other how to help the dreamer give more specific or more feeling responses, the dreamer, who is now off the hot seat, may relax and be able and willing to help his interviewers by being more forthcoming. If the interviewers summarize their work so far and discuss possible directions for the next part of the interview, the dreamer may be able to recognize a direction that he feels would be most promising. You will probably find many uses for this strategy, which, without making direct demands upon the dreamer, often encourages and inspires him to help his interviewers.

WHEN TO END AN INTERVIEW IN PARTNER AND GROUP SETTINGS

A common problem for new dream workers is knowing when to stop. Overworking a dream kills its life and sometimes confuses, threatens, or alienates the dreamer. If your dreamer seems bored with the interview, she may be resisting exploration, and her feelings may have gone underground. Or your style may be too ponderous. Are you bored? If your efforts to liven up the interview by injecting humor or challenge yield no greater interest, you could ask the dreamer if she feels bored and if she would like to continue or end the interview for now.

The dreamer may be satisfied with the progress she has made with the dream before you finish the interview. She may say this in so many words, but more likely she will communicate it by showing greater and greater resistance in the form of distracting and tangential comments. Ask your dreamer if she is satisfied and would like to stop there.

Sometimes dreamers can suffer from feeling or insight overload before you finish the dream. Check with a dreamer who seems to be dealing with material that is painful or difficult as you go along, and let her know that you can stop whenever she feels she has done enough work.

Groups can be unwittingly cruel when, at the end of an interview, each member wants to get her two cents in either by suggesting new areas of exploration or by hinting at alternative interpretations. This thinly veiled interpretive bombardment of the dreamer is often overwhelming as well as disorienting. After a good interview, a dreamer is often pleased with her work, but also fatigued by it. There comes a point when the dreamer simply cannot respond to new input. If an interviewer has ideas about the dream that she has not been able to explore via the interview, it is often best to save them for the next meeting, after the dreamer has had a chance to consider the work she has already completed.

GROUP DREAM REVIEWS

Regularly scheduled sessions for the discussion of journal reviews not only help members consolidate and appreciate their gains in dream-generated insights and in their dream skills, but also may highlight important patterns. For example, dreamers notice their own and other members' repetitive dream images and motifs. New layers of meaning surface that relate to the developmental roots of problems presented in dreams. Dreamers find that reviews enrich their appreciation of the broader ramifications of a given problem or insight when they see how another member's dream has come to shed light on several areas of his or her life not originally recognized as related to the dream.

The group also uses reviews to see if, as a group or as individuals, they have been avoiding discussing certain types of dreams with each other, and if they want to alter such patterns. Most groups simply note the phenomenon of omission if it exists and leave it to the individual dreamers to bring in awkward dreams if and when they choose. Some groups discover that they freely discuss all sorts of dreams except ones that the dreamers judge as ordinary or dull. In these cases, they often set aside one session to bring in such dreams and explore them briefly to see if they are as ordinary as they seem. Jung's statement that "one learns more from ordinary dreams"[3] is sometimes hard to accept if one was, for example, introduced to dreams through a system that emphasized the exotic or the "spiritual." Recognizing the tremendous value in ordinary dreams can be an important liberation for dreamers who think their dreams are inadequate in comparison to the flashy dreams described in books and lectures.

During reviews, dreamers notice whether their dreams seem stuck and repetitive, or if they are developing basic themes and introducing new ones. These changes—or lack thereof—always parallel the dreamer's waking progress in dealing with the issues raised by the dreams. If a dreamer seems caught in a pattern that repeats itself with little or no change, this might be an indication that she needs help in incorporating her insights and may benefit from some psychotherapy. If the dreamer is able to integrate her discoveries and make necessary and desirable changes in her life, this will be clearly reflected in her dreams. The time it takes to see changes in waking and dream life varies enormously with each dreamer, but it almost always takes longer than the dreamer would like. Nevertheless, most dreamers will be able to see encouraging changes in their dreams and in their lives by the time of the first six-month review, and this usually leads to a round of congratulations and a well-deserved celebration.

Eight Steps to Better Recall

We all dream from four to twenty times a night. We dream those dreams in color and in wonderful vividness. But upon awakening it is easy to forget the freshness and the glory of a dream. Here are some very simple ways you can hold on to the immediacy and the aliveness of your dreams:

1. Keep a pen and paper at your bedside.

2. Get enough sleep. Most of us really do need eight or more hours to feel our best and recall our dreams easily. If you need an alarm to wake you or a cup of coffee to feel good in the morning, you probably are not getting enough sleep.

3. Before sleep, write out your day notes in your journal—just four lines about what you did and felt that day. This will greatly increase your recall in the morning.

4. Wake up naturally. This way, you will usually awaken right after your longest dream of the night. If you are getting enough sleep, you won't have to be battered awake by an alarm clock.

5. Lie still for a moment and learn to ask yourself, "What was just going through my mind?" Form the habit of thinking this thought before you ask yourself what day it is or what you have to do today.

6. Take your time and write out your dream in any way you remember it. If you are rushed, jot down a few notes. They may suffice to bring back the dream when you have more time.

7. If you don't remember a dream, force yourself to write out one sentence about whatever you were feeling or whatever first came into your mind as you awoke. In time this habit will convince your memory that forgetting a dream will not get you out of the necessity of putting pen to paper. Within one or two weeks of using these steps, almost everyone I have ever worked with starts recalling dreams. If this does not work for you, read another book on dreams, and ask yourself if you are for some reason anxious about remembering your dreams. Most likely you are not following one of these steps.

8. If, as is much more likely, you start remembering too many dreams, decide how many you want to recall and how many you want to record. One dream a week is plenty if you interview yourself and learn from it. Later, when you are a more efficient interviewer, you will find that you can easily process a dream every day if you care to.

Recording Your Dreams

The difficulty most people have who follow these simple instructions for a week or two is not in recalling too few dreams, but in remembering too many.[1] If this happens to you, decide how many dreams you care to record per week, and let the rest go. One dream a day is usually enough to satisfy most people, and one dream a week is enough to keep you busy if you study it closely.

Recording your dreams can be a pleasure, and if you include the information suggested below, your dream journal will assist you in understanding your dreams. At our Dream Center, students all use the following format:

Date

Day Notes
At night before going to sleep, record here three or four lines describing what you did and felt today. Emphasize the emotional highlights of the day.

Title of Dream
Leave a blank line between your day notes and the dream you record in the morning. After you have recorded your dream, give it a simple title that will help you to remember the dream at a glance when you review your journal. Dream titles will be a great help to you when you study your dreams in series and look for recurring themes.

The Dream

Write down every detail and feeling you can recall and have time to record.

< *Commentary*

Use this space to record any thoughts or feelings you have in the last moment of the dream or immediately upon awakening. Also write down any feelings or impressions you have about the dream as you awake. Later you can use this space and additional pages to make notes about your interview of yourself or with a dream partner. Include any comparisons you might like to draw with other dreams, or with waking-life experiences.

The pound sign (#) placed in the margin beside each dream entry and the less-than sign (<) placed in the margin beside your commentary will help to organize your journal and make it easier to locate specific sections as you review your dreams. Here is an example of a page from the journal of Bertrand, a cabinetmaker who would like to be a writer as well.

August 1

Day Notes: Long day in the shop. How can I change my circumstances so I can write rather than make cabinets all day long? I feel paralyzed and frustrated. Had fun playing with my children, Ian and Natalie, this evening. What is preventing me from creating the life I want?

Boss on My Back

\# I'm carrying my boss on my back, piggyback style. We are in a visually stunning scene of meadow and ravine surrounded by rolling hills and mountains. I'm going downhill with my boss on my back. I'm attempting to run, but he is too heavy for me. I'm trying to be careful and strong. My boss says, "That's why I liked using those five Green Bay Packers." As he says that, implying that I am not as strong as they, I stumble and go to the ground on my belly slightly. As I get back up I ask, "When did you use the Packers?"

< It felt awful to have my boss put me down. In our group session interview, I realized how much like my dad this critical and very demanding boss is. So I'm still carrying my critical self-judgments learned from my father on my back. Small wonder I lose my confidence if I compare myself to FIVE Green Bay Packers! The beautiful scene reminds me of the beauty of creative writing, and of how I stumble when I lose my confidence.

If you use a new, dated page for each dream you recall, you will have plenty of space to write your commentary—at the time you recall the dream, after an interview, or during a monthly or yearly review of your dream journal. Brief but careful day notes will be a great aid in recalling the specific waking context that led to a particular dream. Frequently, the issues you outline in your day notes are the very ones you will dream about that night.

If you are beginning your dream journal, you might like to start by recording the dreams you remember from childhood, as well as any particularly vivid or recurring dreams and nightmares you recall from your youth and adult life. These will give you a variety of important dreams to reflect upon as you study your dreams.

Introduction

1. For enlightening discussions on the best research and arguments regarding these issues, I refer you to the work of Ramon Greenberg and Chester Pearlman, Harry Fiss, Milton Kramer, Rosalind Cartwright, and others.

2. Thomas French and Erika Fromm, *Dream Interpretation: A New Approach* (New York: Basic Books, 1964), 28–36.

3. Portions of the following section on the theory behind the Dream Interview Method were first published in my book *Breakthrough Dreaming: How to Tap the Power of Your 24-Hour Mind* (New York: Bantam Books, 1991), pp. 68–75.

4. Louis Breger, Ian Hunter, and Ron Lane, *The Effect of Stress on Dreams* (New York: International Universities Press, 1971), 191.

5. For a discussion of this point, see John Beebe, "A Jungian Approach to Working with Dreams," in *New Directions in Dream Interpretation,* ed. Gayle Delaney (Albany: State Univ. of New York Press, 1993), 77–102; C. G. Jung, *Dream Analysis: Notes of the Seminar Given in 1928–1930* (Princeton, NJ: Princeton Univ. Press, 1984); and C. G. Jung, *Modern Man in Search of a Soul* (New York: Harcourt, Brace & World, 1933).

6. See C. G. Jung, "General Aspects of Dream Psychology," in *Dreams* (Princeton, NJ: Princeton Univ. Press, 1974), 25–30, for his discussion of the necessity of interpretation from a twofold point of view: causality and finality. Jung proposes that although one must try to understand the cause of a dream, one must also try to understand the sense of purpose inherent in the dream, as in all psychological phenomena. He distinguishes finality from the concept of teleology by defining finality as "the immanent psychological striving for a goal," which might be as simple as the emotional reaction of anger over an insult that has the purpose of revenge.

7. Medard Boss, *"I Dreamt Last Night . . . ,"* trans. Stephen Conway (New York: Gardner Press, 1977), 171.

8. Quoted in Richard Jones, *The New Psychology of Dreaming* (New York: Viking Press, 1974), 102.

9. Boss, "*I Dreamt Last Night . . . ,*" 168.

Chapter 1

1. Barbara Tedlock, "Dreaming and Dream Research," in *Dreaming: Anthropological and Psychological Interpretations,* ed. Barbara Tedlock (Cambridge: Cambridge Univ. Press, 1987), 1–30.

2. Ibid., 2.

3. Ibid.

4. See James Frazer, *The Golden Bough: A Study of Magic and Religion,* 3d ed. (New York: Macmillan, 1936); Lucien Levy-Bruhl, *Primitive Mentality* (New York: Macmillan, 1923); and J. Lincoln, *The Dream in Primitive Cultures* (Baltimore: Williams and Wilkins, 1935).

5. J. Donald Hughes, "The Psychological Role of Dreams in Hippocrates, Plato, and Aristotle" (unpublished paper, Univ. of Denver, December 1984).

6. Aristotle, *On Prophesying by Dreams.*

7. Aristotle, *On Dreams.*

8. Francis Bacon, *Novum Organum,* in *Great Books of the Western World*, vol. 30 (Chicago: Univ. of Chicago Press, 1952), 105–195.

9. Other writers such as Barbara Tedlock ("Dreaming and Dream Research") and Carl W. O'Nell (*Dreams, Culture, and the Individual* [Novato, CA: Chandler & Sharp, 1976]) have pointed to René Descartes, the seventeenth-century geometrician-philosopher, as the man most responsible for this consignment of dream imagery to the world of the unreal. Descartes credited his dreams of the night of Saint Martin's Eve, November 10, 1619, with having revealed to him a fundamental truth about the unity of the sciences, the consequences of which would be his life's work to demonstrate not only in geometry, but in all fields of knowledge. Although it is true that Cartesian dualism, as it came to be understood by many, contributed greatly to the discounting of both the reality and the meaningfulness of dream imagery, Descartes's personal life and his work left room for revelation through dreams and a belief in God and the world of the spirit. The empiricists, who insisted upon an increasingly experimental mode of inquiry, had, I think, an even greater impact on our Western disbelief in the reality and the usefulness of dream imagery.

For discussions on the dreams and philosophy of Descartes, see Jack Vrooman, *René Descartes, a Biography* (New York: G. P. Putnam's Sons, 1970); Jacques Maritain, *The Dream of Descartes* (New York: Philosophical Library, 1944); and Maxime Leroy, *Descartes: Le philosophe au masque* (Paris: Editions Reider, 1929).

In Descartes's *Philosophical Essays* (New York: Bobbs-Merrill, 1964), in the meditation "Of the Nature of the Human Mind, and That It Is More Easily Known Than the Body," Descartes does disparage the usefulness of dreams and the imagination as a means to knowledge, but his overall insistence that God exists and his manner of proving this leave much more room for the reality of a non–physically oriented world than did the attitudes expressed in the first few centuries of the empiricist worldview after Bacon.

For a surprising, and to some a rather amusing, old-school psychoanalytic (Kleinian) interpretation of Descartes's dream, see Stephen Schönberger, "A Dream of Descartes: Reflections on the Unconscious Determinants of the Sciences," *International Journal of Psychoanalysis* 20, no. 1 (1939): 43–57. For a more sensitive discussion of how Descartes's dreams relate to his philosophy, see Allen R. Dyer, "The Dreams of Descartes: Notes on the Origins of Scientific Thinking," *Psychoanalysis and Science*, April 1985.

10. For a detailed and fascinating history of dream interpretation, see J. Donald Hughes's unpublished essay "A History of Dream Interpretation in Western Civilization from the Earliest Times Through the Middle Ages." Hughes is a professor of history at the University of Denver. I have drawn extensively from his work in this chapter.

11. Waldemar Bogoras, *The Chukchee,* Publications of the Jesup North Pacific Expedition, vol. 7 (Leiden, NY: E. J. Brill, Ltd., 1907): 333.

12. Geza Roheim, *The Gates of the Dream* (New York: International Universities Press, 1952), 163.

13. Robert Van de Castle, *The Psychology of Dreaming* (Morristown, NJ: General Learning Press, 1971), 8. See also *Dreams and Dreaming,* ed. S. Lee and A. Mayes (Baltimore: Penguin Books, 1973).

14. John Cawte, "The 'Ordinary' Dreams of the Yolngu in Arnhem Land," *Australian and New Zealand Journal of Psychiatry* 18 (September 1984): 236–243.

15. Ibid., 238. Cawte is here referring to the nocturnal dreams of the Yolngu, not to the often confusing terms *dreaming* and *dreamtime*, which, he says, "are used in Aboriginal Australia for the religious construct of the creative epoch, the time when legendary heroes and ancestors walked the earth, making its features as known today. An essential feature of 'the dreaming' is that it is eternal, now present around us and continuing into the future. In some of the dreams recorded by us, a legendary figure is present but the dreamer clearly distinguishes between the dreaming and his own dream." Ibid., 237. Cawte also makes a point of noting that neither he nor the Yolngu he interviewed "had any difficulty in differentiating dreams from visions or hallucinations while awake." Ibid., 237.

16. Ibid., 243.

17. Ibid., 239.

18. The Hindu *Treatise on Dreams* contained in the Atharva Veda comes from a carefully memorized oral tradition that may go back further in time (1500–1000 B.C.E.) and that is more

sophisticated in that it provides principles of interpretation in addition to symbolic equivalents; however, it was not written down until the twelfth century A.D.

19. Norman MacKenzie, *Dreams and Dreaming* (New York: Vanguard Press, 1965), 31.

20. Hughes, "A History of Dream Interpretation," 8–9.

21. MacKenzie, *Dreams and Dreaming*, 29.

22. Ibid., 26.

23. Ibid., 30.

24. Hughes, "A History of Dream Interpretation," 8.

25. Ibid.

26. Ibid., 13.

27. MacKenzie, *Dreams and Dreaming*, 30.

28. Marielene Putscher, "Dreams and Dream Interpretation in the Bible," *Israel Journal of Psychiatry and Related Sciences* 19 (1982): 152–153.

29. Gen. 28:13–15. For an interesting discussion of Jacob's dream, see Allen P. Ross, "Studies in the Life of Jacob, Part I: Jacob's Vision: The Founding of Bethel," *Bibliotheca Sacra*, July–September 1985, 224–237.

30. Gen. 15:1–14.

31. Putscher, "Dreams and Dream Interpretation," 152.

32. For an interesting treatment of Joseph's interpretive skills, and what I think is a somewhat exaggerated estimate of the role of unconscious motivation in the biblical dreamers, see Janet Hadda, "Joseph: Ancestor of Psychoanalysis," *Conservative Judaism* 37 (spring 1984): 17–21.

33. The first treatise has been lost, and only parts of the third have survived, but Philo's ideas on dreams are found easily in the remaining parts of the trilogy.

34. Philo, *De Somniis*, quoted and discussed in a fascinating article by Jouette M. Bassler, "Philo on Joseph," *Journal for the Study of Judaism* 16, no. 2: 248.

35. Ibid., 249.

36. Ibid.

37. Sandor Lorand, "Dream Interpretation in the Talmud," in *The New World of Dreams,* ed. Ralph L. Woods and Herbert B. Greenhouse (New York: Macmillan, 1974), 150.

38. "Discourse on Good and Bad Dreams," trans. Rev. A. Cohen, in *The World of Dreams,* ed. Ralph L. Woods (New York: Random House, 1947), 125. Robert Van de Castle was probably referring to this passage when he wrote, "He [Rabbi Hisda] also said that bad dreams were preferable to good dreams because the pain they caused would be sufficient to cause the dreamer to prevent their

fulfillment, and they had, therefore, a more transforming effect." Van de Castle, *The Psychology of Dreaming*, 6. The word *transforming* may lead to the misconception that the Talmudic dream theorists believed that the pain from bad dreams could bring about psychological transformation through insight, which they did not in fact propose. Keep in mind the fact that the writers of this Talmud who had an interest in dreams, like those in all preceding civilizations, looked to dreams for prophecy of future events, not for psychological growth. Transformation was considered to be a spiritual affair, due either to God's inspiration communicated in the dream (as in the case of the "good" dream of Jacob's ladder) or to God's inspiration of the interpreter, as in the case of Daniel, who foretold more than transformed Nebuchadnezzar's future. In the passage quoted here, Rabbi Hisda is clearly referring to dreams only as omens of the future. He expresses concern that good dreams are not as valuable as bad dreams because the good they foretell is frustrated by their cheerfulness and thus they are unlikely to come true. There is therefore a net loss in good fortune if one has a good dream about a future event that becomes less likely to be fulfilled now that the dream has caused the cheerfulness. The dreamer, however, profits from the bad dream that foretells an undesired event, because the pain he feels may act to mitigate the chances of the fulfillment of the omen. See Lorand, "Dream Interpretation in the Talmud"; Robert Karl Gnuse, *The Dream Theophany of Samuel: Its Structure in Relation to Ancient Near Eastern Dreams and Its Theological Significance* (New York: Univ. Press of America, 1984); Ross, "Studies in the Life of Jacob"; and Bassler, "Philo on Joseph."

39. "Discourse on Good and Bad Dreams," 126–127.

40. Lorand, "Dream Interpretation in the Talmud," 150–158. This article was originally published under the same title in the *International Journal of Psychoanalysis* 38 (1957). Exactly what Lorand means by "personality" is unclear. In reading his and other's examples of dreams interpreted in the Talmud, I have not come across any that reflect the interpreter's appreciation for the dreamer's individual personality or temperament. Cf. Meir's Jungian interpretation of Artemidorus's dictum that the interpreter must know the dreamer's occupation, status, health, local customs and beliefs, and mood before sleep, discussed later in this chapter.

41. "Discourse on Good and Bad Dreams," 127–128. Source's brackets.

42. Quoted in Raymond De Becker, *The Understanding of Dreams*, trans. Michael Heron (New York: Bell Publishing, 1968), 191; originally published as *Les machinations de la nuit* (Paris: Edition Planete, 1965).

43. Ibid., 192.

44. Yoram Bilu and Henry Abramovitch, "In Search of the Saddig: Visitational Dreams Among Moroccan Jews in Israel," *Psychiatry* 48 (February 1985): 84.

45. Ibid., 85.

46. Ibid., 92.

47. Ibid., 89. Source's brackets and italics, except the first set of brackets.

48. Ibid. Source's italics.

49. Quoted in "Maine Rabbi's Specialty Is Helping Counselors," *New York Times,* July 15, 1989.

50. Scholars are not in agreement about the dating of the Vedas. For example, Roger Caillois writes that the Artharva Veda is usually attributed to the fifth century B.C.E. "Logical and Philosophical Problems of the Dream," in *The Dream in Human Societies,* ed. G. E. von Grunebaum and Roger Caillois (Berkeley: Univ. of California Press, 1966), 23.

51. De Becker, *The Understanding of Dreams,* 184–187.

52. Ibid., 186–187.

53. Ibid., 185.

54. Ibid., 185–186.

55. Robert Ernest Hume, *The Thirteen Principal Upanishads, with an Outline of the Philosophy of the Upanishads* (Oxford: Oxford Univ. Press, 1971), 2.

56. Swami Prabhavananda, *The Spiritual Heritage of India* (New York: Anchor Books, 1964), 39. Compare Aristotle's view that in dreams what the mind sees are images caused by the activity of the blood in the sense organs. (This view is described in the section on Greek dream traditions later in this chapter.)

57. Hume, *The Thirteen Principal Upanishads,* 134.

58. Ibid., 136–137.

59. Ibid., 138.

60. Andrew O. Fort, "Dreaming in Advaita Vedanta," *Philosophy East and West* 35 (October 1985). Source's italics.

61. Ibid. Source's brackets and italics.

62. Sri Aurobindo, "An Unpublished Letter of Sri Aurobindo," *Sri Aurobindo Mandir Annual* (Calcutta), no. 35 (August 15, 1976): 1–2.

63. For example, a "railway-journey is always in vital dreams a symbol of a journey or progress of the inner being" (ibid., 4) and "the rain is a symbol of a descent from some other consciousness" (ibid., 5).

64. Sri Aurobindo, "Sleep and Dreams," *Sri Aurobindo Circle* 26: 118.

65. Michel Soymié, "Les songes et leur interprétation en Chine," in *Les songes et leur interprétations: Sources orientales* (Paris: Seuil, 1959), 276–305.

66. Michel Strickmann, "Dreamwork of Psycho-Sinologists: Doctors, Taoists, and Monks," in *Psycho-Sinology: The Universe of Dreams in Chinese Culture,* ed. Carolyn T. Brown (Lanham, MD: Univ. Press of America, 1988), 24.

67. One might add that diviners interpret along the lines of prognostication, and modern psychotherapists along introspective, psychodynamic lines.

68. Strickmann, "Dreamwork of Psycho-Sinologists," 26.

69. William Nienhauser, Jr., "Floating Clouds and Dreams in Liu Tsung-Yüan's Yung-Chou Exile Writings," *Journal of the American Oriental Society* 106.1 (1986): 169–181.

70. Strickmann, "Dreamwork of Psycho-Sinologists," 26.

71. Soymié, "Les songes et leur interprétation," 284.

72. Ibid.

73. Ibid., 282–283.

74. Strickmann, "Dreamwork of Psycho-Sinologists," 28.

75. De Becker, *The Understanding of Dreams,* 188.

76. Soymié, "Les songes et leur interprétation," 295.

77. De Becker, *The Understanding of Dreams,* 190.

78. Soymié, "Les songes et leur interprétation, 297–298.

79. Lie-tseu, quoted in Soymié, "Les songes et leur interprétation," 297; also quoted and translated in De Becker, *The Understanding of Dreams,* 204.

80. Wei Hsiang-shu, Han-sung-t', and Yung-yen, in *The Interpretation of Dreams in Ancient China,* ed. Roberto K. Ong (Bochum, Germany: Studienverlag Brockmeyer, 1985), 62.

81. Ibid., 61.

82. Terese Tse Bartholomew, *Myths and Rebuses in Chinese Art* (San Francisco: Asian Art Museum of San Francisco, 1988).

83. Hughes, "A History of Dream Interpretation," 18.

84. Dreams in which the dreamer reports that a being comes to the place where the dreamer is sleeping and delivers a message (i.e., the dreams of Gudea, Thutmose IV, Jacob, and Solomon, to name a few) lend themselves to an interesting discussion of Jaynes's conception of the bicameral mind. See Julian Jaynes, *The Origin of Consciousness in the Breakdown of the Bicameral Mind* (Boston: Houghton Mifflin, 1982).

85. Hughes, "A History of Dream Interpretation," 18–19.

86. Quoted in Hughes, "A History of Dream Interpretation," 20.

87. Ibid., 21.

88. Carl A. Meier, "The Dream in Ancient Greece and Its Use in Temple Cures (Incubation)," in *The Dream and Human Societies,* ed. G. E. von Grunebaum and Roger Caillois (Berkeley: Univ. of California Press, 1966), 303–318.

89. Ibid., 314–316.

90. Robert Rousselle, "Healing Cults in Antiquity: The Dream Cures of Asclepius of Epidaurus," *Journal of Psychohistory* 12 (winter 1985): 339–352.

91. Ibid., 341.

92. Ibid., 340. Some have suggested that the temple priests used hypnotic induction in the incubation ritual. There are many ways to describe what constitutes hypnotic induction. I would propose that the priests simply profited from the suggestive effects of purposely petitioning a god for aid in a dream, of sleeping in a special place, and of hearing and reading of previous cures. For an interesting critique of the popular contention that hypnosis was unwittingly used in these temples, see Henderikus J. Stam and Nicholas Spanos, "The Asclepian Dream Healings and Hypnosis: A Critique," *International Journal of Clinical and Experimental Hypnosis* 30 (1982): 9–22.

93. The name Hippocrates will be used throughout this chapter to refer to the author of *On Dreams*, although whether the author was Hippocrates or one of his students is a matter of debate among scholars.

94. Hughes, "A History of Dream Interpretation," 24–27.

95. Democritus (460?–352? B.C.E.) wrote that dream images were created by the soul, which received from the dreamer's pores (especially from those of the sensory organs) atoms that emanate from all the objects in the waking world. See Angel J. Cappelletti, "El sueño y los sueños en la filosofia prearistotelica," *Revue de Filosofia de la Universidad de Costa Rica* 23 (1985): 71–81.

96. Hughes, "The Psychological Role of Dreams," 1.

97. Ibid., 2. Compare Carl A. Meier's "psychopomorphic" attempt to cast Hippocrates and many of the Greeks as foreshadowing a Jungian approach to dreams in Meier, "The Dream in Ancient Greece," 303–319.

98. Hippocrates, *On Dreams*, trans. W. H. S. Jones (Cambridge: Harvard Univ. Press, 1931), 4:420–447, quoted in Hughes, "A History of Dream Interpretation," 25.

99. Hippocrates, *Regimen (On Dreams)*, quoted in Hughes, "A History of Dream Interpretation," 26.

100. Hughes, "A History of Dream Interpretation," 26.

101. Paul Chabaneïx, *Le subconcient chez les artistes, les savants, et les écrivains* (Paris: J.-B. Baillière & Fils, 1897), 62.

102. For descriptions of the pre-Socratics, see Kathleen Freeman, *The Pre-Socratic Philosophers* (Cambridge: Harvard Univ. Press, 1966); Philip Wheelwright, *The Presocratics* (New York: Odyssey Press, 1966); and Cappelletti, "El sueño y los sueños." For a more detailed discussion of the attitudes toward dreams of the major Greek philosophers, see Hughes, "A History of Dream Interpretation."

103. Plato, *Republic* 9.572.

104. Ibid., 9.571–572.

105. See Cappelletti, "El sueño y los sueños," 74–75, for his argument that Democritus also saw dreams as expressing desires. Freud wrote in *The Interpretation of Dreams* (ed. and trans. James Strachey [New York: Avon Books, 1966], 165–166) that the Ptolemaic physician Herophilus was one of the early writers on dreams to anticipate his belief in the wish-fulfilling nature of dreams. But Freud notes that neither Herophilus nor a nineteenth-century writer, Scherner, gave sufficient weight to the importance of wishes in dream formation, nor did they relate wishes to the "essential nature of dreaming" as he did. I suspect that from earliest times many if not all writers on dreams who did not think of dreams exclusively as omens assumed that some dreams expressed the fulfillment of wishes. It is hard to believe that there was ever a time when humankind did not recognize the cause of a dream of abundant food or water, or sex, or honors, that came at a time when these things were greatly desired.

106. Hughes, "A History of Dream Interpretation," 27–29.

107. Aristotle, *On Dreams;* Hughes, "A History of Dream Interpretation."

108. Aristotle, *On Prophesying by Dreams* 462b.20.

109. Hughes, "The Psychological Role of Dreams," 7.

110. Aristotle, *On Dreams* 463a.25.

111. J. Donald Hughes, "The Dreams of Alexander the Great," *Journal of Psychohistory* 12 (fall 1984): 168–192.

112. Virgil, *Aeneid* 7.81 ff., quoted in Hughes, "A History of Dream Interpretation," 33.

113. Quoted in Sheila McNally, "Ariadne and Others: Images of Sleep in Greek and Early Roman Art," *Classical Antiquity* 4 (fall 1985): 174. This article gives a fascinating account of its subject as portrayed in statues, vases, pediments, drawings, and other art objects of the period.

114. Claudian, *Contra Europa* 1.312–313, cited in De Becker, *The Understanding of Dreams,* 146.

115. MacKenzie, *Dreams and Dreaming,* 50.

116. Ibid.

117. Ibid., 50–51.

118. Ibid., 51.

119. Cicero, *On Divination,* from Cicero, "Argument Against Taking Dreams Seriously," in *The World of Dreams,* ed. Ralph L. Woods (New York: Random House, 1947), 201.

120. Hughes, "A History of Dream Interpretation," 34.

121. Cicero, *On Divination,* quoted in Hughes, "A History of Dream Interpretation," 34.

122. Cicero, *On Divination,* in *The World of Dreams,* 202.

123. Ibid., 203.

124. Ibid., 204.

125. Artemidorus, *Oneirocritica*, trans. Robert J. White (Park Ridge, NJ: Noyes Press, 1975), 4.2. The commentary by White makes this book especially helpful in understanding the dream practices of the period.

126. Ibid., 4.22.

127. For example, see Meier, "The Dream in Ancient Greece," 311 and passim. Meier writes: "But keep in mind that he [Artemidorus] carefully investigated the dreamers' personal circumstances as well as the outcome (anamnesis, catamnesis, and epicrisis)" (311). And later he writes that Artemidorus held that the interpreter must know the dreamer's character (312). Looking back seventeen hundred years, one is greatly tempted to read into *Oneirocritica* our modern conceptions of character and introspective conceptions of personality. But Artemidorus's suggestions that the interpreter inform himself regarding the dreamer's name, occupation, social and financial status, age, state of health, and mood before sleep is a far, far cry from suggesting that the interpreter assess the character of the dreamer or that he take a careful emotional personal history (anamnesis) of the dreamer.

128. Artemidorus, *Oneirocritica* 4.184–185. See also S. R. F. Price, "The Future of Dreams: From Freud to Artemidorus," *Past and Present* 113 (1986): 3–37, for an instructive rebuttal to recent efforts by some to read into Artemidorus's work an introspective approach to dreaming.

129. Artemidorus, *Oneirocritica* 4.20.

130. Price, "The Future of Dreams," 24.

131. Artemidorus, *Oneirocritica* 3.60.

132. Ibid., 1.8–9.

133. Freud, *The Interpretation of Dreams*, 130. Source's emphasis.

134. Artemidorus, *Oneirocritica* 3.66.

135. Ibid., 1.79.

136. Ibid., 4.23.

137. Ibid., 4.20.

138. Price, "The Future of Dreams," 31–32.

139. For more detailed accounts of New Testament and early Christian dreams by Christian authors, see Lois Hendricks, *Discovering My Biblical Dream Heritage* (San Jose, CA: Resource Publications, 1989); Morton T. Kelsey, *God, Dreams, and Revelation* (Minneapolis: Augsburg Publishing, 1974); and John Sanford, *Dreams: God's Forgotten Language* (Philadelphia: Lippincott, 1968).

140. Tertullian, *De Anima* 46.

141. Kelsey, *God, Dreams, and Revelation,* 113–114.

142. Tertullian, *De Anima* 47.

143. Ibid., 45.

144. Louis M. Savary, Patricia H. Berne, and Strephon Kaplan Williams, *Dreams and Spiritual Growth: A Christian Approach to Dreamwork* (New York: Paulist Press, 1984), 38–39.

145. Kelsey, *God, Dreams, and Revelation,* 142. See also Augustine Fitzgerald, *The Essays and Hymns of Synesius of Cyrene* (London: Oxford Univ. Press, 1930).

146. Kelsey, *God, Dreams, and Revelation,* 143.

147. Synesius of Cyrene, "Dreams Take the Soul to 'The Superior Region,'" trans. Isaac Myer, in *The World of Dreams,* ed. Ralph L. Woods (New York: Random House, 1947), 136–137. Woods suggests that Synesius's belief in divination, being unusually unguarded and enthusiastic for a bishop of the time, might have been part of a deal he made with the church authorities who invited him to become a bishop in spite of the fact that he had a wife (134).

148. Kelsey, *God, Dreams, and Revelation,* 143.

149. Ibid.

150. Hughes, "A History of Dream Interpretation," 42.

151. Kelsey, *God, Dreams, and Revelation,* 144.

152. *Encyclopaedia Britannica,* 1965 ed., 20:754–757.

153. Alison M. Peden, "Macrobius and Mediaeval Dream Literature," *Medium Ævum* 1:59–73.

154. *Comprehensive Textbook of Psychiatry,* ed. Alfred Freedman and Harold Kaplan (Baltimore: Williams and Wilkins, 1967), 11.

155. Elaine Pagels, *Adam, Eve, and the Serpent* (New York: Random House, 1988); Lois E. Nesbitt, "The Faith with a Thousand Faces," *Princeton Alumni Weekly,* 22 February 1989, 9.

156. Peden, "Macrobius and Mediaeval Dream Literature," 64.

157. Peden ("Macrobius and Mediaeval Dream Literature") writes that William of Conches's commentary on Macrobius is still unpublished and must be located in libraries, but that for a general discussion on Conches's work one might consult J. Le Goff, "Les rêves dans la culture et la psychologie collective de l'Occident médiéval," in *Pour un autre moyen âge* (Paris, 1977), 305–306.

Peden also notes that Conches offered a physiological interpretation of the incubus, as did Paschalis Romanus of Constantinople. "Macrobius and Mediaeval Dream Literature," 64–65. These explanations, like the first written one by Galen, were physiological fantasies rather than the physiological science for which they passed. For example, Paschalis Romanus described this terrifying experience of feeling the weight of a creature on one's chest as the result of "blood gathering around the heart or pressure on parts of the brain." Ibid., 65.

158. Ibid.

159. *Encyclopaedia Britannica,* 1965 ed., 4:643–654, 12:663–681.

160. Toufy Fahd, "Les songes et leur interprétation selon l'Islam," *Sources Orientales* 2 (1959; special issue, ed. A.-M. Esnoul, P. Garelli, et al. and titled *Les songes et leur interprétation*): 125–158.

161. Toufy Fahd, "The Dream in Medieval Islamic Society," in *The Dream and Human Societies,* ed. G. E. von Grunebaum and Roger Caillois (Berkeley: Univ. of California Press, 1966), 351.

162. Jean Lecerf, "The Dream in Popular Culture: Arabic and Islamic," in *The Dream and Human Societies,* ed. G. E. von Grunebaum and Roger Caillois (Berkeley: Univ. of California Press, 1966), 365.

163. Fritz Meier, "Some Aspects of Inspiration by Demons in Islam," in *The Dream and Human Societies,* ed. G. E. von Grunebaum and Roger Caillois (Berkeley: Univ. of California Press, 1966), 421.

164. Nathaniel Bland, "Muhammedan Tâbír, or Dream Interpretation," in *The World of Dreams,* ed. Ralph L. Woods (New York: Random House, 1947), 72.

165. Meier, "Some Aspects of Inspiration," 423.

166. Koran 12:6.

167. G. E. von Grunebaum, "The Cultural Function of the Dream as Illustrated by Classical Islam," in *The Dream and Human Societies,* ed. G. E. von Grunebaum and Roger Caillois (Berkeley: Univ. of California Press, 1966), 7.

168. Ibid., 3–21.

169. Bland, "Muhammedan Tâbír," 75.

170. De Becker, *The Understanding of Dreams,* 216–217.

171. John Calvin, *Commentaries on the Book of Daniel,* excerpted under the title "The Operation of a Divine Agency in Dreams," in *The World of Dreams,* ed. Ralph L. Woods (New York: Random House, 1947), 149–151.

172. Fritjof Capra, *The Turning Point* (New York: Simon & Schuster, 1981), 56.

173. Benvenuto Cellini, *The Autobiography of Benvenuto Cellini,* trans. J. Addington Symonds (New York: P. F. Collier, 1910), 245–246.

174. This essay, *Olympica,* has been lost, but it is summarized by his biographer, A. Baillet, in *Vie de Monsieur Descartes* (Paris: Table Ronde, 1946).

175. Blaise Pascal, "How Can We Tell We Are Awake?" from *Provincial Letters and Thoughts*, trans. A. Moliner, in *The World of Dreams*, ed. Ralph L. Woods (New York: Random House, 1947), 212.

176. Leroy Loemker, *Struggle for Synthesis* (Cambridge: Harvard Univ. Press, 1972), 238.

177. Leroy Loemker, ed., *Leibniz: Philosophical Papers and Letters*, vol. 2 (Chicago: Univ. of Chicago Press, 1956), 1041.

178. Loemker, *Struggle for Synthesis*, 239.

179. Peretz Lavie and J. Allan Hobson, "Origin of Dreams: Anticipation of Modern Theories in the Philosophy and Physiology of the Eighteenth and Nineteenth Centuries," *Psychological Bulletin* 100 (1986): 231. See also Gottfried Wilhelm Leibniz, *New Essay Concerning Human Understanding*, trans. A. G. Langley (La Salle, IL: Open Court Publishing, 1949), 115.

180. Lavie and Hobson, "Origin of Dreams."

181. MacKenzie, *Dreams and Dreaming*, 81.

182. *Encyclopaedia Britannica*, 1965 ed., 7:390.

183. Ibid.

184. Ibid., 391.

185. Ibid.

186. Jacques Chouillet, "La poétique du rêve dans les salons de Diderot," *Stanford French Review* 8 (fall 1984): 245–256.

187. Voltaire, "Somnambulists and Dreamers," from *Philosophical Dictionary*, in *The World of Dreams*, ed. Ralph L. Woods (New York: Random House, 1947), 232.

188. Ibid., 230.

189. Ibid., 230–231.

190. Ibid., 230. In *Dreams and Dreaming*, MacKenzie writes that Voltaire "argued that dreams were purely physiological in origin" and that he (along with Hobbes) "dismissed the idea that dreams might offer significant clues to the . . . problems that confronted him [the dreamer] in waking life" (87–88). In the present chapter, I have chosen generally not to point out such inaccuracies, but to get on with the story of the history of dream interpretation in as straightforward and accurate a fashion as possible. I have no desire to detract from such a fine book as MacKenzie's, and in presenting the facts as I understand them, I hope to adequately inform the reader without dragging her or him through endless little corrections and differences of opinion.

191. MacKenzie, *Dreams and Dreaming*, 91.

192. David Hartley, *Observations on Man*, quoted in MacKenzie, *Dreams and Dreaming*, 91.

193. Ibid. For a review of the precursors of modern theories of the concept of dreaming as an endogenous product of brain activity, see Lavie and Hobson, "Origin of Dreams," 229–240.

194. W. Robert, *Der Traum als Naturnotwendigkeit erklärt* (Hamburg, 1886), quoted in Freud, *The Interpretation of Dreams*, 111–112.

195. Francis Crick and Graeme Mitchison, "The Function of Dream Sleep," *Nature* 304 (14 July 1983): 111–114.

196. MacKenzie, *Dreams and Dreaming*, 92–98.

197. Henri F. Ellenberger, *The Discovery of the Unconscious: The History and Evolution of Dynamic Psychiatry* (New York: Basic Books, 1970), 145–147.

198. Ibid., 206.

199. Carl Gustav Carus, *Psyche, zur Entwicklungsgeschichte der Seele* (Pforzheim: Flamer and Hoffman, 1846), quoted in Ellenberger, *The Discovery of the Unconscious*, 207.

200. Ellenberger, *The Discovery of the Unconscious*, 207.

201. Ibid., 208–209.

202. Chabaneïx, *Le subconscient chez les artistes*, 73.

203. Ellenberger, *The Discovery of the Unconscious*, 214–215.

204. Ibid., 205.

205. Ibid., 225.

206. Ibid., 223–226.

207. Ibid., 306.

208. Hervey de Saint-Denys, *Dreams and How to Guide Them*, ed. Morton Schatzman, trans. Nicholas Fry (Worcester and London: Duckworth, 1982); originally published as *Les rêves et les moyens de les diriger* (1867).

209. Ellenberger, *The Discovery of the Unconscious*, 304–305.

Chapter 2

1. Ellenberger, *The Discovery of the Unconscious*, 321.

2. Ellenberger, *The Discovery of the Unconscious*, 543. Source's brackets. In 1925, Freud wrote that Nietzsche was "a philosopher 'whose guesses and intuitions often agree in the most astonishing way with the laborious findings of psychoanalysis,' adding that for a long time he avoided reading Nietzsche on that very account, in order to keep his mind free from external influences." Ibid., 277.

3. McGinn, personal communication with author. For more information on this topic, see Friedrich Nietzsche, *The Gay Science*, trans. Walter Kaufmann (New York: Random House, 1974).

4. Contrary to popular belief, Freud did *not* define dreams as symptoms of pathology, although he used them to diagnose and treat pathology: "A dream, however, is no pathological phenomenon; it presupposes no disturbance of psychical equilibrium; it leaves behind no loss of efficiency . . .

"[Dreams] have proved that *what is suppressed continues to exist in normal people as well as abnormal, and remains capable of psychical functioning.* Dreams themselves are among the manifestations of this suppressed material; this is so theoretically in every case, and it can be observed empirically in a great number of cases at least." Freud, *The Interpretation of Dreams*, 646–647.

5. Ibid., 160.

6. Ibid., 362–363.

7. Ibid., 363.

8. Ibid.

9. Ibid., 151, 152.

10. The manifest dream is the dream as the dreamer recalls it, as opposed to the latent or hidden meaning, which is disguised by the manifest dream.

11. Freud, *The Interpretation of Dreams*, 419–420 and passim.

12. Ibid., 429.

13. Ibid., 430.

14. Ibid., 395.

15. Ibid., 407.

16. Ibid., 130–131.

17. Ibid., 130. As we have seen, Artemidorus did not in fact take into account the character of the dreamer. This and Freud's implication that Artemidorus did not consider the interpretation of a given image in the context of the dream as a whole—which Artemidorus in fact often did by describing different meanings for the same image in different dream contexts—leads me to believe that Freud may not have read *Oneirocritica* very carefully, or that he may not have had access to the book.

18. Freud, *The Interpretation of Dreams*, 435.

19. Ibid., 431.

20. Ellenberger, *The Discovery of the Unconscious*, 292.

21. Freud, *The Interpretation of Dreams*, 97.

22. Ibid., 603.

23. Ellenberger, *The Discovery of the Unconscious*, 657.

24. Ibid., 711.

25. C. G. Jung, *Dreams* (Princeton, NJ: Princeton Univ. Press, 1974), 63.

26. Jung, "The Practical Use of Dream-Analysis," in *Dreams*, 90.

27. Ellenberger, *The Discovery of the Unconscious*, 728.

28. Jung, *Dreams*, 55.

29. Jung, "General Aspects of Dream Psychology," in *Dreams*, 34–35.

30. As we shall see, Boss does not require a thorough understanding of the waking situation, believing that aspects of it that are relevant to the dream will surface in the dream and its explication. I would suggest that it is hazardous to assume that one can construct an accurate picture of a person's waking situation from his reports. This has become abundantly clear to most therapists trained in couples and family therapy. Further, it is easy to read into the interpretation of a dream meanings that support your theory. In the case of Freud all dreams had to be interpreted as fulfillments of wishes, and in the case of Jung almost all dreams had to be interpreted, at least in part, as compensating for a waking attitude.

31. I have worked with three Jungian analysts, one in New York and two in Zurich, and have known quite well a good number of Jungian analysands and analysts, none of whom practices "taking up the context" in quite the way Jung suggests. I have yet to find a written account of a Jungian dream analysis that demonstrates this approach.

32. Jung, *Modern Man*, 12–14.

33. In suggesting that the dreamer provide a description and history of an image, Jung does not specifically ask for a description of its function, nor does he ever ask for a definition of objects in dreams. In his presentations of his patients' dreams, Jung does not recount instances in which he asked for descriptions from his dreamer, but he does present cases in which he provides his own descriptions, apparently assuming that his descriptions would be an adequate summation of what the dreamer would say if asked. He then bases his interpretations upon his descriptive impression of an image, rather than upon that of the patient. For example, see Jung, *Dream Analysis*, 37, 109, 647.

34. Mary Ann Mattoon, *Applied Dream Analysis: A Jungian Approach* (Washington, DC: V. H. Winston & Sons, 1978).

In Jung's dream seminars of 1928–1930, he gives his own concrete descriptions of several images in the dreams of his patients, but he never says that he ever asked the dreamers for their concrete descriptions, nor does he qualify his own descriptions as not necessarily being those the dreamers might have given. For example, Jung rhetorically asks his students how they would describe a mouse to someone who had never seen one, and he answers, "It is a tiny grey animal, hardly seen in the daytime, which disturbs one at night with disagreeable little noises; they eat all kinds of things and one must always be careful that they don't get at the good things in the kitchen. They live in houses, parasites, and one tries to catch them by means of traps and cats because they are generally a nuisance. . . . Then the mouse often appears in folklore and typically in fairy stories. Now what would it represent psychologically?" Jung, *Dream Analysis*, 535. Jung fishes for the meaning of mice among his class of students and finally gets what he wants: the mouse represents sexuality, Eros. In another dream session, Jung describes a tortoise as cold-blooded and untrustworthy, as apathetic, long-lived, and highly mythological and mysterious. After eliciting several guesses that miss the mark Jung has in mind, Jung pronounces that the tortoise is a symbol of the transcendent function that operates in the human psyche to reconcile pairs of opposites! I wonder what descriptions the dreamers of these images would have offered, and where the words they would have used might have led them. See Jung, *Dream Analysis*, 535–545, 642–650.

35. Jung, *Dreams*, 71–72.

36. Ibid., 76.

37. As an example of the way "taking up the context" has been understood and often confused with amplification, see Mattoon, *Applied Dream Analysis*, 53–56.

38. Jung, *Dreams*, 77–78.

39. I have discussed Jung's method as it is manifested in these seminars in "The Dream Interview," in *New Directions in Dream Interpretation*, ed. Gayle Delaney (Albany: State Univ. of New York Press, 1993), 195–240.

40. Jung, *Dream Analysis*, 125, 138.

41. Ibid., 499; see also 483.

42. For example, the mechanic in dream 19 (ibid., 316) and the sick little girl in dream 1 (ibid., 89–90).

43. For example, after providing his own description of chickens ("Chickens are animals for which we can have no great respect. They are usually panicky, blind, dumb creatures which run into the road just as an automobile comes along. They are an excellent simile for fragmentary tendencies repressed or never come across by us. . . . All the things which escape our control and observation are 'chickens'"), Jung proceeds to interpret the chicken as the dreamer's feeling function. Ibid., 109.

44. In an interview with Erik Craig, Boss stated that he had at least thirty analytic sessions with Freud and that then, because of Freud's cancer, he continued with "another true Freudian," Hans Behn-Eschenburg. At the Berlin Psychoanalytic Institute, Karen Horney was his training and supervisory analyst. Later, while Boss was in private practice, Jung invited him and some five other therapists to biweekly workshops on Jung's work. According to Boss, Jung had developed a following of women and nonmedical men and was looking for a male medical successor to follow his disciple, Carl Meier. Boss said that after ten years of these meetings Jung "had to state that not one of us was converted." Erik Craig, "An Encounter with Medard Boss," *Humanistic Psychologist* 16 (spring 1988; special issue, ed. Erik Craig and titled *Psychotherapy for Freedom*): 34–35.

45. *Dasein*, literally translated as "being-there," is a term that is used by Heidegger to denote individual human existence in relation to the world. *Daseinsanalysis* is the analysis of human exis-

tence as it relates to phenomena while waking and sleeping, as opposed to the more mechanistic intrapsychic formulations of classical psychoanalysis.

46. Craig, "An Encounter with Medard Boss," 28.

47. Boss, *"I Dreamt Last Night . . . ,"* 24.

48. Ibid.

49. Ibid., 199.

50. Ibid., 208–209.

51. Ibid., 214.

52. Ibid., 32.

53. Ibid., 31–32.

54. Ibid., 32.

55. Ibid., 83.

56. Ibid., 84.

57. Medard Boss, *Psychoanalysis and Daseinsanalysis,* trans. Ludwig B. Lefebre (New York: Dacapo Press, 1982), 264.

58. Ibid., 264–265.

59. Boss, *"I Dreamt Last Night . . . ,"* 212.

60. Ellenberger, *The Discovery of the Unconscious,* 255.

Chapter 3

1. This chapter is an expansion of an address I gave to the American Psychological Association in Boston in 1992, which was later published under the title "The Changing Roles of Dream Interpreters in the Understanding of Dreams" in the *International Journal of Psychosomatics* 40, nos. 1–4 (1993): 6–8.

Chapter 4

1. Ilona Marshall, a San Francisco Bay Area dream worker and former student of mine, has drawn on her language-teaching skills to devise an elaborate diagramming system that indicates descriptive phrases, warnings, unpleasant images, significant concepts, positive messages, and brilliant ideas. You might like to develop your own system of markings.

2. Paul J. Stern, *In Praise of Madness* (New York: W. W. Norton & Co., 1972), 43.

3. Gayle Delaney, *Sensual Dreaming: How to Understand and Interpret Your Erotic Dreams* (New York: Fawcett, 1994), 69–70.

4. Gayle Delaney, *Living Your Dreams* (San Francisco: HarperSanFrancisco, 1996), 188–192.

Chapter 5

1. Earlier versions of the dream interviewer's cue card have been published in the 1979, 1981, and 1988 editions of my book *Living Your Dreams*, as well as in my books *Breakthrough Dreaming, New Directions in Dream Interpretation, The Dream Kit, Sensual Dreaming,* and *In Your Dreams.*

Chapter 6

1. Gayle Delaney, *In Your Dreams: Falling, Flying and Other Dream Themes* (San Francisco: HarperSanFrancisco, 1997).

2. This section on examination dreams comes from one of my "Exploring Your Dreams" columns, titled "Making the Grade," in *New Realities Magazine*, July/August 1989, 7.

3. This section on nightmares was first published, in a slightly different form, in one of my "Exploring Your Dreams" columns, titled "Nightmares," in *New Realities Magazine*, March/April 1985, 6.

Chapter 7

1. *A Popular History of American Invention*, ed. W. B. Kaempffert (New York: Scribners Sons, 1924), 381–388.

2. B. M. Kedrov, "On the Question of Scientific Creativity," *Voprosy Psikhologie* 3 (1957): 105–106.

3. James Strachey, editor's introduction to Freud, *The Interpretation of Dreams*, xvii.

4. W. B. Cannon, *The Way of an Investigator: A Scientist's Experiences in Medical Research* (New York: W. W. Norton, 1945), 61.

5. Ibid., 59–60.

6. Ibid., 57–58.

7. Quoted in Naomi Epel, *Writers Dreaming: Twenty-Six Writers Talk About Their Dreams and the Creative Process* (New York: Vintage Books, 1993), 60.

8. Quoted in Epel, *Writers Dreaming*, 138.

9. Dr. Loma K. Flowers, "The Use of Presleep Instructions and Dreams in Psychosomatic Disorders," *Psychotherapy and Psychosomatics* 64 (1995): 173–177; quoted in Delaney, *Living Your Dreams*, 149–150.

10. Gayle Delaney, "Secular Dream Incubation" (master's thesis, Sonoma State Univ., 1974).

Later, after Henry and I had broken up and I had moved to San Francisco in 1973, he developed a method of incubation that fit his personality better. It was ritualistic and involved sleeping in a special place after a four-to-six-hour discussion session with Henry as a guide. I'm more the streamlined, do-it-yourself type. See Henry Reed, "Dream Incubation: A Ritual in Contemporary Form," *Journal of Humanistic Psychology* 4 (fall 1976): 52–70.

11. Robert Davé, "Effects of Hypnotically Induced Dreams on Creative Problem Solving," *Journal of Abnormal Psychology* 88, no. 3 (1979): 293–302.

12. Morton Schatzman, "Sleeping on Problems Can Really Solve Them," *New Scientist*, August 11, 1983, 416–417; and Morton Schatzman, "The Meaning of Dreams," *New Scientist*, December 25, 1986, 38–39.

13. William C. Dement, *Some Must Watch While Some Must Sleep* (San Francisco: W. H. Freeman, 1972), 99–100.

14. Diedre Barrett, "The 'Committee of Sleep': A Study of Dream Incubation for Problem Solving," *Dreaming: Journal of the Association for the Study of Dreams* 3, no. 2 (June 1993): 115–122.

15. Delaney, *Living Your Dreams*, 29–34.

16. Delaney, *Sensual Dreaming*, 193–195.

17. Ibid., 126–127.

18. Sheila Purcell, J. Mullington, Alan Moffitt, Robert Hoffmann, and R. Pigeau, "Dream Self-Reflectiveness as a Learned Cognitive Skill," *Sleep* 9, no. 3 (1986): 423–437.

19. Sheila Purcell, Alan Moffitt, and Robert Hoffmann, "Waking, Dreaming, and Self-Regulation," in *The Functions of Dreaming*, ed. Alan Moffitt, Milton Kramer, and Robert Hoffmann (Albany: State Univ. of New York Press, 1993), 197–260.

20. Jayne Gackenbach and Jane Bosveld, *Control Your Dreams* (New York: Harper & Row, 1989).

21. Ibid., 31–33. See also two Tholey references cited on p. 218 of this book: P. Tholey, "Techniques for Inducing and Manipulating Lucid Dreams," *Perceptual and Motor Skills* 57 (1983): 79–90; and P. Tholey, "Psychotherapeutic Application of Lucid Dreaming," in *Conscious Mind, Sleeping Brain: Perspectives on Lucid Dreaming*, ed. J. I. Gackenbach and S. LaBerge (New York: Plenum, 1988).

22. Quoted in Gackenbach and Bosveld, *Control Your Dreams*, 33.

23. Ibid., 67–68.

24. Ibid., 65.

25. Purcell, Moffitt, and Hoffmann, "Waking, Dreaming, and Self-Regulation," 237–238.

26. Rosalind Cartwright and Lynne Lamberg, *Crisis Dreaming: Using Your Dreams to Solve Your Problems* (New York: HarperCollins, 1992).

27. Ibid., 105–106.

28. Ibid., 107–108.

29. Ibid., 111–113.

30. Barry Krakow, M.D., and Joseph Neidhardt, M.D., *Conquering Bad Dreams and Nightmares* (New York: Berkley Books, 1992), 215–216.

Chapter 8

1. V. S. Rotenberg, "REM Sleep and Dreams," in *The Functions of Dreaming,* ed. Alan Moffitt, Milton Kramer, and Robert Hoffmann (Albany: State Univ. of New York Press, 1993), 273.

2. Ibid., 261–292.

3. See James E. Schrager and Julian Gresser, "Going Public, Japanese Style," *Wall Street Journal,* Western ed., May 2, 1988.

4. Anjali Hazarika, *Daring to Dream: Cultivating Corporate Through Dreamwork* (New Delhi, Thousand Oaks, CA, and London: Sage Publications, in press).

5. Ibid.

6. *Inc. Magazine,* May 1988, 110. This section on EMC was originally published in one of my "Exploring Your Dreams" columns, titled "Sleeping on the Job," in *New Realities Magazine,* September/October 1988, 48.

7. Delaney, *Living Your Dreams,* chap. 8.

8. August Kekulé, address to the German Chemical Society in Berlin, 1890, published in *Berichte der deutschen chemischen Gesellschaft* 23 (1890), 1306–1307; translated for author by Jürgen Weber. For a lively exchange of articles, letters, and barbs between a chemist and a historian of science who believe Kekulé's dream account, and a couple of positivistic scientists who discount it, see John Wotiz and Susanna Rudofsky, "Kekulé's Dreams: Fact or Fiction?" *Chemistry in Britain* 20 (August 1984): 720–723; B. Ramsay and A. J. Rocke, "Kekulé's Dreams: Separating the Fiction from the Fact," *Chemistry in Britain* 20 (December 1984): 1093–1094; Richard Seltzer, "Influence of Kekulé Dream on Benzene Structure Disputed," *Chemical and Engineering News* 63 (November 4,

1985): 22–23; A. J. Rocke, John Wotiz, and Susanna Rudofsky, letters to the editor in *Chemical and Engineering News* 64 (January 20, 1986): 58–59; and Pierre Thullier, "Du rêve à la science: Le serpent de Kekulé," *La Recherche* 17, no. 175 (March 1986): 386–391.

9. James R. Newman, "Srinivasa Ramanujan," *Scientific American* 178, no. 6 (June 1948): 54–57.

10. Elmer Tory, letter to author, November 7, 1985.

11. Maritain, *The Dream of Descartes,* 9–23; Leroy, *Descartes,* 79–96.

12. Leibniz, *Philosophical Papers and Letters,* 2:1041.

13. Chabaneïx, *Le subconscient chez les artistes,* 73.

14. Ibid., 53.

15. Friedrich Nietzsche, *Beyond Good and Evil,* trans. Walter Kaufmann (New York: Random House, 1966), 106.

16. Ronald Clark, *The Life of Bertrand Russell* (New York: Knopf, 1976), 393–394; and *The Collected Stories of Bertrand Russell,* ed. Barry Feinberg (New York: Simon & Schuster, 1973).

17. Bertrand Russell to Lady Ottoline Morrell, 20 March 1921, reprinted in Clark, *The Life of Bertrand Russell,* 33.

18. *Oxford English Dictionary* (Oxford: Oxford University Press, 1971), 3481.

19. Leon Edel, *Stuff of Sleep and Dreams: Experiments in Literary Psychology* (New York: Avon Books, 1982), 14.

20. Coleridge wrote that while taking a nap, and having had some opium, he dreamt two or three hundred lines of *Kubla Khan,* but that while he was writing them down, he was interrupted by a visitor and could remember only eight or ten lines of his masterpiece. Lawrence Hanson, *The Life of Samuel Taylor Coleridge* (New York: Russell & Russell, 1962). It has been rumored that Coleridge had made notes on the poem before this dream, suggesting that his dream was not the first source for his inspiration. Investigating this, Steve Goldsmith, an English professor at the University of California at Berkeley, asked the British Museum if it had any manuscripts related to the poem. The museum, which holds the only page of the original poem, reported that there was no other material in their catalog box, which should contain any extant notes.

21. Edel, *Stuff of Sleep and Dreams,* 15.

22. See Michael R. Katz, *Dreams and the Unconscious in Nineteenth-Century Russian Fiction* (Hanover, NH: Univ. Press of New England, 1984).

23. Alexander Gilchrist, *The Life of William Blake* (London: J. M. Dent & Sons, 1945; 1st ed., 1863); and Mona Wilson, *The Life of William Blake* (Oxford: Oxford Univ. Press, 1971).

24. Epel, *Writers Dreaming.* This book is exciting to read because it tells you what some of our best writers have to say not only about dreaming, but about the creative state of mind as well.

25. Ibid., 9.

26. Ibid., 39.

27. Ibid., 134–143.

28. Ibid., 162.

29. Ibid., 190.

30. Ibid., 196.

31. Ibid., 201.

32. Ibid.

33. Quoted in Paul McKellar, *Imagination and Thinking* (New York: Basic Books, 1957), 56.

34. Cellini, *Autobiography,* 245–246.

35. Stig Bjorkman, Torsten Mams, and Jonas Sima, *Interviews with Ingmar Bergman* (New York: Simon & Schuster, 1970), 44.

36. Quoted in George S. Bozarth, program notes for the San Francisco Symphony, 1985. Bozarth is the director of the American Brahms Society Archives in Seattle, Washington.

37. Quoted in Walter Ductoux, "Das Rheingold," *San Francisco Opera Magazine,* October 1977.

38. Mel Graves, program notes for Kronos Quartet, 1985–1986 season, 17.

39. Tim Page, *San Francisco Chronicle,* July 21, 1985, 43 (excerpted from the *New York Times Magazine,* 1985).

40. Hippocrates, *On Dreams,* quoted in Hughes, "The Psychological Role of Dreams."

41. Robert C. Smith, "A Possible Biologic Role of Dreaming," *Psychotherapy and Psychosomatics* 41 (1984): 167–176; Robert C. Smith, "Evaluating Dream Function: Emphasizing the Study of Patients with Organic Disease," in *Cognition and Dream Research,* ed. R. Haskell (New York: Institute of Mind and Behavior, 1986), 267–280; and Robert C. Smith, "Traumatic Dreams as an Early Warning of Health Problems," in *Dreamtime and Dreamwork,* ed. Stanley Krippner (Los Angeles: Jeremy P. Tarcher, 1990), 224–232.

42. Bernard Siegel and Barbara Siegel, "A Surgeon's Experience with Dreams and Spontaneous Drawings," *Dream Network Bulletin* 2, no. 2 (February 1983): 1.

43. Victoria Macdonald, "How Nightmares Can Predict Illness," *Sunday Telegraph,* January 19, 1997, 7.

44. Loma K. Flowers and Joan E. Zweben, "The Dream Interview Method in Addiction Recovery: A Treatment Guide," *Journal of Substance Abuse Treatment* 13, no. 2 (1966): 99–105.

45. Loma K. Flowers and Joan E. Zweben, "The Changing Role of 'Using' Dreams in Addiction Recovery," *Journal of Substance Abuse Treatment*, in press.

46. Ibid.

47. Dement, *Some Must Watch*, 102.

48. Epel, *Writers Dreaming*, 261.

Chapter 9

1. Montague Ullman and Nan Zimmerman, *Working with Dreams* (New York: Delacorte Press, 1979).

2. Delaney, *Breakthrough Dreaming*, 393–409. This book may be difficult to find. If you visit my Web site, *www.gdelaney.com,* you will find out where you can obtain a copy. It is a good handbook for solo and group study of the dream-interview process.

3. Jung, *Dream Analysis*, 4.

Appendix

1. The section on dream recording was originally printed in my book *Breakthrough Dreaming*, pp. 19–22.

For the rest of your life, every single night you will create and experience dreams that deal with every important issue that concerns you. These dreams will constitute some of the most honest, creative, and insightful thinking and feeling you will ever do. Take advantage of your dreams. Spend a little time now, and enjoy the fruits of your interpretive skills for the rest of your life.

Tools and Books for Solo and Group Dream Study

I've been working for years to create tools that will enable people to understand their own dreams. Here they are:

THE DREAM KIT: AN ALL-IN-ONE TOOL KIT FOR UNDERSTANDING YOUR DREAMS (HARPERSANFRANCISCO, 1995)

This tool kit includes a workbook that shows you how to recognize patterns in your dreams and provides nightly, weekly, monthly, and yearly review sheets. It also includes instructions for incubating or targeting your dreams for specific problem solving (how to "sleep on it"). Included is an audiocassette on how to work with your dreams and how to put yourself to sleep listening to the last ten minutes of the tape. In recording this tape, I had in mind that an avid dreamer could give it to a spouse who thinks dreams are silly and say, "Sweetheart, listen to this tape. After you have listened to it, you will be a little better informed about the subject, and I will be happy then to discuss it with you." This tape should relieve you from having to defend your interest in dreaming. The best part of the kit is a pack of cue cards that you can hold in your hands as you work with your own or a partner's dream. These cards cue you to ask appropriate interview questions at the right time and really speed your learning. We use the cards in my study groups and at large workshops and lectures with great success.

LIVING YOUR DREAMS (HARPERSANFRANCISCO, 1996)

This book shows you how to target your dreams on a given night to help you understand and solve a practical, emotional, or creative problem. It provides many ideas about how you can put your dreams to work to improve your problem-assessment and problem-solving skills in many areas of your personal and professional life. I first wrote this book in 1977, and since then it has been used in business schools and training programs around the country and in Europe, India, and Asia to teach people how to tap their nocturnal problem-solving abilities. This is a good introduction to dream interpretation and a classic in the use of dream incubation for practical problem solving.

IN YOUR DREAMS: FALLING, FLYING, AND OTHER DREAM THEMES (HARPERSANFRANCISCO, 1997)

This new kind of dream dictionary lets you go right to a particular theme or image, but respects your intelligence and does not give you silly, fixed interpretations. Instead you will find sample dream interpretations and a list of questions relevant to a particular type of dream. Interpretations offered by various dream analysts are briefly described to demonstrate the necessity of tailoring each interpretation to your specific dream no matter how many people have reported the same one!

BREAKTHROUGH DREAMING: HOW TO TAP THE POWER OF YOUR 24-HOUR MIND (BANTAM BOOKS, 1991)

Of all my books this is my personal favorite, a thorough step-by-step manual for people interested in becoming really good dream interviewers. It is very helpful for people working on their own. This is the basic handbook used to teach dream interviewing to amateurs and professionals in schools and training centers, and is used as a manual in dream study groups around the country that use my approach. It includes instructions on conducting dream groups and an extensive bibliography with commentary. It is temporarily out of print, and at press time it is not clear who will be republishing it. You can ask your bookseller to look it up in *Books in Print*, or you can check in at my Web site, *www.gdelaney.com*, for the latest news.

BREAKTHROUGH DREAMING: FIVE CASSETTES AND A WORKBOOK (1995)

This program in dream study consists of five tapes and a workbook on dream incubation and interviewing. I have included a brief history of dreaming. A wonderful gift for people who want an easy introduction to dream work. Available via mail order from Nightingale Conant; call 1-800-323-5552.

BREAKTHROUGH DREAMING: THE TWO-TAPE VERSION (SIMON & SCHUSTER, 1996)

Simon & Schuster has produced a two-tape version of the five-tape *Breakthrough Dreaming* (1995), available in bookstores. If you have friends who do not understand or appreciate your interest in dreaming, you can usually get them to react less superficially and think more deeply by having them listen to these two tapes.

SENSUAL DREAMING: HOW TO UNDERSTAND AND INTERPRET THE EROTIC CONTENT OF YOUR DREAMS (FAWCETT, 1994; ORIGINALLY PUBLISHED UNDER THE TITLE SEXUAL DREAMS)

Well, don't you think it's about time we take a contemporary look at what our sexual dreams are all about? These can be powerfully liberating dreams that help us understand our sexual inhibitions, our conflicts, and, in some cases, our wounds. Men love this book. If you have a boyfriend you would like to interest in dreaming and in opening up his heart, this may be a temptation he won't turn down. Available from Ballantine Books; call 1-800-733-3000.

NEW DIRECTIONS IN DREAM INTERPRETATION (STATE UNIVERSITY OF NEW YORK PRESS, 1991)

This book presents eight different approaches to dream interpretation, with chapters written by the colleagues I most admire. Each author presents a modern version of his or her approach and emphasizes method, telling what he or she actually *does* rather than simply reciting theories of interpretation. This book will allow you to make meaningful comparisons between different methods. Bookstores will special-order it if you insist, or you can call SUNY Press at 1-800-666-2211.

BRING ME A DREAM

On this videocassette Dr. Loma Flowers and I discuss and demonstrate the use of dreams for specific problem solving with four students. Available from the Delaney & Flowers Dream Center; call 415-587-3424.

More Great Books

Crisis Dreaming: Using Your Dreams to Solve Your Problems, by Rosalind Cartwright and Lynne Lamberg (New York: HarperCollins, 1992).

Some Must Watch While Some Must Sleep, by William C. Dement (San Francisco: W. H. Freeman, 1974).

Writers Dreaming, by Naomi Epel (New York: Vintage Books, 1993).

Hypnotic Realities: The Introduction of Clinical Hypnosis and Forms of Indirect Suggestion, by Milton Erickson, Ernest Rossi, and Sheila Rossi (New York: Irvington Publishers, 1981).

Control Your Dreams, by Jayne Gackenbach and Jane Bosveld (New York: Harper & Row, 1989).

Conquering Bad Dreams and Nightmares, by Barry Krakow, M.D., and Joseph Neidhardt, M.D. (New York: Berkley Books, 1992).

The Nightmare, by Ernest Hartman (New York: Basic Books, 1984).

Dream Working: How to Use Your Dreams for Creative Problem Solving, by Stanley Krippner and Joseph Dillard (Buffalo, NY: Bearly, Ltd., 1988).

The Dreambody, by Arnold Mindell (Santa Monica, CA: Sigo Press, 1982).

The Functions of Dreaming, edited by Alan Moffitt, Milton Kramer, and Robert Hoffmann (Albany: State Univ. of New York Press, 1993).

Dreams and Dream Groups: Messages from the Interior, by Eva Renée Neu (Freedom, CA: Crossing Press, 1988).

Dream Solutions, by Henry Reed (San Rafael, CA: New World Library, 1991).

Dream Reader, by Anthony Shafton (Albany: State Univ. of New York Press, 1995).

Sleeping, Dreaming, and Dying: Conversations on Consciousness with the Dalai Lama, edited and narrated by Francisco Varella (Boulder, CO: Wisdom Books, 1997).

Web Sites for Serious Dreamers

WWW.GDELANEY.COM

At this site, designed by Richard McWilliams, you will find articles on dreaming, notices about projects you can participate in such as a survey on sexual dreams, and calls for contributions to my future books. You will be able to write in questions on dreaming, which I shall try to answer in weekly columns. There will also be hot buttons to other good sites on dreams and to stores where you can buy my books on-line. Once I find funding for it, I shall have a chat room and conduct live dream classes once a week.

WWW.DREAMGATE.COM/DREAM/LIBRARY

Created by Richard Wilkerson, the energetic and generous Internet wizard of the Association for the Study of Dreams, this site provides a resource directory for dream-related sites on-line. You will also find connections to on-line dream classes conducted by Richard, as well as a wealth of other information.

WWW.OUTREACH.ORG/DREAMS
Here you will find "Unlocking the Secret of Your Dreams," an on-line course on dreams written and taught by Jayne Gackenbach, who has for years been a prime mover in the Association for the Study of Dreams. The course offers five lessons, with assignments to bring your dream study to life. The site also offers an on-line dream group.

Dream Study Centers

THE DELANEY & FLOWERS DREAM CENTER
In 1981 Dr. Loma Flowers and I began offering classes and programs to professionals and amateurs who want to develop their dream skills. We have programs for local and out-of-town students at all levels of expertise, and offer a diploma program as well. Our Brief Intensive Program is designed for out-of-town dreamers who come to the Dream Center for individually scheduled series of dream sessions. A BIP can be as short as four hours over a weekend, or may be a six- to twelve-hour program in a five-day week, or may last a year. We help BIP students find less expensive housing at bed-and-breakfasts and in the homes of people who like to board people interesting enough to come to the San Francisco area to study their dreams. We conduct individual, pair, and group classes throughout the year. For the last decade or so, we have held a regular open workshop at 6:30 to 8:30 every fourth Tuesday of the month. Be sure to call for the special address of this workshop.

We work with some students by phone, and teach around the country and in Europe whenever we can. (Gayle speaks and works in French and Italian.) For those dreamers who prefer to simply understand their dreams without necessarily learning how to do it for themselves, I also provide dream-interview sessions on an hourly basis. To receive our brochures, send a self-addressed, stamped (with postage to cover two ounces; currently, fifty-five cents) envelope to The Delaney & Flowers Dream Center, P.O. Box 320402, San Francisco, CA 94132. To schedule an appointment by phone or in person, call us at 415-587-3424. Our e-mail address is Dreams@gdelaney.com.

THE SANTA FE CENTER FOR THE STUDY OF DREAMS
Dr. Erik Craig, one of the kindest, most alive people I know, directs this center. Erik is extraordinarily well versed in humanistic and existential psychology, and has a private practice in Santa Fe as well. He is a master dream interviewer, and teaches classes and conducts dream study groups as well as individual dream sessions. Erik also conducts dream seminars and individual sessions regularly in Detroit and Boston. You can contact him at 113 Camino Escondido #3, Santa Fe, NM 87501. His toll-free phone number is 888-986-8666; his local number is 505-986-8666. His e-mail address is DreamsSFNM @aol.com.

THE ASSOCIATION FOR THE STUDY OF DREAMS

Come to the association's conferences and meet hundreds of dreamers from all over the United States and the world. Presentations range from experiential workshops to lectures by therapists, researchers, authors, artists, and people from the most diverse fields who have a keen interest in dreaming. On Saturday night of our annual five-day conference we have a Dream Ball to which all are invited to come as a character from a dream or costumed as Freud or Jung or some other legend in the field. We learn a lot and have enormous fun at our conferences. Many of the dream specialists I cite in this book are members and organizers of the association. By attending the conferences you will be able to meet these people, as well as discuss dreams and dance and play with them. The ASD also publishes a regular newsletter that is more like a magazine, and a journal called *Dreaming*. This is a very creative group that has done much to forward the academic and public awareness of the importance of dreams. By the way, Loma Flowers was our first chairman, and I the founding president, back in 1982–1984. Write to The Association for the Study of Dreams, P.O. Box 1600, Vienna, VA 22183 (sending a self-addressed, stamped envelope when you ask for information is a big help); telephone: 703-242-8888; Web site: *www.outreach.org/gmcc/asd*.

INDEX

Abercrombie, John, 61

Abramovitch, Henry, 22

"Act of intuitive imagination," 3

Action/plot of dreams, 110–11; descriptions and bridges, 132–33

Addictions and dreams, 248–50

Adler, Alfred, 74, 164

Alexander the Great, 38

Allen, Steve, 246

Allende, Isabel, 241–42

American Plains Indians, 12

Amplification method, 78–79, 82, 92

Anderson, Bill, 235

Animals, in dreams: adjectives about, helping the dreamer use, 127; bridging to a person or force in dreamer's life/aspect of self, 128; common dreams, 189–94; cue card questions for, 129–30

Anxiety, 69, 164

Applied Dream Analysis: A Jungian Approach (Mattoon), 77

Aristotle, 10, 11, 35, 36, 37–38, 51, 55, 246

Artemidorus, 40–47, 56, 70–71, 79

Association for the Study of Dreams, 231, 247, 261

Associative method, 93–94; experience-near associations, 94

Augustine, 51

Aurobindo, Yogi, 27–28

Avecenna, 51, 52

Bach, Richard, 243

Bacon, Francis, 10, 11, 55–56

Bad dreams, 213–14. *See also* Nightmares

Barker, Clive, 242

Barrett, Diedre, 203, 204

Bassler, Jouette M., 19

Beatty papyrus, 14–15, 91–92

Being chased dreams 148–49

Benefits of dreaming, 2, 4–5, 7, 86, 228–50. *See also* Dream Interview Method

Bergman, Ingmar, 244

Bilu, Yoram, 22

Blaise, Clark, 242

Blake, William, 241

Bogzarin, Fariba, 218

Bonime, Walter, 94, 98

Book of the Dead, 16

Boss, Medard, 65, 80–87; differs from Freud, 83, 84, 143; differs from Jung, 84, 85, 143; on dream interview, 4; on dream state, 5; examples of method, 83–85; phenomenological (Daseinanalytic) approach, 80–81, 100, 143

Brahms, Johannes, 245

Breakthrough Dreaming (Delaney), 260, 262

Breger, Louis, 4

Brücke, Ernst, 199

Calvin, John, 54

Cannon, W. B., 199–200

Capra, Fritjof, 55
Caquot, M., 21
Car dreams, 177–79
Cartwright, Rosalind, 94, 220
Carus, Carl Gustav, 62
Castle, Bob, 120
Cats, dreams containing, 190–92
Causes of dreams, 1; Chinese tradition, 30–31; day-residue, 68; demons, 31, 48–49, 54, 56; desires, repressed, 36–37, 51, 62, 67, 68–69, 73; disease, 11, 20, 34, 35, 49–50, 246–48; divine source, 15, 19, 38–39, 40–41, 48–49, 54; external sensory stimuli, 63, 68; Hartley's view, 60; Jungian view, 74–76
Cawte, John, 13–14
Cellini, Benvenuto, 56–57, 244
Censor, unconscious, in dreams, 57, 66, 74–75
Chinese dream traditions, 28–32
Chou Li, 30
Christian Church and dream, 47–52; dreams in New Testament, 47–48; revelatory power of dreams, 48
Chrysostom, John, 49
Chuang Tzu, 57
Chuckchee people, Siberia, 12
Cicero, 39–40
Clairvoyant/revelatory dreams, 11; Aristotle on, 38; Cellini, 57; Christian tradition, 48; Descartes, 57; of King Thutmose, 15; miraculous births, 29
Coleridge, Samuel Taylor, 241
Confucius, 28–29
Control Your Dreams (Gackenbach and Bosveld), 214
Craig, Erik, 94, 260
Creativity in Business (Ray and Myers), 230
Crick, Francis, 61
Crisis Dreaming (Cartwright), 220–22

Cue cards, 123–41, 257; adjectives, helping the dreamer use, 127; animals: descriptions and bridges, 129–30; example of process, 135–41; feelings: descriptions and bridges, 131–32; "like," using the word, 126; objects: descriptions and bridges, 130–31; people: descriptions and bridges, 126–29; settings: descriptions and bridges, 125–26; summary, 133–35; warm-up questions, 124
Cultural-formula method, 91–92
Cunningham, Jane, 263

Dane, Joseph, 217
Daring to Dream (Hazarika), 232
Darwin, Charles, 66
Davé, Robert, 202–3
De Becker, Raymond, 21, 24
Delaney & Flowers Dream Center, 105, 124, 175–76, 204, 212, 215, 229, 258, 260
Dement, William, 203, 249–50
Demons or evil spirits, as cause of dreams, 31, 48–49, 54, 56
Denial, 114
Descartes, René, 57, 58, 239
Desires, repressed, in dreams, 36–37, 51, 62, 67, 68–69, 73, 89
De Somniis (Philo), 19
Diagnosis of disease, through dreams, 11, 20, 34, 35, 49–50, 246–48; mental illness, 34, 35
Dickens, Charles, 241
Diderot, Denis, 58–59
Dipsychism, 61
Directing dreams. See Incubation
Dramatic structure of dreams: and Artemidorus, 46–47. See also Dream Interview Method
Dream Analysis: Notes of the Seminar Given in 1928–1930 (Jung), 79
Dream analyst, how to choose, 253–5

Dreambody (Mindell), 97

Dream books: Beatty papyrus, 14–15, 91–92; Chinese, 30; limitations, 20; Roman, 40–47; Taoist, 30

Dream dictionaries, 7, 56, 146

Dream elements, 105–6

Dream in Clinical Practice, The (Natterson), 98–99

Dream Interview Method, 100–122; basic strategies, 141–44; bridging, 104, 112–13, 122; considering options for action, 121–22; cue card, 123–41; description, 103–4, 108–11, 122; diagramming your dream, 105–7; dream elements (six), 105–6; example of author's dream, 115–21; example of diagramming, 106–7; example of interview, 114–15; example of reflection, 115; experience-near associations, 94; four steps of a dream interview, 108–15; high-lighting the feelings in the dream, 108; home-work for dreamer, 115; interviewer as visitor from another planet, 77, 101, 103–4, 123, 147; outlining your dream, 107–8; past, not focusing on, 126; preparing for, 104–5; reflecting on the dream and the dream interview, 115–22; restatement, 104, 111–12, 126; summary, 104, 113–14; theoretical basis, 100–101

Dream Kit, The (Delaney), 124, 252, 258

Dream partner. *See* Partnership for dream work

Dreams and Dreaming (MacKenzie), 16

Dreams and the Growth of Personality (Rossi), 116, 119

Dreams and How to Guide Them (Saint-Denys), 64

Dreams, common types, 145–97; animals, 190–94; customized, 146; how to interpret any animal, 189–90; how to interpret any object, 176–77; how to interpret any person, 171–72; how to interpret any setting, 183–84; how to interpret any theme, 146–48; nightmares, 195–97; objects, 177–83; people, 172–76; themes, 148. *See also* specific dreams

Dreams of a Spirit Seer (Kant), 239

Drugs, cigarettes, or alcohol, dreaming about, 179–83

Egyptian dream traditions, 14–17, 91

Ellenberger, Henri F., 61, 63, 71

EMC Corporation, 234–35

Emotion-focusing method, 95–97

Empiricists, on dreams, 10–11, 42

Enlightenment, Age of, and dreams, 58–63

Enlightenment (spiritual), and dreaming, 25–26, 59

Epel, Naomi, 241–42

Erikson, Erik, 6

Essays by a Hidden Man (Wang Fu), 29–30

Examination dreams, 160–66

External sensory stimuli, 63, 68

Fahd, Toufy, 52

Falling dreams, 69, 145

Faraday, Ann, 98

Feelings, 46, 105; Boss viewpoint, 82; cue card questions, 131–32; during dreams, 79–80, 110; and pitfall of emotion-focusing method, 96–97; role in Dream Interview Method, 101; role in traditional interpretation methods, 43–44, 50, 77, 90–91, 93–94. *See also* Dream Interview Method

Fiss, Harry, 94

Fixed-symbol substitution, 4, 5, 6; Chinese, 30; cultural approach to dream interpretation, 92–93; dangers of, 6; psychotheoretical approach, 93–94; Roman, 40–47. *See also* Freud, Sigmund; Jung, Carl

Flowers, Loma, 94, 100–101, 105,

200–201, 248–49, 260
Flying dreams, 69; 166–71
French, Thomas, 3
Freud, Sigmund, 64, 65–72, 83, 228; and anamnesis, 143; curative effect of understanding dreams, 30, 66, 86; day-residue, 68; desires, repressed, 62, 67, 68–69; diagnosis of mental illness through dreams, 35; dream symbolism, 69–70, 71, 79, 89, 92; "dream work," 66, 68, 82; on examination dreams, 164, 165; free association, 5, 66–67, 68, 82, 89, 93–94, 143; reversal, 67–68, 80; and role of dreamer, 90, 93–94; symbol substitution, 5, 80, 89
Fromm, Erika, 3

Gackenbach, Jayne, 214, 215, 218
Galen of Pergamon, 35–36, 39, 246
Gestalt approach, 95
God(s) and dreaming: cause of dreams, 15, 19, 38–39, 40–41, 48–49, 54; as communication with mortals, 49; and guidance, 43; mystical union with dreamer, 19. *See also* Predictive dreams; Revelatory dreams; Visitational dreaming
Gotthilf, Heinrich von Schubert, 61–62
Grafton, Sue, 200
Graves, Mel, 245
Greek tradition and dreaming, 32–38
Greenberg, Raymond, 196
Group dream work: collaborative versus authoritarian, 99; dream reviews by, 267–68; ending an interview, 266–67; Gestalt approach (role playing), 95; how to join, 259–60; how to organize, 260–63; personal projection, 99, 100; role of leader or coach, 263–64; strategies to follow, 264–66
Grunebaum, von, G. E., 53

Hallowell, Irving, 10

Hartley, David, 60
Hartman, Ernest, 196
Hastings, Arthur, 144
Hazarika, Anjali, 232
Healing through dreaming: ancient world, 14, 16–17, 28–29, 31, 33–34, 35–36; Greece, modern, 36; Israel, modern, 22–23; U.S., modern, 247
Hegel, G. W. F., 66
Heidigger, Martin, 80
Helmholtz, von, Hermann, 199
Henry, Dan, 121
Herophilus of Alexandria, 35
Hindu dream traditions, India, 23–28
Hippocrates, 34–35, 55, 246
Hobbes, Thomas, 58
Hoffmann, Robert, 203, 213, 219
Houses, dreams about parents', other relatives', 184–87
Howe, Elias, 198–99, 236
Hughes, Donald, 12, 15, 32, 33, 38
Hunter, Ian, 4

"*I Dreamt Last Night . . .*" (Boss), 100
Illiad (Homer), 32
Imprisonment dreams, 42
In Your Dreams (Delaney), 146
Incubation of dreams, 16, 85, 198–227, 229; in *Book of the Dead*, 16; Delaney method, 202, 204–9; 230–36; Delaney short version and very short version, 209; examples of impressive, 198–201; fasting, 12, 20; Greek temples for, 33; Jewish practices, 17–18, 20; lucid dreaming, 212–20; meditation, 37; prayer, 12, 20; Romans, 38; samples, 209–12; and visitational dreams, 22
Individuation, 72–73, 92
Inquiries Concerning the Intellectual Powers, and the Investigation of Truth (Abercrombie), 61
Interpretation of dreams, 5, 88–101;

Artemidorus's approach, 42–43, 70–71, 79; associative method, 93–94; collaborative vs. authoritative, 98, 99; cultural-formula method, 91–92; divergent, 3–4, 88, 102; dreamer's role in, 43–44, 50, 77; Dream Interview Method, 94, 100–122; emotion-focusing method, 95–97; Freudian approach, 69–70, 88, 93; Jewish tradition, 21; Jungian approach, 70, 89, 92; levels of meaning, 4; personal-projection method, 98–100; phenomenological method, 100–101; psychotheoretical-formula method, 92–93; questions to ask about different forms of dream analysis, 90. *See also* Dream Interview Method

Interpretation of Dreams, The (Freud), 72

Intuition, 3, 98

Islam and dreams, 52–54; Muhammad's, 53, 228

Jewish dream beliefs, 17–23; Babylonian Talmud, 20–23; incubation, 17–18, 20; interpretation, 21, 43; modern interpreters, 23; Moroccan Jews, 22; respect for individualized nature of dreams, 21; visitations and healing, 22–23

Johns, Jasper, 243, 244

Jung, Carl, 65, 72–80, 88–89; amplification, 78–79, 82, 92; and anamnesis, 143; archetypes, 73–74, 92; on dream interviews, 4; focus associations, 143; individuation, 72–73, 92; method, 76–79, 83; mythology and folklore, symbols from, 6, 50, 78–79; on ordinary dreams, 267; subjective interpretation of dream images, 75; symbol substitution, 5, 75, 89; "taking up the context," 77–78; thrivalist approach, 72, 86, 89; and the unconscious, 62, 74–76

Kant, Immanuel, 239

Karkow, Barry, 224–26

Kekulé, August, 236–37

Kelsey, Morton, 49

King, Johanna, 94

King, Stephen, 200, 242

Klee, Paul, 243

Krippner, Stanley, 94, 98

Language of dreams, 1, 2–3; objective (Freud), 84; Boss's view, 81; subjective approach to imagery, 75, 84; symbolism in, 64, 69–70, 71, 75, 78–79. *See also* Dream Interview Method

Lane, Ron, 4

Laurie, Norman, 234

LeBerge, Stephen, 214–15, 217

Leibniz, Gottfried Wilhelm, 57–58, 239

Lelouche, Claude, 244

Lie-Tseu, 30–31

Life of the Dream, The (Scherner), 64

Living Your Dreams (Delaney), 212, 218, 230, 233, 235, 241, 262

Locke, John, 58

Loemker, Leroy, 57

Lorand, Sandor, 21

Losing purse or wallet dreams, 156–58

Lucid dreaming, 212–20; hypnotic induction, 217; MILD technique, 214–15; Tholey's method, 215–17

MacKenzie, Norman, 16, 36, 38–39

Mafiosi, Nazis, fascists, and dictators in dreams, 174–76

Man, Medicine, and Miracles (Siegel), 247

Manifest dream, 100

Marshal, Ilona, 232–33

Mattoon, Mary Ann, 5, 77

Maury, Alfred, 63

McGinn, Robert, 66

Meditation, presleep, 37

Meditations on the First Philosophy

(Descartes), 239

Men and dreams: and authoritarian culture, 86; male psyche, 3

Mendeleyev, Dmitry, 199, 236

Menezes, Francis, 231–32

Mesmer, Franz, 61

Mindell, Arnold, 97

Mitchison, Graeme, 61

Moffitt, Alan, 213, 219

Moral responsibility for dreams, 49

Moss, Rick, 244

Movie and TV stars, dreams with, 172–74

Mukerjee, Bharati, 242

Muslim tradition, 21

Myers, Michelle, 230

Myths and dreaming, 6, 50. *See also* Jung, Carl

Nahmani, Rabbi, 21

Naked in public dreams, 151–53

Natterson, Joseph, 98–99

Neidhardt, Joseph, 224–26

New Age therapists, 92

New Directions in Dream Interpretation (Delaney), 100

New rooms in a house dreams, 89, 159–60

Nietzsche, Friedrich, 66, 72, 239–40

Nightmare, The (Hartman), 196

Nightmares and bad dreams: Chinese spells to ward off, 9; common, 195–96, 214; gods who chase away, 31–32; Krakow and Neidhardt method of nightmare control, 224–26; RISC, 220–24; stopping, 197, 220–27; value of, 32, 196, 213–14, 227

Objects, 110; common dreams of, 176–83; cue card questions, 130–31

Observations on Man (Hartley), 60

Odyssey (Homer), 32

Ogala Sioux, 12

Old Testament: Abraham's dream, 17; Daniel's interpretation of Nebuchandnezzar's, 18–19; Jacob's dream, 17, 19; Joseph's dreams, 18, 19–20; Joseph's interpretation of butler's, baker's, and pharaoh's dreams, 19, 91–92; Solomon's dream, 18

On Divination (Cicero), 39–40

On Dreams (Hippocrates), 34, 246

Oneirocritica: The Interpretation of Dreams (Artemidorus), 40–47, 56

Out of body experience, during dreaming, 13, 23

Parkinson, D. B., 236

Partnership for dream work: ending an interview, 266–67; finding a partner, 254–55; pointers for forming, 255–59

Pascal, Blaise, 57

People and animals in dreams, 105, 110; adjectives about, helping the dreamer use, 127; bridging to a person or force in dreamer's life/aspect of self, 128; common dreams about people, 171–76; cue card questions for, 126–29; "like," using the word, 126; question never to ask, 110; Perls, Fritz, 95; Personal-projection method, 98–100

Petronius, 39

"Phenomenological Challenges for the Clinical Use of Dreams" (Craig and Walsh), 100

Phenomenological method, 100–101

Philo, 19

Physiological aspects of dreaming, 1; Aristotle, 37; early Christian, 52; Diderot, 59; Hindu tradition, 24; Plato, 35, 36–37; Plutarch, 38

Polypsychism (dissociated personalities), 61

Positivism and dreams, 63–64

Prelutsky, Jack, 242–43

Price, Reynolds, 243

Price, S. R. F., 47

Problem-solving in dreams, 57, 71–72, 228–46; and addictions, 248–50; in business world, 230–36; examples of impressive, 198–201; inventions and designs, 236–38; musicians, 245; painters, sculptors, moviemakers, 243–44; in philosophy, 239–41; and REM sleep, 230; and writers, 241–43

Prometheus Bound (Aeschylus), 33

Prophetic/predictive dreams, 13, 19, 33, 34–35, 38, 41, 43, 48–49, 56, 62

Psychodynamic explorations of dreams, 55, 61–62

Psychological aspects of dreaming, 1; Hebrew's recognition of, 18; Hindu tradition, 24; Psycho-theoretical-formula method, 92–93. *See also* Boss, Medard; Freud, Sigmund; Jung, Carl

Psychotherapy, early, 62–63

Purcell, Sheila, 213, 219

Putscher, Marielene, 18

Puységur, de, Marquis, 61

Ragsdale, Floyd, 234

Ramanujan, Srinivasa, 237

Ray, Michael, 230

Reality of dreams, 10–11; Hindu India, 26; primal societies, 10, 12–14

Recall of dreams: eight steps to, 269–70; Hindu tradition, 24; loss of, OT explanation, 19

Recording your dreams, 270–72

Reed, Henry, 202

Reil, J., 61

Reversal, in dream interpretation, 67–68

Robert, W., 60–61

Roheim, Geza, 12

Roman tradition and dreams, 38–47

Rosengren, Bob, 218–19

Rotenberg, V. S., 230

Rousselle, Robert, 34

Royston, Robert, 248

Russell, Bertrand, 240–41

Saint-Denys, de, Marquis Hervey, 64

Saint visitation in dreams, 22–23

Santa Fe Center for the Study of Dreams, 100, 248

Schatzman, Morton, 203

Scherner, Karl, 64

Schopenhauer, Arthur, 62, 239

Schrager, James, 231

Sensual Dreams (Delaney), 155

Settings, 105, 109–10; cue card questions, 125–26

Sexual dreams: Artemidorus, 44–46, 49; as devil's doing, 49; former lovers, 156; and Freud, 44, 69–71; helpful hints, 155; intercourse with mother, 42, 44–46; issues in, 114–15; making love to an unexpected partner, 154–56; and Plato, 36, 49

Shakespeare, William, 55

Shamans, use of dreams by, 12, 13

Shimeon Bar-Yohai , 22–23

Siegel, Bernard, 247–48

Sky, Rabbi, temple Beth El, ME, 23

Sleep and Dreams (Maury), 63

Smith, Kent, 232–33

Smith, Robert, 247

Snake dreams, 192–94

Solo dream study, 251–52

Somatic theory of dreams, 58

Some Must Watch While Some Must Sleep (William Dement), 203

Sommer, Tana, 243

Soymié, Michel, 30

Stafford, Harry, 71

Stanford University Graduate School of Business, Delaney method at, 230–31

Stern, Paul, 111

Stone, Robert, 250
Strategies, basic dream interview, 141–42; amplifying the feelings, 142; corralling the dreamer, 143; guessing the absurd, or the opposite, 142; "how is it different from," 143; restatement, 144; sheepdogging, 144
Strickmann, Michel, 28
Strindberg, August, 243
Summary, 104, 113–14; cue card questions, 133–35
Symbol substitution, 5, 80, 89
Symbolic nature of dreams. *See* Language of dreams
Symbolism of Dreams, The (Gotthilf),61
Synesius of Cyrene, 49–50

Tape recorder, use of, 115, 257
Tedlock, Barbara, 10
Teeth falling out dreams, 150–51
Tertullian, 48–49
Thought, continuation of conscious, in dreams, 59–60. *See also* Problem-solving dreams
Tory, Elmer M., 237–38
Town, cities, states, or countries, dreams about, 187–89
Transpersonal Psychology Institute, 144
Treatise on Dreams (Atharva Veda), 24
Tylor, Edward B., 10

Ullman, Montague, 98, 99
Unable to run dreams, 153–54
Unconscious mind and dreaming, 2, 51, 62, 66, 73; Boss denial of, 81

Understanding of Dreams, The (De Becker), 24
Upanishads on dreaming, 24–25

Van de Castle, Robert, 12
Virgil, 38
Visitational dreams: Cellini, 57; Chinese, 28–29, 31; dead souls appear, 59; Egyptian, 16–17; Greeks, 33–34; Hebrew, 22–23
Voltaire, 59–60, 239

Wagner, Richard, 245
Wang Fu, 29–30
Web site, 212
Webster, Guy, 246
Webster, Paul Frances, 246
Wei Hsiang-shu, 31
William of Conches, 52
Winfrey, Ophrah, 218
Wishes. *See* Desires
Women: discounted in dream history, 12–13; dream interpretation and authoritarian culture, 86; female psyche and dreaming, 3; and Freud, 71; and Jungian approach, 92–93; and saints' visitations, Israel, 22–23; in Switzerland, 86, 92
Writers Dreaming (Epel), 241

Yolngu people, Australia, 13–14

Zhong Kui, 31
Zimmerman, Nan, 99
Zweben, Joan E., 248–49
Zwilich, Ellen, 245–46